MISSIONARIES AND MANDARINS

Missionaries and Mandarins

*Feminist engagement
with development institutions*

Edited by
CAROL MILLER and SHAHRA RAZAVI

INTERMEDIATE TECHNOLOGY PUBLICATIONS
In association with the
UNITED NATIONS RESEARCH INSTITUTE FOR
SOCIAL DEVELOPMENT 1998

Intermediate Technology Publications Ltd
103–105 Southampton Row
London WC1B 4HH, UK

© UNRISD 1998

A CIP catalogue record for this book is available from the British
Library

ISBN 1 85339 434 3

Typeset by Dorwyn Ltd, Rowlands Castle, Hants
Printed in the UK by SRP, Exeter

Contents

Notes on Contributors

Anne Marie Goetz is a Fellow at the Institute of Development Studies, Sussex, UK. She has written extensively on gender and institutions, including *Getting Institutions Right For Women in Development* (Zed, 1997). She has also done research on the gender implications of credit programmes in rural Bangladesh.

Linda Mayoux is a Research Fellow at the Open University, Milton Keynes, UK. She has done extensive research and published on gender issues in micro-enterprises, income-generating projects, co-operatives and, more recently, NGOs in developing countries. She is currently developing a research programme on Empowerment, Sustainability and Micro-finance.

Carol Miller is Research Associate, Gender Programme, United Nations Institute for Social Development (UNRISD), Geneva. She has written on gender and development and on gender and international institutions, including historical research on women's issues and the League of Nations. She is also an Associate Lecturer at the Open University, a long-distance learning institution based in the UK.

Rabéa Naciri is a Professor of Geography at the Faculté des Lettres et Sciences Humaines, University of Rabat. She has written widely on the status of women in Morocco. She is also actively involved in a number of Moroccan women's organizations, and is currently Executive Director of Collectif 95 Maghreb Egalité.

Shahra Razavi is Co-ordinator of the Gender Programme, United Nations Institute for Social Development (UNRISD), Geneva, where she manages two inter-regional projects, Technical Co-operation and Women's Lives: Integrating Gender into Development Policy and Gender, Poverty and Well-being. A specialist in agrarian and development issues, she is the author of numerous publications on gender and development.

Marian Sawyer is Associate Professor in Politics at the Australian National University, Canberra, Australia. She has published extensively on the women's movement and the state in Australia, including *Sisters in Suits: Women and Public Policy in Australia* (Allen and Unwin, 1990). More recently she has become interested in comparative research on women's policy machinery in western industrialized states.

Preface

Over the past three decades there has been a growing recognition by feminist scholars and activists of the role played by a range of institutions in sustaining gender inequalities. The feminist project of de-institutionalizing male bias involves a number of hotly contested political and discursive strategies. The main political strategy explored in the volume is "entryism" whereby feminists attempt to enter and transform host institutions from within, through the promotion of gender-sensitive bureaucratic structures and practices. "Entryism" is just one of the strategies referred to under the umbrella of feminist "engagement" with institutions. Another is political pressure exercised by women's movements on development institutions, pressure that is crucial to promoting gender transformative policy. Chapters in this volume suggest that feminist policy advocacy within state (and other) bureaucracies should be seen as a complement and not an alternative to women's organizations and activism on the outside. The relationship between femocrats (insiders) and organized women's movements (outsiders) is contextualized within broader themes of state-civil society relations, the growth of the international women's movement, as well as the apparent decentralization of development institutions and their claims to apply participatory approaches to policy formulation.

Feminist engagement with institutions also leads to the adoption of a variety of discursive strategies to present gender concerns as legitimate policy issues. One of the central tensions that emerges is between feminists who highlight the positive pay offs of gender equity for other developmental goals (economic efficiency, poverty reduction, environmental concerns) and those using more confrontational discourses. Engagement with institutions, as the contributors to this volume attest, inevitably brings to the fore issues of co-optation and instrumentalism, as well as concerns about the risks of neutralizing the transformative nature of the feminist agenda.

The title of this volume thus derives from the challenges of pursuing transformative change (as missionaries) while dealing with the constraints imposed by working within bureaucracies (as mandarins). Despite the inherent trade-offs, there is consensus among the contributors that the role of powerful institutions in determining development discourse and practice makes them simply too important to ignore.

This volume brings together research that was carried out between 1993–1997 in connection with the UNRISD/UNDP project, Technical Co-operation and Women's Lives: Integrating Gender into Development Policy. The aim of this project was to strengthen national efforts to bring women's concerns into the process of economic policy making. One component involved a gender analysis of development policy-making institutions in order to understand why they prove so resistant to women and their interests. In exploring the efforts of these institutions to "mainstream" gender concerns into their policy-making processes, attention was paid to the impact of external pressures for policy change, new institutional structures and practices for integrating gender concerns, as well as to discursive and practical strategies adopted by internal gender advocates. Case studies included multilateral organizations (the ILO, the UNDP and the World Bank) and several states (Bangladesh, Chile, Jamaica, Mali, Morocco, Uganda and Vietnam). To provide a further comparative perspective, a paper exploring the women's policies machineries in Australia, Canada and New Zealand—generally considered to be among the most developed in the world—was commissioned. In view of the assumed advantages of non-governmental organizations (NGOs) in providing a conducive environment for gender policy, another paper was commissioned to present a critical analysis of the experience of gender mainstreaming in national and international NGOs in India, Bangladesh and the UK. The research was carried out by national researchers in the participating countries, external consultants and UNRISD staff.

Acknowledgements

The editors would like to acknowledge the support of the United Nations Development Programme (UNDP), which funded the UNRISD-implemented project Technical Co-operation and Women's Lives: Integrating Gender into Development Policy out of which many of the papers in this volume emerged. At UNRISD, we are grateful to Yusuf Bangura, Dharam Ghai, Cynthia Hewitt de Alcántara, and Peter Utting for providing useful comments on earlier versions of various chapters. Also at UNRISD, special thanks go to the following interns and research assistants who patiently agreed to our seemingly endless requests for support in library searches, checking references and proof-reading: Christine Bourgeois, Melissa Gleckel, Uzma Hashmi, Louise Richmond, Aimee Solway, Cynthia Wierzbicki and Rose Winton. Jenifer Freedman and Erika Drucker also provided assistance with editing and translation. Outside UNRISD, we would like to thank Nüket Kardam for her comments on earlier drafts of various chapters.

The fact that the UNRISD/UNDP project was initiated in the first place owes to the initiative of Ingrid Palmer, who deserves a special acknowledgement.

Acronyms

ACFODE	Action for Development (Uganda)
BJMS	Bangladesh *Jatiyo Mahila Sangstha* (National Women's Association)
BNP	Bangladesh National Party
BPPS	Bureau for Programme and Policy Support (UNDP)
CAPOW	Coalition of Actively Participating Organisations of Women
CAS	Country Assistance Strategy paper (World Bank)
CEDAW	Convention on the Elimination of All Forms of Discrimination Against Women
CIDA	Canadian International Development Agency
CNMD	*Concerlación Nacional de Mujeres por la Democracia* (National Coalition of Women for Democracy, Chile)
CRIAW	Canadian Research Institute for the Advancement of Women
CSN	Country Strategy Note (UNDP)
CSW	Commission on the Status of Women (UN)
DANIDA	Danish International Development Assistance
DAW	Division for the Advancement of Women (UN)
DAWN	Development Alternatives with Women for a New Era
DGIS	Directorate General for International Co-operation (the Netherlands)
DWA	Department of Women's Affairs (Bangladesh)
ECOSOC	Economic and Social Council (UN)
EEO	Equal Employment Opportunity (New Zealand)
EGALITE	Equality of Rights Branch (ILO)
ESP	Education and Social Policy Department (World Bank)
ESW	economic and sector work (World Bank)
FEMMES	Office for Women Workers' Questions (ILO)
FHH	female-headed households
FIDA-U	Ugandan Association of Women Lawyers
G7	Group of Seven (leading industrial countries)
GAD	gender and development
GAP	Gender Analysis and Policy (World Bank)
GB	Grameen Bank, Bangladesh
GIDP	Gender in Development Programme (UNDP)
GOB	Government of Bangladesh
GOJ	Government of Jamaica
GOM	Government of Morocco
GOU	Government of Uganda
GRO	grassroots member organizations
GSO	grassroots support organizations
HDR	Human Development Report (UNDP)
ICPD	International Conference on Population and Development

IFAD	International Fund for Agricultural Development
ILO	International Labour Organisation/Office
IMF	International Monetary Fund
INGO	international non-government organization
INSTRAW	International Research and Training Institute for the Advancement of Women
IWY	International Women's Year
MDT	multidisciplinary teams (World Bank)
MFEP	Ministry of Finance and Economic Planning (Uganda)
NAC	National Action Committee on the Status of Women (Canada)
NGO	non-governmental organization
NRC	National Resistance Council (Uganda)
NRM	National Resistance Movement (Uganda)
NWC	National Women's Council (Uganda)
NWCC	National Women's Consultative Council (Australia)
OECD	Organization for Economic Co-operation and Development
OED	Operations Evaluation Department (World Bank)
OSW	Office of the Status of Women (Australia)
PHRWD	Population and Human Resources Department (World Bank)
PRA	participatory rural appraisal
RC	Resistance Council (Uganda)
SDPED	Social Development and Poverty Elimination Division (UNDP)
SERNAM	National Service for Women (Chile)
SEWA	Self-employed Women's Association
UNCED	United Nations Conference on Environment and Development
UNDP	United Nations Development Programme
UNFPA	United Nations Population Fund
UNICEF	United Nations Children's Fund
UNIFEM	United Nations Development Fund for Women
UNRISD	United Nations Research Institute for Social Development
UWFCT	Uganda Women's Finance and Credit Trust
VWU	Vietnamese Women's Union
WEL	Women's Electoral Lobby (Australia and New Zealand)
WID	women in development
WINGO	women's international non-governmental organization
WWF	Working Women's Forum (India)

The United Nations Research Institute for Social Development (UN-RISD) is an autonomous agency engaging in multi-disciplinary research on the social dimensions of contemporary problems affecting development. Its work is guided by the conviction that, for effective development policies to be formulated, an understanding of the social and political context is crucial. The Institute attempts to provide governments, development agencies, grassroots organizations and scholars with a better understanding of how development policies and processes of economic, social and environmental change affect different social groups. Working through an extensive network of national research centres, UNRISD aims to promote original research and strengthen research capacity in developing countries.

Current research programmes include: Business Responsibility for Sustainable Development; Emerging Mass Tourism in the South; Gender, Poverty and Well-Being; Globalization and Citizenship; Grassroots Initiatives and Knowledge Networks for Land Reform in Developing Countries; New Information and Communication Technologies; Public Sector Reform and Crisis-Ridden States; Technical Co-operation and Women's Lives: Integrating Gender into Development Policy; Volunteer Action and Local Democracy: A Partnership for a Better Urban Future; and the War-torn Societies Project. Recent research programmes have included: Crisis, Adjustment and Social Change; Culture and Development; Environment, Sustainable Development and Social Change; Ethnic Conflict and Development; Participation and Changes in Property Relations in Communist and Post-Communist Societies; Political Violence and Social Movements; Social Policy, Institutional Reform and Globalization; and Socio-Economic and Political Consequences of the International Trade in Illicit Drugs. UNRISD research projects focused on the 1995 World Summit for Social Development included: Economic Restructuring and Social Policy; Ethnic Diversity and Public Policies; Rethinking Social Development in the 1990s; and Social Integration at the Grassroots: The Urban Dimension.

A list of the Institute's free and priced publications can be obtained by contacting the Reference Centre at: the United Nations Research Institute for Social Development, Palais des Nations, 1211 Geneva 10, Switzerland; Tel (41 22) 798 84 00/798 58 50; Fax (41 22) 740 07 91; Telex 41.29.62 UNO CH; e-mail: info@unrisd.org; World Wide Web Site: http://www.unrisd.org

1

Introduction

CAROL MILLER and SHAHRA RAZAVI

OVER THE PAST three decades a wide spectrum of organizations working in the development field have been scrutinized by feminist activists and scholars for their gender inequitable structures, procedures, and policy outcomes. A point made repeatedly in the early Women in Development (WID) evaluations of development projects was the inability of agricultural innovation practices and extension services to meet their own objectives of increasing rural productivity and incomes because the relevant policymaking institutions systematically overlooked women's roles in the production process (Staudt, 1978; Dey, 1981). Male farmers tended to receive inputs and extension advice for crops that only women grew. At the same time, women were constructed as needy beneficiaries of under-funded, residual welfare programmes in their roles as homemakers, reproducers, and child rearers (Buvinic, 1986). But institutionalized bias of this kind is by no means restricted to development organizations. Observers of the US welfare system have identified a similar dualistic structure with a corresponding gender sub-text: a masculine sub-system consisting of social insurance schemes that position recipients as right-bearers and citizens, and a feminine 'relief', means-tested sub-system that constructs the recipients as 'clients of public charity' (Fraser, 1989).

Abstracting from these findings, it is no longer acceptable to see the household as the sole bastion of patriarchy. While much of the focus of the early gender and development literature was on domestic institutions where gender relations are most explicit, since the mid-1980s increasing attention has been directed at the ways in which 'familial norms and values are constantly drawn on to construct the terms on which women and men enter, and participate, in public life and in the marketplace' (Kabeer, 1994:61). The burden of this new genre of feminist analysis has been to demonstrate the extent to which gender operates as a pervasive organizational principle across 'impersonal' institutional arenas. In modern industrial firms and in agribusiness ventures, for example, definitions of 'skill' and of tasks tend to institutionalize a hierarchical and gendered labour force, each with its own areas of work, wages, patterns of recruitment, and promotion prospects (Humphrey, 1987; Mackintosh, 1989). Similarly, a 'gendered archeology of organizations' illuminates the gendered sub-texts of apparently neutral organizing structures, practices, and ideologies to help explain why they prove so resistant to women and their interests (Goetz, 1995).

At the same time, as Naila Kabeer (1994) aptly goes on to argue, because different social institutions are organized around quite specific objectives with their own idiosyncratic set of rules and procedures, gender hierarchies are not uniformly woven into institutional structures, but produced dynamically through the interactions of gender/familial ideologies and distinct institutional practices. Institutions are understood to be 'the rules of the game ... the humanly devised constraints that shape human interaction' (North, 1990:3), or 'the operation of tradition, custom or legal constraint' which tends to create 'durable and routinized patterns of behaviour' (Hodgson, 1988:10). In other words, social institutions impose certain parameters on human behaviour which lead to routinized (and thus predictable) patterns of social interaction.

In the context of the policymaking organizations considered in this volume, what we are concerned with are the rules, incentives, constraints, and 'meanings'[1] which contribute to the systematic diversion of resources, values, and power away from women and towards men. To give a simple example, the common notion that women are housewives dependent on a male 'breadwinner', has tended to deny them a wide range of rights (employment, child custody) and resources (full wage, land, credit), thereby depriving them of the power and status that comes with having full citizenship. The feminist project of de-institutionalizing male bias involves a simultaneous struggle on at least three main fronts: at the discursive level, where women's interests and needs are constructed and contested; at the institutional level, in defining the rules and procedures which shape the practices of bureaucratic actors; and finally, at the level of resource allocation—'the struggle over the satisfaction of the need' (Fraser, 1989:164).

A central question that arises in this context is the choice of institutional strategy. An interesting feature accompanying some strands of feminist critique of development organizations has been the political strategy of 'entryism' (Bangura, 1997)—a sustained attempt to enter and gradually transform the host organization from within, changing its procedures, goals, and culture along lines that are more gender-equitable.[2]

The dynamics of pursuing transformative agendas from within established bureaucracies—of being 'missionaries' while adapting to the techniques and practices of the bureaucracy as 'mandarins' would have to do—is one of the central themes of this volume.[3] Several chapters describe the process of 'institutionalizing' gender-equitable bureaucratic practices in state-level institutions (Goetz and Sawer), multilateral organizations (Miller), and non-governmental organizations (NGOs) (Mayoux). These chapters explore the national and international forces that have led to the creation of new institutional structures and procedures.[4] These changes are meant to adjust organizational practice in such a way as to ensure that bureaucratic outcomes (projects, programmes, policies) are routinely free of male bias. None the less, as several chapters indicate, rarely have the necessary resources been forthcoming to translate feminist policy ambitions into concrete outcomes.

A further set of issues that is hotly debated by the contributors is the choice of discursive strategy. One of the central tensions is between feminists advocating 'win–win' scenarios that highlight the outcomes of their policies in terms of the 'common good' (very often in the language of liberal individualism), and those using confrontational discourses (that tend to be rooted in a more structuralist

2

understanding of women's subordination). Issues of co-optation and instrument-alism, as well as the risks of neutralizing the transformative nature of the feminist agenda, are raised in several chapters. Others, however, provide a more positive assessment of these discursive strategies, and see the contestation over concepts like 'efficiency' as a way of subverting the dominant neo-liberal discourse. This is considered to be particularly significant as feminists enter parts of the policy establishment that speak the language of economics.

All of the above can be seen as aspects of a feminist 'engagement' strategy, the aim of which is to promote change within existing bureaucratic structures, even if it is recognized that change will be incremental. In view of the tremendous influence exercised by the state and a range of other institutions over every facet of women's lives—and the gender biases around which their programmes and policies are constructed—these institutions are considered too important to ignore. As Reinelt (1995) puts it, the 'politics of engagement' views mainstream institutions as key terrains of political struggle. This approach has been contrasted with the alternative—'disengagement' strategy—which is skeptical of the ability of bureaucracies to promote women's concerns (Ferguson, 1984). According to this latter approach, feminism, like all forms of oppositional discourses, 'is endangered by too-close contact with bureaucratic linguistic and institutional forms' (Ferguson, 1984:180). The hierarchical and technocratic rationale of modern bureaucracies are seen to be fundamentally opposed to feminist goals. Moreover, from this perspective, the requirements of conformity and loyalty suppress and defuse feminist voices as they enter bureaucracies.

While the feminist strategies described in the chapters of this volume tend to subscribe to an 'engagement' approach, they are grounded in a recognition of the gendered nature of bureaucratic structures and of the role played by powerful institutions in determining development practice and discourse. They reject the view, however, that bureaucracies are monolithic and impermeable. As several chapters illustrate, feminist policy advocates have made greater incursions into institutions or parts of institutions that are more amenable to gender concerns. Miller, for example, suggests that it has been easier to argue the case for attention to gender concerns in an organization like the International Labour Office, that is committed to social justice, than in the World Bank, with its emphasis on economic efficiency and growth. Similarly, the parts of bureaucracies that deal with social issues have been more penetrable than those that focus on economic policy. Over the past decade, feminist policy advocates have sought to infiltrate the more resistant institutional structures, including those concerned with economic policy, with varying degrees of success, as the chapters by Goetz, Sawer, Razavi, and Miller illustrate.

State–civil society relations

Notwithstanding the processes of globalization and democratization referred to in several chapters of this volume, the state remains the main forum of national decision-making. It continues to play a central role in laying down the parameters for the institutional and market frameworks which govern citizens' social, political, and economic options (Joekes, 1995). It is not surprising, therefore, that women's movements over the past century have targeted the state and continue to do so. In describing feminist 'engagement' with state institutions, the chapters in this volume nonetheless present a contradictory picture of how women's groups view the state.

On the one hand, Goetz and Naciri observe a reticence on the part of some women's groups about direct involvement with the state and political parties. Such a view is underpinned by more than a decade of feminist theorizing about the role of the state in perpetuating gender disadvantage (Connell, 1990; Cockburn, 1991). As noted earlier, public policies in modern welfare states have constructed women's identity around social relations of dependency on male income-earners with far-reaching implications for women's position as rights-bearers and citizens (Fraser, 1989). Similarly, state institutions and legal systems in both the North and the South have upheld women's structurally unequal position in the family by sanctioning gender-differentiated practices in political and economic participation, and inheritance rights, and by tacitly condoning domestic and sexual violence against women. On the other hand, as several chapters in this volume demonstrate (including those by Goetz and Naciri), feminist practice in many countries has demonstrated achievements from working through state institutions.

The debate between feminist 'engagement' and 'disengagement' strategies is in many ways rooted in the conflicting views of the state: a vehicle for social justice versus a protector of male interests. Recent feminist formulations have attempted to re-conceptualize this ambivalence about the state, pointing to its *contradictory* role in constructing *and* de-constructing gender disadvantage. Waylen (1995) sees the state as another institutional site of political struggle around the construction of women's interests and identities. She argues, however, that the state should not be seen as a unitary structure but a differentiated set of institutions and practices that are the product of a particular historical and political conjuncture. As such, the relationship between the state and gender relations is not fixed or immutable. While the state can reinforce gender disadvantage, opportunity structures exist within it that can be used by women's movements to challenge unequal gender relations. It follows, therefore, that feminist analyses of state–civil society relations must be historically, culturally, and politically grounded. Feminist engagement with the state in any given context will be shaped by historical legacies and political traditions, the nature of the state and its basis of legitimacy, the openness of civil society and the relative power of its constituent parts, and the relations between the state and civil society.[5]

The comparative country case studies of state–civil society relations included in this volume confirm the importance of historically and contextually grounded analyses. Chapters by Goetz and Naciri point to the historical legacies of political liberation movements in shaping the discursive and practical strategies of

4

women's movements in selected Southern countries. In the chapter by Sawer, the history of feminist engagement with the state in Australia, Canada, and New Zealand is located within the political tradition of social liberalism shared by these countries. The chapter traces the challenges posed to feminist advocacy in the fiscally conservative 1980s and 1990s as these countries experienced a fundamental rethinking of the role of the state. Interestingly, Sawer points out that feminist theorizing about the state emerged in the United States and the United Kingdom, both countries where feminists' interventions in the state were relatively underdeveloped. She contrasts this with the experience in Australia, Canada, and New Zealand, where women's movements have tended to see the state as a vehicle for social justice; the 1970s feminist ideology and practice that emerged out of the American women's liberation movement—summed up in the slogan 'women and revolution' not 'women and bureaucracy'—have never been fully embraced in these countries. These examples also provide an interesting contrast with the experiences of many Southern countries described in other chapters.

In her chapter, Goetz demonstrates that changes in political systems—such as the transitions from military dictatorships to democracies in Uganda and Chile—also provide opportunities for articulating women's interests and furthering feminist agendas. With the exception of Vietnam, the process of democratization in all of the country case studies has provided new openings for women to mobilize and put pressure on the state, although the degree to which autonomous women's organizations have emerged as a political force varies from country to country. Feminist scholarship on women's movements has shown that even where women have organized alongside men in oppositional politics to bring about regime changes and greater democratization, they have often been unable to sustain their visibility in the new power configurations that emerge or to organize effectively around women's interests (Jacquette, 1994). While the country case studies provided in chapters by Goetz and Naciri tend to support this thesis, there is some evidence of women's constituency building and the consolidation of women's political influence. For the reasons outlined in Goetz's chapter, however, the process of liberalization in Vietnam—as in other transitional economies—has tended to undermine women's political participation and, thus far, there has been very little political space available to nurture autonomous civil society groups. As such, policy advocacy on women's issues is still largely the purview of state or party institutions, in particular the Vietnamese Women's Union, the Communist Party's mass organization of women.

Naciri's chapter locates contemporary feminist politics in Morocco within a momentous conjuncture of a variety of political forces: the process of democratization; the increased political prominence of Islamic fundamentalist interests; and the state's search for (economic and political) legitimacy in the eyes of the international community. This chapter provides a rich analysis of the way these forces have conditioned the constraints and 'opportunity structures' available to the women's movement in its efforts to influence the state. Indeed, a variety of

5

strategies have been pursued by the women's movement, many of which are not mutually exclusive. Some women's organizations have sought a *rapprochement* with secular, leftist political parties in order to help counteract Islamic political interests. Similarly, they have endeavoured to exploit the contradictions evident in the self-declared modernism of the state (including a commitment to women's rights) and its efforts to appease traditional political elements by marginalizing the feminist agenda.

At the same time, in view of the fact that the discourse on women's issues in Morocco has been shaped by religious and cultural traditions, even within the parties of the left, some women's groups have sought to engage Islam directly and to make it more inclusive, for example through an egalitarian reinterpretation of the Koran. For other women, especially from poorer social groups, Islam has been adopted as a 'strategy of resistence', symbolized most vividly by the donning of *le hijab* (the veil) which, Naciri argues, provides a certain status and more freedom of movement in an otherwise oppressive social and economic environment. A similar point is made by Waylen (1992) in her analysis of the widespread mobilization around very traditional pronouncements about women and motherhood that was one of the many forms of political action undertaken by Chilean women under Pinochet's regime. By placing the Moroccan women's movement within its national political/religious context, Naciri's chapter illuminates the highly diverse forms of political action by women which can be seen to constitute feminist politics.

Working within and against the state

More specifically, a key dimension of state–civil society relations that chapters in this volume explore is the relationship between femocrats[6] (insiders) and organized women's movements (outsiders). Feminist 'engagement' strategies involve both 'entryism', as described, for example, in Sawer's chapter on femocrats within state institutions, and continuous pressure from the women's movement(s) on the outside, a point made most forcefully in the chapter by Goetz. In the chapters in this volume, feminist policy advocacy within state (and other) bureaucracies is viewed as a complement and not an alternative to women's organization and activism on the outside. Even in the context of 'disengagement' strategies, where feminists work solely through independent women's organizations, some form of engagement with the state and mainstream institutions is unavoidable (Reinelt, 1995). Women's organizations are often shaped and mobilized in response to the policies of state institutions that are seen to be antithetical to women's interests; it follows that feminist activism involves challenging the structure and practices of these institutions (Gelb, 1995). It is for these reasons that women's movements have sought to develop structures of interest articulation and representation within state institutions. Strategically positioned within the state, femocrats are, in theory, well situated to identify and take advantage of the political opportunity spaces to push forward a feminist agenda. But their position working 'within and against the state' (London-Edinburgh Weekend Return Group, 1979) raises questions of 'legitimacy' in the eyes of both their colleagues within the bureaucracy and the women's movement on the outside.[7]

The strategy of implementing change 'from within' demands a wide range of skills on the part of gender advocates or 'femocrats', which can be most usefully summarized under the headings of 'technical' and 'political'. Polsby (1985) refers to these internal advocates as 'policy entrepreneurs' in order to draw attention to the innovative nature of their work in identifying new issues, skilfully mobilizing facts about them which can serve as a justification for action, and cultivating internal allies whose support can help promote policy change. As several of the contributions to this volume demonstrate, tampering with the nuts and bolts of a bureaucracy in the context of a highly sophisticated policy development process requires an in-depth understanding of how the bureaucratic machinery works. Gender advocates also need to have astute political skills in order to identify where the strategic points of leverage in the policy establishment are and how allies can be cultivated despite the distrust of traditional bureaucrats.

One policy area that has been particularly resistant to feminist incursions has been macro-economic decision-making—the purview of powerful Ministries of Finance. Gender machineries in both national and international agencies still have difficulty making inroads in this field, which continues to be dominated by men schooled in 'gender-blind' neo-classical economics. But having the competence and confidence to both understand and question economic policy requires fluency and skill in economic analysis (Pearson, 1995). The growing body of work by feminist economists provides a potential resource that gender machineries can use to help them to focus on the design of policy reforms and to facilitate communication with the economists who dominate macro-economic policy-making (Elson and McGee, 1995). The gender machineries in a number of governments and international agencies have begun to use this body of knowledge in their efforts to integrate a gender perspective into programme and policy assistance (Pearson, 1995; Miller and Razavi, this volume).

And finally, as highlighted in the contribution by Goetz, to ensure that policy commitments to women do not remain trapped on paper, gender advocates need financial analysis skills which can tie those policy commitments to budget allocations. In Australia innovative Women's Budget Statements, which require all government departments and agencies to account for the impact of their activities on women, have been introduced by gender machineries, but the utility of this model in other contexts where the budgetary process is less reliable and established and the public administration weakened by severe financial strain, is questioned by Goetz.

While some gender machineries manage to demonstrate considerable dexterity in both budgetary and policy analysis, many of those described in this volume suffer from skill shortages. The fact that in most cases gender machineries remain

7

under-staffed and under-resourced accentuates this problem. In many Southern countries, concerns for fiscal prudence and economic stabilization have, over the course of the past two decades, significantly weakened the capacity of the public administration to carry out its remaining areas of responsibility (Bangura, 1994; UNICEF/UNDP, 1995). The phenomenon of 'moonlighting' by civil servants is a stark indication of the changing orientation of bureaucrats in such contexts. In the face of deeply entrenched bureaucratic malaise in many countries, 'getting institutions right for women' (IDS, 1995) is a formidable challenge.

In addition to the skills needed to foster alliances and establish legitimacy within the bureaucracy, women in public administration need a range of skills to maintain legitimacy in the eyes of the women's movement. This is a crucial part of their policy advocacy work, for as Sawer's chapter demonstrates, organized external pressure has played an indispensable role in pushing through feminist policy initiatives in Australia, Canada, and New Zealand. Several chapters in this volume confirm that internal policy advocacy is underpinned by an effective external political base. Aware of this fact, femocrats have developed political skills and strategies for 'bridge-building' with the women's movement in order to foster external pressure. Bridge-building has taken a number of forms including consultation mechanisms, information sharing and, in some cases, resourcing the women's movement. A comment by a femocrat from New Zealand, quoted by Sawer, neatly captures femocrats' understanding that achieving feminist policy goals depends on concerted public action in support of these goals by the women's movement: 'I don't feel threatened by those women outside who say that we aren't doing enough'.

In several of the case studies described by Goetz, the iterative relationship between women's units in public administration and women's constituencies in civil society has proven more difficult to establish or exploit. Women's NGOs often demonstrate a reluctance to become too closely associated with WID/Gender and Development (GAD) bureaucrats, which in itself reflects a healthy concern about retaining autonomy, but makes strategic collaboration difficult. Again, it is useful to locate such concerns in the broader history of state–civil society relations. Women's groups, particularly national umbrella organizations, have been vulnerable to political co-optation. In several countries, the energy of the women's movement was largely co-opted by political parties and channelled into the liberation movements of the 1970s and 1980s. More recently, as Goetz argues, the WID/GAD agenda has been used by dominant political parties as a means either of demonstrating their progressive attitudes to the international community or of reinforcing their political support base to include women's constituencies. These factors, in addition to the visibility of wives or female relatives of national leaders in high political positions, have led to a certain wariness about mainstream politics and party-linked WID units or women's associations.

Similarly, femocrats who are career civil servants and have not therefore 'cut their teeth' in the women's movement are often viewed with suspicion by those on the outside. An example cited in Sawer's chapter is instructive. During the 1980s, relations between the Australian women's movement and the Office of the Status of Women reached a low point when an economist, without a background in the women's movement, headed the Office and was perceived by outsiders to have capitulated on key policy issues. Conversely, feminist activists who move into the bureaucracy are often accused of co-optation (Sawer and Groves, 1994b). The migration of the leaders of the women's movement into the state can also have the effect of decimating the women's movement, as was observed in Chile after the downfall of Pinochet (Waylen, 1995) and more recently, in post-apartheid South Africa (Meer, 1997), thus undermining the political base for internal gender advocacy.

At the same time, the perception that femocrats have little legitimacy within state institutions can also impact negatively on insider–outsider relations. In Morocco, for example, where women's policy machinery is the least developed amongst the countries described in this volume, the women's movement seems to bypass women in public administration and to work primarily on the outside or through alliances with political parties. In fact, the WID/GAD bureaucratics within government departments mentioned in the chapter by Goetz are not even referred to in Naciri's chapter, reinforcing the view that in Morocco they are not perceived by the women's movement as key players. Overall, then, the chapters in this volume point to the importance of strong external women's constitutencies to support internal gender policy advocacy; at the same time they depict the complex and often mutually distrustful nature of relations between insiders and outsiders, a theme we will explore further.

Instrumentalism and co-optation

Several of the chapters in this volume reflect on the issues of co-optation and instrumentalism which are inevitably raised when feminists make public policy claims—either as femocrats working 'inside' mainstream bureaucracies, or even as activists/scholars sitting outside the policy establishment but engaging with it through advocacy work that takes their discursive politics into the public arena. In many instances femocrats and activists alike have tended to make the tactical choice of framing their policy goals in universalist—rather than confrontational— terms. They have demonstrated positive spin-offs from their policy recommendations in order to increase the appeal of their campaign to a broader public and to press their claims successfully against rival claimants. As Katzenstein puts it, 'feminist interest groups are often very word conscious, usually out of calculated instrumentality as to what phraseologies will "work"' (1995:36). A cursory glance at WID's short history would show that a dominant theme in its advocacy has been to highlight the 'high pay-offs of investing in women' (Goetz, 1994; Razavi and Miller, 1995a). The phrase coined by the *Human Development Report* (UNDP, 1995:1), 'development, if not engendered, is endangered' succinctly captures the type of 'win–win scenario' that WID advocates have been promoting.

9

This strategy, however, takes on a particularly problematic turn in the context of the economic rationalist arguments that have dominated national and international policy agendas over the past two decades. As several of the contributors to this volume observe, with the growing influence of the neo-liberal philosophy which is inherently opposed to policy interventionism aimed at achieving social equity, feminist policy advocates have been persuaded to make a range of instrumental arguments that link gender equity to more 'legitimate' policy concerns, such as growth and market efficiency. Razavi looks at a new genre of feminist scholarship/advocacy that engages with mainstream economists on their own terms using neo-classical efficiency discourse. Many of the demands that have been raised traditionally by equal rights activists as human rights issues, are now re-framed as 'gender-based distortions' (to parallel the neo-classical obsession with 'price distortions') causing allocative inefficiency. Discrimination against women in land and credit markets, for example, is constructed as a 'gender-based market distortion' because resources are not free to go to those who can make best economic use of them (Palmer, 1991). Similarly, Sawer discusses the temptation on the part of femocrats in Australia to justify even basic human rights issues, such as domestic violence, in terms of its economic costs. Arguments like these, their advocates suggest, may be 'heard' more readily by those bent on promoting economic growth and removing market distortions than would equity-based discourses. But are some critical items on the feminist agenda lost in the process of making this political choice?

The contributors to this volume provide divergent interpretations of instrumentalism and its consequences. A critical understanding of instrumental strategies is voiced by both Goetz and Mayoux. The reframing of gender equity concerns in terms of social and economic efficiency gains, they argue, has the effect of de-politicizing the issue and runs the risk of making women more perfectly exploitable for development. As it has been argued elsewhere, the tendency to highlight the usefulness (for development) of investing in women can mean an intensification of women's work-loads as the onus shifts to them to extend their unpaid work as feeders, healers, and teachers of children to include the provision of basic services to the community (Kandiyoti, 1990; Goetz, 1994).

Some of the other contributors, however, adopt a more agnostic approach. Razavi argues that in the world of 'real'—as opposed to 'abstract'—politics, strategic alliances, compromises, and instrumental arguments are not aberrations; they are part of the everyday reality that constitutes feminist politics worldwide and have allowed gender concerns to be brought into bureaucracies immured intractably in particular procedural and cognitive mind sets—albeit not always in their purest form. The feminist effort to re-define the meaning of 'efficiency' along lines that can encompass items on the WID/GAD agenda can be seen as an attempt to subvert the neo-liberal agenda using its own tools. As Nancy Fraser aptly observes, policymaking institutions tend to depoliticize certain matters by economizing them: 'the issues in question here are cast as impersonal market imperatives, or as "private" ownership prerogatives, or as technical problems for managers and planners, all in contradistinction to political matters' (1989:168). Seen in this light, the struggle over the meaning of concepts like 'efficiency' and 'market distortions' politicizes the supposedly neutral (and technical) space occupied by economics, and turns it into a key terrain of political struggle.

But it is not just the 'technical' discourse of economics that feminists have sought to reinterpret and reformulate. Feminists—both lay and religious—have also been actively engaged in the reinterpretation of religious texts and doctrines. In several Muslim countries where women's civil and political rights have been repeatedly infringed under the feeble pretext that equal rights is a Western import, a critical site of feminist struggle has been to reinterpret the Koran and the *Shari'a* (Islamic law) in an effort to rupture the monopoly that patriarchal institutions have thus far exercised over the interpretation of religious texts (Mernissi, 1991). In her analysis of Moroccan feminist politics, Naciri sees an important role for feminist researchers who seek to show that an alternative interpretation of the Koran is not only possible but also desirable in order to bring Islam up to date with the exigencies of the contemporary world. Similarly, within the American Catholic Church, feminists have created a strong counterdiscourse in response to the words, rituals, and symbols that emanate from the Vatican (Katzenstein, 1995).

A more general point about the feminist concern with instrumentalism, as Naciri reminds us, is that women are not 'instruments'. In Morocco, for example, women have used education to pursue their own agendas in ways that were not necessarily expected or desired by nationalists who initially advocated female education on highly instrumental grounds. Along similar lines, Sawer illustrates how an instrumental interest in women's votes was exploited by femocrats to obtain large childcare commitments from the Labor Party in Australia before the 1984 and 1993 federal elections. In both instances the instrumentalist policies and strategies of decision-makers (often male) have been confounded by women who, either as individuals or in an organized manner, have pursued their own agendas and priorities.

Nevertheless, the tension between wanting to live up to feminist ideals and having to appeal to a wider public is one that both feminist activists and practitioners confront on a daily basis. In some instances these political actors have been able to increase the appeal of their campaign to a broader public by deliberately choosing universalist discourses, but without compromising the feminist goals for which they are striving. In other words, instrumentalist discourses need not automatically lead to co-optation and a watering down of feminist demands. An example from feminist strategies in the US during the 1980s when the antifeminist backlash was at its worst clarifies this point:

Despite the intrinsic radicalness of the feminization of power concept, the Feminist Majority have been able to package the idea as a liberal concern with equality. The effectiveness of this liberal packaging has been the true genius of

11

the Feminist Majority ... The undertones of policy overhaul and radical change in the way society is structured are to be found in the Feminist Majority literature, but only if one is really looking for them. As a result the Feminist Majority have clearly been able to combine an appeal to both liberal and radical sections within the populace (cited in Spalter-Roth and Schreiber, 1995:118).

Rethinking the insider–outsider dynamics

A number of forces gathering momentum in recent years—the increasing permeability of national boundaries and the consequent weakening of the state, as well as the growing importance of civil society organizations operating at both national and international levels—are changing the parameters within which *insiders* and *outsiders* operate. On the one hand, as discussed below, the growing prominence of the 'international women's movement', underpinned by a wide range of formal and informal mechanisms at the international level, provides greater opportunities for enforcing state accountability to its female constituents. At the same time North–South tensions complicate the task of national women's movements in using these international linkages to strengthen their position *vis-à-vis* the state. On the other hand, the weakening and ideological discrediting of the state has created unrealistic expectations of what the 'NGO sector' is capable of delivering—particularly to women. As we see below, a better recognition of the institutionalized male bias within many NGOs, and of the implausibility of substituting the leading role of the state (in mobilizing resources and setting standards for major social service and development programmes) with patchy and unco-ordinated NGO services, highlight the importance of continued feminist engagement with the state.

The international women's movement and globalization

Many of the chapters in this volume refer to the role played by the international women's movement in getting gender issues on the global agenda, both in relation to the general principles affirmed in international human rights' instruments and the commitments emerging out of the main UN conferences of the past two decades. Chapters by Goetz and Sawer explore the way in which women's organizations can strategically exploit governments' international commitments. For example, when governments ratify international legislation or express support for principles agreed upon at UN world conferences, they set themselves up for international scrutiny and for comparison with other nations. Since most countries wish to protect their reputations *vis-à-vis* the international community, femocrats are able to use this sensitivity both to promote gender equity at the international level and to press their own governments to implement relevant international obligations. A recent analysis of NGO activity at UN conferences also indicates that NGOs take advantage of the ease of access to senior government officials at these international events and use the opportunity to pursue their on-going domestic lobbying as well as to influence their government's position in conference negotiations (Krut, 1997)—a point that Sawer's discussion on the Australian efforts at the Fourth World Conference on Women, held in Beijing appears to confirm.

Contributions to this volume thus illustrate how the intersection of international and domestic pressure and networking has advanced the feminist agenda within different institutional contexts. Despite the diversity of the institutions discussed here—from Southern NGOs (Mayoux) and states (Goetz), to Northern states (Sawer) and international organizations (Miller)—the instruments used for promoting change have been remarkably uniform. Mayoux, for example, refers to the 'convergence' in language and approach to gender issues evident in the work of NGOs, governments and multilateral institutions. This is perhaps an indication of the strength of the international women's movement in setting norms and in providing a medium for interaction, negotiation, and the exchange of lessons across national boundaries. The uniformity of approach, however, begs the question of how far there is a uni-directional flow of information and ideas from the North to the South. A case in point is the term 'gender' which, as Goetz observes, derives from an Anglo-American understanding of the social construction of gender difference and fails to translate easily into other languages.

On the issue of interlinkages among different levels of feminist activity, Miller's chapter considers the impact of the international women's movement and supportive bilateral donors on the way gender issues have been taken up in selected multilateral organizations and are reflected in the programmes these organizations support in developing countries. The chapter by Goetz confirms that the international development community has played an important role in supporting and resourcing national-level gender initiatives. The influence of external pressure, she argues, including that from multilateral organizations, has served a useful purpose in the absence of strong national women's constituencies and/or of national resources for gender and development activities. Mayoux's chapter indicates that funding from external donors—multilateral and bilateral organizations and international non-governmental organizations (INGOs)—has also played a role in supporting the efforts of national and local NGOs to make governments more responsive to women's needs.

At the same time, several chapters in this volume suggest that a donor-driven WID/GAD agenda may have adverse long-term implications for the legitimacy of gender issues at the national level. Chapters by Goetz and Naciri refer to ambiguities over commitment to a feminist agenda in contexts where governments take up gender issues primarily to demonstrate their progressive attitudes to the international community and/or in response to financial incentives provided by foreign donors. Reliance on external resourcing also raises problems of sustainability once funding is cut back. More importantly, external funding lends to the idea that the feminist agenda embodied in activities promoted by international development organizations is a foreign import, thereby stigmatizing and undermining efforts of indigenous women's movements. The problem is wider than government accusations of 'cultural imperialism'. As the chapter by Goetz suggests, WID bureaucrats express frustration at the lack of 'national ownership' over the WID/GAD agenda, implying that it is imposed by Northern donors and often fails to reflect the realities of women's lives in a particular country context. A striking example of the lack of fit between donor approaches to WID/GAD and local realities is the focus on small-scale and informal sector income-generating projects found in the activities of the Bureau of Women's Affairs in Jamaica. Income-generating projects may be popular with donors but seem out of place in a country with extremely high rates of female participation in formal employment.

The lack of 'national ownership' over the WID/GAD agenda raises the related issue of North–South divides in feminism, particularly the claim that the feminist agendas of Northern donors reflect only the concerns of Northern feminists. Since the 1970s there have been tensions between feminists in the North and South on how the problem of women in development should be conceptualized. Women of the South have been instrumental, though not alone, in framing women's search for equity and social justice within an analysis of the unequal political and economic structures within which women were located (Beneria and Sen, 1981; Sen and Grown, 1988; Elson and Pearson, 1981). Through a structuralist analysis of class and gender relations, attention has been drawn to the highly varied, and often polarizing, implications of development, especially in the context of the spread of the global market economy. As described elsewhere, this contrasted sharply with the liberal feminist quest for formal equality with men and the WID preoccupation with integrating women into market-led development (Kabeer, 1994; Razavi and Miller, 1995a). Chapters in this volume (particularly that by Razavi) suggest that this tension continues to characterize current feminist approaches to gender and development. North–South tensions are likely to continue to manifest themselves as long as the development policies pursued by Northern institutions are seen to perpetuate structural inequalities between the North and the South. North–South tensions are also fuelled by 'identity' politics, which remain a powerful factor in shaping the relations between Northern and Southern NGOs.

Mayoux (in this volume) observes that, in working with women from the South, Northern INGOs have learned to avoid assuming a common agenda. Where commonalities of interest can be identified—for example, around issues concerning women's human rights—shared agendas for action have been agreed and form part of the INGOs' programmes in the South. Even those wary of the influence Northern perspectives exercise over the international agenda point to the importance of finding common ground for advocacy work—with the caveat that differences need to be recognized and handled in a positive way (Jain, 1996; Ronquillo-Nemenzo, 1996). Networks and alliances established in connection with the recent UN world conferences (UNCED, the Vienna Conference on Human Rights, the Social Summit, ICPD, and Beijing) indicate the tremendous potential for solidarity and united action by the international women's movement (Jain, 1996).

Gita Sen (1996:4) refers to this process as the 'globalization of feminist politics', and argues that the weakening of the nation state and globalization provide new possibilities for political mobilization and global action around women's rights. One example she gives concerns the recent debate on reproductive and sexual rights, which worked itself from the local or national to the global level. This made it possible to clarify and expand understandings in a more inclusive manner and to embrace 'not only the commonality but also the diversity of women's concerns worldwide'. The expanded meanings—affirming women's rights to control their bodies and to express female sexuality—influenced the discourse on reproductive and sexual rights in the UN conferences in Cairo and Beijing and were reflected in the official documents emerging from these events.

Sen's analysis suggests that real exchange of ideas and information between Northern and Southern feminists is possible. A survey of NGOs active in recent UN conferences suggests a similar conclusion. The findings indicate that many NGOs attend these international events, not only to influence governments, but also to influence other NGOs, and define linkages with other NGOs as their major success stories. Their strategy has been two-pronged: to learn as much as possible about the issues; and to lobby larger, Northern NGOs with better and more effective access to funding and to sympathetic governments (Krut, 1997). Although the chapters in this volume diverge over the extent to which the global feminist agenda represents an equal exchange of ideas among constituent groups of the international women's movement, they tend to support the thesis that globalization presents new opportunities to be seized in making the process more inclusive.

Participation, decentralization and NGOs

'Participatory', or 'bottom-up', development is not a new item on the development agenda. Interest in 'participatory approaches' has nevertheless been rekindled in recent years and major donor organizations have taken steps to change their centralized top-down working procedures, in some cases by working more intensively through NGOs. In many countries the political transition from military dictatorships to pluralist and democratic political set-ups has provided the setting for the emergence of an active and vibrant civil society, including women's groups and NGOs. Also influential at this juncture has been the shrinkage of state resources and the ideological discrediting of bureaucratized state services (especially in the poorer countries), which in some instances has meant that NGOs are the last option for meeting needs previously considered to be the responsibility of the state (Wolfe, 1994). A consensus thus seems to be emerging which confirms the relative advantages of participatory approaches, and of NGOs as agents most capable of realizing the assumed advantages.[8] Not surprisingly, the optimism regarding NGOs' abilities to solve major social problems in an efficient, participatory and innovative manner has been questioned by some of those on the outside, as well as by some NGOs themselves.

One of the implicit assumptions in this consensus, about which there has been much recent controversy, is that through participatory approaches women are more likely to be *heard*, and also the needs that *they* identify are more likely to be met (Jackson, 1996; Kabeer, 1996a; IDS Bulletin, 1997). And following from that, given the assumed advantages of NGOs in carrying out participatory work—their greater flexibility in reaching the poor and the socially marginalized, and their innovativeness—they are seen as potentially more responsive to women's needs and also more likely to challenge underlying gender inequalities. In other words, the assumption seems to be that NGOs, unlike other development organizations, do not confront institutionalized forms of male bias, centralized decision-making procedures, or an over-reliance on standardized solutions. In addition to the chapter by Mayoux, which deals extensively with the politics of participatory development in the NGO sector, several other chapters in this volume provide insights into the different dimensions of this complex set of issues.

Any assessment of NGOs will have to begin with Mayoux's reminder that the NGO sector is large, diverse, and changing rapidly. Moreover, the category of organizations generally referred to by the acronym NGO overlaps with interest-group organizations, issue-oriented organizations, and religious movements (Wolfe, 1994). In fact many of the presumed advantages attributed to NGOs, in particular their more participatory credentials, seem to be based partly on the frequent inclusion of small local grassroots membership organizations (GROs) within the definition of NGOs. It is nevertheless notable that a number of NGOs have been at the forefront of developing participatory methodological techniques—including 'gender needs assessments' and Participatory Rural Appraisal (PRA)—which enable women and other marginalized groups to voice their choices, perceptions, and needs. To assume, however, that participatory techniques will automatically give 'voice' to those who have been hitherto excluded through complex forms of social inequality and discrimination seems unduly optimistic.

As Jackson has argued, 'For women who are excluded from dominant world views and male vocabularies (Ardener, 1975) it is not wise to assume that they can, or will, simply express their priorities as PRA assumes' (1996:500). Mayoux draws attention to the nature of gender (and class) politics at the grassroots level, which tend to constrain the ability of women—poor women in particular—to publicly express their needs and interests, especially in group situations. Even where some grassroots organizations have made a considerable effort to create the space to enlist poor women's views, the forms and aims of women's participation have been ultimately determined by male priorities through a process of co-optation.

While populist claims about representing poor women's voices through participatory research methods have to be approached with caution, it would be equally problematic to assume that women cannot voice their true demands. As Mayoux points out, while women tend to internalize the stereotypes of ideal womanly and feminine behaviour and express them in initial consultative meetings (especially in the presence of men), these may not be as representative of their interests as those expressed after women have had time to reflect or think, or once they have greater awareness of other options. This nuanced understanding of the politics of communication which draws attention to the context-specficity of verbal exchanges between 'us' (the practitioner/researcher) and 'them' (the subjects of PRA) confirms the point made by Kabeer, namely that participatory assessment, like any other research tool, is as gender-blind or as gender-aware as its practitioner (1996a).

Participatory methods of information-generation, even if 'properly' implemented, will have little impact on policy design unless there are also participatory structures through which grassroots constituencies and field staff can influence policy decision-making. The problem of geographical and social distance between the 'grassroots' and the centres of decision-making is particularly acute in the case of INGOs. In many of these large INGOs, like the multilateral agencies described by Miller, the main move towards increasing participation has taken the form of regional decentralization to INGO offices overseas and partner NGOs.

Does decentralization bode well for the representation of women's interests within the policymaking process? Decentralization in the context of multilateral organizations has been driven in part by the realization that national contexts and national priorities have tended to be inadequately reflected in development assistance. In response, organizations like the UNDP and the ILO are taking major steps to decentralize further their operations. Miller, however, raises questions about whether strong system-wide WID/gender procedures are in place to ensure that field structures will be responsive to gender issues, and whether there is enough national-level commitment to the WID/gender mandate to keep the issue on the agenda.

Some of the same questions seem to be relevant to INGOs undergoing decentralization. According to institutional insiders, in the short term, at least, the process of organizational decentralization seems to have slowed down the implementation of gender policy in some of the larger INGOs. Whether there will be positive spin-offs in the long term, in the form of increased grassroots participation in decision-making, is hard to predict. A number of factors are nevertheless likely to affect the outcome of these on-going efforts to increase grassroots participation in policy design. Most crucially, the pressures of bureaucratic growth (scaling-up), the emphasis on speedy delivery, and the competition for external funding are all likely to reduce the incentives for carrying out participatory methods of needs assessment and planning (which tend to be time- and resource-consuming), while they strengthen the incentives for imposing standardized, 'blue-print' solutions. Moreover, as convincingly argued by Mayoux, increasing women's (or men's) participation in decision-making does not always lead to the emergence of an explicit or coherent strategy for change; nor can it be assumed to be unambiguously beneficial or 'efficient' for the women concerned.

Another critical question that emerges from several contributions to this volume is the potential tension between the service delivery and advocacy roles of NGOs, and the important part played by funding agents in fostering the former and muting the latter tendencies. There has been widespread controversy over donor-driven reform strategies that involve NGOs in the delivery of social services, in particular regarding implications for social sector provisioning, the role of the state, and the social dimensions of citizenship (Vivian, 1995). Approaching the problem from the vantage point of poor women, Mayoux voices the concern that some of the current policy interest in NGOs, and the increasing funding at their disposal, may be merely substituting one inadequate and unresponsive system of service and welfare provision for women (i.e. the state system) with another system which is even less well-resourced, less co-ordinated, and even more dependent on women's own unpaid 'participatory' labour input. This is a far cry from the oft-mentioned claim that as 'conduits of local democracy', NGOs have the potential to ensure that institutions become more accountable and more responsive to the needs of ordinary people (Clark, 1991).

In her discussion of participatory efforts in the World Bank, which has involved increasing collaboration with NGOs, Siddharth (1995) argues that thus far there has been a tendency for NGOs (both domestic and international) to act as intermediaries implementing projects, rather than policy advocates challenging policy priorities, influencing resource allocation and changing Bank practice. There are signs, however, of NGOs taking on a greater policy advocacy role. It is also in this latter sense—as policy advocates or 'adversaries' *vis-à-vis* the state and private sector institutions—that Elson (1992) sees a critical place for women's NGOs in bringing about real policy reform and resource allocation in women's favour. This is very much the lobbying mode in which 'peak bodies' such as the National Action Committee on the Status of Women (NAC) in Canada and the Coalition of Actively Participating Organizations of Women (CAPOW) in Australia function (Sawer). Other examples of attempts by the state to enlist the views of women's organizations in important matters of national concern emerge from Uganda, where an unprecedented process of consultation with women was put in place in 1990 at the initiative of the WID/gender machinery, to collect their views on the country's constitution (Goetz).

Notwithstanding the important policy advocacy role that women's organizations and NGOs can play, the choice between lobbying and service delivery cannot be seen as unproblematic. As Mayoux points out, in some organizations (e.g. SEWA) there is emerging disquiet amongst the grassroots women members about the amount of time and organizational resources spent by the leadership on issues which are seen as being of no direct and immediate benefit to them. In some Southern NGOs the tension over priorities is seen in class terms—as one between urban middle class women and poor women—where the latter group seem to prefer practical interventions (such as tube-wells) as opposed to gender advocacy and lobbying. Ultimately the gains made by the international women's movement through lobbying and political action at the global level—as has been described by Sen (see above)—will have to take into account the tensions that this is causing within some organizations.

2

Becoming multilingual:
the challenges of feminist policy advocacy*

SHAHRA RAZAVI

Most observers would agree that since the beginning of the United Nations Decade for Women (1976) gender issues have become more visible within a wide range of policymaking institutions. As several chapters in this volume demonstrate, new bureaucratic structures have been set up with an explicit mandate to bring women's interests into the policymaking process. A great deal of effort has gone into rescuing gender from the 'project trap' and demonstrating its relevance to fiscal, monetary, and trade policies. In response to a range of pressures from the international and national women's movements, a growing number of development agencies are beginning to raise gender issues at the programme level (Elson and McGee, 1995), and several Northern and Southern country governments have taken steps to include gender considerations in their national development plans and strategic economic policies.

Yet moving gender from the margins of development practice to the centre (or near centre) has been a major challenge for all those who have been at the forefront of this effort—whether as activists, scholars, or internal advocates.[1] Feminist accounts of institutional politics document the dogged resistance that internal advocates encountered as they struggled to bring gender into organizations with mandates that hardly mesh with gender equity or with bureaucratic procedures that border on inflexibility, and how they had to rely on the co-operation of bureaucrats (often male) who seemed to be at best indifferent, but more often hostile to what they perceived to be irrelevant political incursions into their professional boundaries and personal lives (Goetz, 1992; Kardam, 1991; Staudt, 1985; Sawer, 1996). The accounts speak of struggles made and battles won, as well as of low ebbs and severe constraints that seem to question the very *raison d'être* of the internal advocate in the bureaucracy. In the process strategic alliances and compromises have had to be made to ensure 'least worst scenarios', with the inevitable outcome that the content of gender policy has been very often watered down—some would say irrevocably.

The analysis of gender policy discourses in this chapter is set within the context of a changing national and international political economy. Ironically, by the

*Useful comments were made on an earlier draft by Nilüfer Cajatay, Naila Kabeer and Carol Miller.

time gender policy advocacy had picked up and was in full force, the Golden Age of Keynesian economics had given way to a neo-liberal philosophy inherently opposed to all kinds of interventionism because of its faith in markets as self-optimizing mechanisms.[2] Not surprisingly, the arguments of gender advocates for a level playing field brought them into an uneasy relationship with neo-liberal advocates of market-led growth. Part of their response was to make a range of instrumental arguments that linked gender equity to more 'legitimate' policy concerns, such as market efficiency, growth, and human resource development—a strategy that has been criticized persistently by feminist scholars (Goetz, 1994; Jackson, 1996; Kandiyoti, 1990; Moser, 1989). The other part was to make alliances with like-minded internal advocates who seemed to be pursuing parallel objectives: social development, poverty alleviation, and environmental sustainability.

By the early 1990s some distinct changes in the dominant paradigm were discernible. As the complexity of the adjustment process became evident, simple market prescriptions were looking increasingly anomalous. The tone of mainstream development discourse had mellowed: poverty alleviation and social dimensions were once again on the development agenda, creating a more conducive policy environment for gender advocacy. It is within this changing discursive context that the feminist critiques of the 'poverty trap' are beginning to be heard: an argument that sees poverty analyses and policies as not necessarily appropriate for tackling gender issues because women's subordination is not caused by poverty (Jackson, 1996). Gender disadvantage, they argue, works on a different axis and has a different logic from poverty.

Our starting point in this chapter is that sensitivity to gender issues in development has been conceptualized in a number of different ways; some of these have been captured in Moser's (1989) schema under the labels of 'equity', 'poverty', 'efficiency' and so forth. Only certain strands of feminist thinking have been taken up by policymaking institutions, while others have been neglected or abandoned. This selective take-up of gender presents useful insights into the way development institutions work. It also hints at the political dilemmas facing feminist advocates: entering the mainstream entails making alliances and compromises, and modifying one's agenda and language. Some feminist critics have argued that 'the game is not worth the candle', in other words, that what has been lost in the process of assimilation has been so central to the feminist agenda, that there seems to be little reason to pursue the same strategies any further.

This chapter argues that while the criticisms of instrumentalism are valid and potentially useful for the internal advocate, they show little understanding of the constraints within which gender policy is formulated; the discourses emanating from policymaking institutions are, in part at least, the outcome of political manoeuvres by internal advocates who seek to highlight the relevance of gender to their host organizations in a language that is familiar and accepted. In other words, the specific goals, procedures and culture/ideology of each organization

21

shape the way in which a new issue is taken up. One should not, however, see the response to a new issue in deterministic terms, since the internal advocate does exercise a degree of choice in this process.

Policy advocates use both new information and political clout to promote a new issue. They exercise choice by deciding what kind of bargaining and discursive strategies to use to bring about change. But as Kardam reminds us, 'they do not choose the circumstances in which they make decisions, rather they intervene within a particular context' (Kardam, 1991:6). Three critical sets of issues are likely to impact on the way institutions respond to outside pressures for change: firstly, the organization's degree of independence from external pressures, determined by its governance structure and accountability mechanisms; secondly, organizational mandate, ideology and procedures; and thirdly, the existence and capacity of internal advocates (Kardam, 1993, 1995). 'Thus policy outcomes are best seen as the result of an interaction between individual choice and structural conditions' (Kardam, 1991:6).

The development arena includes organizations with widely varying mandates and cultures. The discursive strategies adopted by internal advocates in one context may not necessarily be the most appropriate for other institutional settings. Comparative analyses of international organizations reveal that these discursive strategies are highly context specific. As Miller (Chapter 6) argues, while the dominance of the economics discourse within the World Bank may have made it imperative for gender advocates in that institution to make their arguments for policy attention to women in terms of economic efficiency, the strategies of gender advocates in the ILO have not been shaped by the same set of constraints. In general, ILO's social justice mandate has provided greater scope for advocates to draw attention to women workers' concerns on the grounds of gender justice and equity.

The role of the internal advocate is thus inevitably conservative, as she works within the constraints posed by her institution. Her work can only become transformative if and when institutional outsiders—activists and scholars—through political pressure and/or new knowledge, facilitate a re-definition of the organization's strategies for achieving its mandate, thereby stretching open those boundaries. As such, the roles of the practitioners and scholars/activists are different, but complementary. What is needed is more tolerance of the different strategies of feminist advocacy, and a clearer recognition of the fact that policy discourses are context specific. Moreover, a radical alternative to these ameliorative measures, with all the compromises that they entail, would be a strategy of disengagement (Stienstra, 1994)—an option that few would consider advisable given the significant influence that mainstream institutions continue to exert over the policy process.

Gender discourses in the development context

This section does not aim to provide an exhaustive account of how gender issues have been conceptualized, nor will it explain the many phases of engagement between WID advocates and the development establishment, since that story has already been told by others (Moser, 1989; Kabeer, 1994). Our discussion has a more limited objective, namely to identify and assess the recent manifestations of two dominant strands of GAD thinking which have justified the case for policy attention to women on the grounds of the presumed pay-offs that it will bring for development: increasing growth rates and economic efficiency, and reducing poverty. Before we turn to these recent gender discourses and the charges of instrumentalism levelled against them, a few words on the earlier debates are in order.

Gender policy discourses: the antecedents

Jacquette (1990) makes a useful distinction between three competing criteria for gender justice: equality, merit, and need. All three criteria have been used by feminist advocates in the development context. The equality criteria, embodied in equal rights feminism, has attracted a good deal of scholarly attention as well as being an important force within feminist politics since the early nineteenth century (Banks, 1981). It is the approach that feminist critics of 'efficiency' tend to support because it values equality for intrinsic, rather than instrumental, reasons. It informs the wide range of international legal instruments dealing with women's rights,[3] the work of the various international agencies and commissions dedicated to promoting and monitoring the advancement of women, as well as the recommendations emerging from the international women's conferences.[4] It is a dominant force within the international women's movement, and the philosophical backbone of women's activism for legal rights in many national settings.

A rather different set of arguments can be made if justice is premised on the market conception of merit, linking rewards to productivity; this is also known as the efficiency approach (Moser, 1989). This style of argument has gained increasing prominence over the past two decades in view of the intensified engagement between gender advocates and the parts of the development establishment that speak the economic language (such as the international financial institutions and the technical agencies). Ester Boserup is very often cited as the pioneer whose work legitimized policy attention to women on the grounds of their equal productivity to men. In *Women's Role in Economic Development* (1970) Boserup constructed a new identity for women, presenting them to policymakers as productive agents contributing to development, rather than 'needy' beneficiaries.[5] It was a decade later, however, that the efficiency argument was fully spelt out. Rather than emphasizing the adverse impact of development on women, Rogers (1980) warned of the adverse consequences for development if women were excluded from planners' frameworks—a pertinent concern at a time when there was a sense of growing economic crisis in the Third World (Kabeer, 1994:25). If resources were to be efficiently allocated, then planners could no longer afford to neglect women's productivity. As is argued below,

23

the same strategy is being pursued in the 'gender efficiency' approach put forward by a new generation of feminist economists.

The third criterion identified by Jacquette is need—the discursive path that Boserup consciously avoided. Despite the many counterclaims, there remains a broad consensus on the legitimacy of claims based on need: 'that a society cannot be just if it treats its weakest and poorest members without compassion' (Jacquette, 1990:62). Individuals, groups and policymaking institutions are often influenced by a combination of powerful motives for wanting to alleviate poverty, motives which range from altruistic/humanistic concerns to political fear and even economic self-interest (Saith, 1996). While the motives are complex and contradictory, and the recipients always subject to the whims of the giver, claims based on need have tended to be persuasive. Yet for a variety of reasons WID advocates like Boserup went to great lengths to distinguish their approach from the 'welfare approach', refusing to resort to the need/poverty criteria.[6] There were other voices making needs-based arguments for gender justice, however, in what has become known as the 'anti-poverty approach to women' (Buvinic, 1983; Moser, 1989).

Early on, Buvinic (1983) made the observation that feminist policy advocates had to resort to poverty arguments because the emphasis on 'poor women', and by implication poor men, made the feminist agenda less threatening to male bureaucrats and programme implementers who were resistant to feminist incursions into the bureaucracy. The anti-poverty approach was thus a 'toned-down version' of the equity approach (Buvinic, 1983), or worse, equity stripped of its gender politics (Jackson, 1996). It needs to be noted, however, that the anti-poverty approach became popular at a time when the development paradigm itself was coming to grips with the failures of trickle-down growth strategies and when new initiatives, like the basic needs approach,[7] were taking shape. It thus seems reasonable to argue that the proponents of the anti-poverty approach were using the paradigm shift *strategically* to push forward the feminist agenda, rather than merely reacting to bureaucratic resistance. They were, however, selective in what they adopted from the new development paradigm, focusing for the most part on the productive work of poor women, 'productive employment', and attaching less weight to the other items on the 'basic needs' agenda that were welfare-oriented.

These early WID discourses have been extensively analysed by feminist scholars; the arguments will not be repeated here. A few brief observations should be sufficient to pave the way for discussion of GAD discourses. The first point to note is WID's productivist bias, which goes hand-in-hand with its relegation of welfare, to which reference has already been made. As others have argued, in accepting the liberal feminist argument for equal opportunities in development, WID advocates were also bound into its normative dualisms (Kabeer, 1994:24). While the neglect of the reproductive sphere was an understandable reaction to the way the 'separate spheres' discourse had been used to subordinate women, it nevertheless replicated the tendency of mainstream development policy to prioritize production over human provisioning. No questions were thus raised about men's and women's different degrees of embodiment in the processes of human reproduction and sustenance; how it impacted on their respective productivities; and most critically, what adjustments were demanded of social and economic policies to create a meaningful level playing field. More recently, feminist macro-economists have been able to address this serious pitfall in WID advocacy by providing a gendered understanding of the linkages between the productive and reproductive spheres, and drawing out the implications for growth strategies (Elson, 1991).

Feminist critics have also highlighted the origins of WID advocacy in Northern feminist movements, especially those of the United States. The productivist bias which informed both the efficiency and the anti-poverty approaches, for example, paralleled the concerns of feminist activists in the United States, who in their own national campaigns for equal rights were highlighting women's productive contributions while they downplayed biological differences and the reproductive sphere (where women were assigned primary responsibility). Given the dominance of Northern feminist voices in WID advocacy, it is not surprising that some of their priorities and biases were carried over into the development discourse.

Another pitfall which stemmed from WID's footing in liberal individualism and which was exacerbated by the absence of Southern women's voices was its uncritical assessment of the development process itself. As feminist scholars have pointed out, WID's analysis of women's subordination was superficial and unsystematic; it held planners' prejudices to blame for women's marginalization, rather than delving deeper into the structural factors endogenous to the development process that were working against women (Beneria and Sen, 1981). As we will see later, the critical writings of feminist scholars (from both North and South) and the emergence of a more coherent voice from feminist activists in the South countered many of these shortcomings, and has been formative in the emergence of an alternative strand of feminist policy advocacy which is rooted in a more structuralist understanding of women's subordination within the development process.

Yet despite these severe shortcomings, the new genre of WID scholarship appealed to feminist activists: by linking in to the concerns of development practitioners it raised the profile of women's issues as a serious development concern deserving the attention of mainstream policymakers. In fact, as far as the encounter between feminist advocates and the development establishment was concerned, the verdict by the end of the decade was that both efficiency and anti-poverty arguments had paid off (Buvinic, 1983; Moser, 1989). Synergistic arguments thus seemed to have worked within the development context by making gender issues *relevant* for policymakers: while synergism may not have constituted a solid foundation for scholarship (Jackson, 1993), it was conducive to gender advocacy.[8] The other side of the coin—the costs of assimilation within mainstream institutions—had not yet become clear, a subject to which we will return later.

By the mid-1980s the neo-liberal policy agenda that had come to dominate development discourse and practice presented feminist advocates with a paradoxical situation. On the one hand, the preoccupation with short-term efficiency goals that characterized the first decade of adjustment bluntly revealed the extent to which progress in gender equity is dependent on a conducive macro-policy environment. The outcome was a significant body of feminist research documenting the negative impact of adjustment policies on women. The central plank of the neo-liberal agenda—economic efficiency—was thus shown to be at odds with gender equity, thereby questioning the 'win–win scenario' that underpinned efficiency arguments for gender justice.

On the other hand, given the importance of maintaining communication with those in the policy formulation process, and the enormous rhetorical appeal of the concept of efficiency, some feminist advocates tried to subvert the neo-liberal agenda by using the efficiency discourse rather than abandoning it (Palmer, 1991, 1992), while others sought a more radical re-formulation of 'efficiency' to bring it in line with a conception of development that is human-centred and conducive to gender equity (Elson, 1991, 1995; Beneria, 1995; Sen and Grown, 1988). In the following sections we will be looking at some of the new ground covered by this genre of politicized feminist scholarship.

Gender efficiency: fitting gender into the mainstream

The aim of this section is to look at a new genre of feminist policy advocacy that engages with mainstream economists in the development establishment *on their own terms*—using neo-classical efficiency discourse. It should come as no surprise that these authors, like many others writing in the 1980s and 1990s, have located their analyses in the context of economies undergoing structural adjustment policies. In fact much of the feminist advocacy of the past decade, in both the North and the South, has taken place within the context of structural adjustment/economic restructuring. In the context of the present discussion one needs to bear in mind the political sub-text of writings on gender and adjustment. There are, for example, a number of neo-classical economists for whom gender is an illustration, or a means for understanding the complexities of a far more important process, namely adjustment (Collier, 1989). For others, however, framing gender within neo-classical discourse, above and beyond any merit it may have in enhancing the overall understanding of adjustment, has a political function—namely that of winning over policymakers.

> Adjustment strategies mean that demands for resources must now be supported by persuasion that there will be an economic dividend ... if it can be argued that *gender issues impact on adjustment* at every turn then it might be easier to persuade policy makers to review gender issues at the earliest stage of planning, before options on overall adjustment strategies are closed off and certainly before policy packages are detailed (Palmer, 1992:70; emphasis in original).

26

The point in making this distinction is to place the work of feminist economists like Ingrid Palmer within their proper historical context: the continuation of a political strategy—albeit analytically more sophisticated than earlier attempts—of putting women on the agenda of policymakers by showing how they can contribute to development. While sharing many features with earlier efficiency discourse (like Boserup's), the novelty of this new version of the argument lies in the way it conceptualizes gender using neo-classical tools of analysis (market distortions, factor market rigidities), juxtaposed against an appreciation of intra-household inequalities and bargaining.[9]

What distinguishes this new genre of writing from some of the other commentaries on gender and adjustment is that rather than focusing on how structural adjustment policies have affected the welfare of women and children, their aim is to show how gender biases and rigidities affect adjustment policies, and can ultimately frustrate them.[10] As in the earlier efficiency approach, the tactic is to demonstrate the *relevance* of gender by showing that it impacts on the concerns of policymakers (e.g. growth, adjustment). The other feature that is different in Palmer's approach is that it interrogates current macro-economic policies from within a neo-classical framework: it accepts the concerns of policymakers about 'price distortions' and their negative impact on allocative efficiency, but then goes on to criticize the existing adjustment policies for not going far enough to remove 'gender-based market distortions' which are also causing allocative inefficiency. This is an interesting political move for it attempts to support feminist objectives with the same tools that have often been used against women.[11]

According to Palmer (1991), these gender-based distortions span a wide range of institutions—the state, the market, and the household—and stem from social and cultural biases.[12] For example, women are often discriminated against in land and credit markets, sometimes exacerbated by gender-biased government policies. Discrimination here represents a market distortion because resources are not free to go to those who can make 'best economic use of them' (ibid.:11). 'Women must be able to raise capital as easily as men if capital resources are to be efficiently distributed. Dynamic efficiency is not compatible with non-homgeneity of the capital market' (ibid.:162).

Similarly at the intra-household level, the lavish application of female labour on men's export crops represents economic waste since that labour could have been employed more productively elsewhere (e.g. women's own plots, or enterprises) (ibid.:157). Thus the exchange of resources between husband and wife is neither equitable nor does it represent an efficient allocation of resources. A similar waste of resources results from the burden of reproductive labour that women have to perform—the 'reproductive tax' (ibid.:12). The impact of this 'tax' is to channel part of women's labour to where market forces would not direct it, thereby limiting their capabilities to engage in remunerative work: women's reproductive work thus 'distorts the "production" labour market' (ibid.:163).

27

As is clear from the above examples, Palmer voices many of the issues raised by gender activists working from within an equal rights framework, such as land rights or public support for women's reproductive work, even though they are framed within a neo-classical efficiency discourse. As such, her work provides a bridge between the gender advocacy literature and the neo-classical paradigm that tends to dominate mainstream policy discourses. The strength of her argument, as Elson (1993) notes, is that it presents these demands within a coherent framework that is systematically linked to the design of adjustment policies, as opposed to drawing up an *ad hoc* 'shopping list' of women's demands unrelated to policy objectives. There are, however, a number of problems in Palmer's analysis and style of advocacy which stem from the neo-classical assumptions that underpin it.

While the critique of gender discrimination within private credit markets, for example, appears to be a description of how 'real markets' operate, some of the policy recommendations are framed within the realm of 'abstract markets' which has been extensively problematized by political economists and sociologists (Hewitt de Alcantara, 1993; Mackintosh, 1990). This depiction of markets as gender-neutral cash nexuses also flies in the face of a substantial body of feminist scholarship that documents the pervasive institutionalization of gender hierarchies within markets. Palmer's controversial argument in favour of large-scale commercial agriculture is a case in point. The solution to the under-valuation of women's labour within smallholder agriculture, we are told, is to be found by encouraging female employment in the large-scale commercial sector because it would increase competition between rural labour markets. While the availability of alternative employment opportunities for women can potentially increase their choices (and their intrahousehold bargaining power), to ignore the way in which definitions of labour (female, migrant, skilled, etc.) are built into the way markets operate seems unduly optimistic. Even though a female labourer does not work in a commercial estate in her capacity as 'wife', her labour is nevertheless defined as 'female', thereby carrying her subordinate status with her into the workplace.[13] The literature on female employment both in the commercial agricultural sector and in industrial establishments provides plenty of insight into how social norms about 'femininity', 'women's work' and 'wifely dependence' operate within these so-called impersonal markets to create separate male and female spheres and distinct gender hierarchies (Humphrey, 1987; Mackintosh, 1989). These gender hierarchies are not of course immutable; they can be challenged through persistent political action on the part of the women workers, and relevant institutions (e.g. governments, NGOs, pressure groups). To assume, however, that markets can automatically provide a 'proper costing' of female labour, ignores the need for public action to regulate them socially.[14]

There are similar pitfalls in the suggestion that women's reproductive work should be 'opened up to market forces' in order to be properly valued. As the available evidence on the segmentation of labour markets clearly shows, where components of women's work have been opened up to market forces, this has not necessarily resolved the problems of under-valuation. Very often segmentation is maintained despite the large numbers of women who have entered the labour force, with some occupations becoming characteristically female while others become male; the case of domestic service clearly illustrates how gender hierarchies are reproduced within markets. Moreover, even if some reproductive services could be provided through markets, only a specific category of women (and men) with sufficient purchasing power would be able to access those services—not necessarily those who would need the services most, such as poorer working mothers with a large number of children. As many have argued, markets are seriously limited in their ability to meet human needs: they respond to demand backed by cash, and not to needs alone (A. Sen, 1981; Mackintosh, 1990).

These observations are admittedly of an analytical nature which is not necessarily the most appropriate criterion by which to assess writings with a strong advocacy content. Policy advocacy requires a language that is different from academic discourse—one that is less complex and nuanced, but more bold and appealing to practitioners who want to respond to a number of competing demands. Although it is not easy to judge the impact these arguments are having on their intended interlocutors—mainstream macro-economists in policy-making positions—it seems reasonable to assume that they will be heard more readily than zero-sum equity arguments for gender justice in institutions pursuing a growth/efficiency mandate, and in certain national contexts where feminist advocacy has to take place within the narrow 'developmental' confines defined by a strong state.[15] As organizational theorists remind us, for a new issue like gender to be taken up by an organization it needs to be moulded into a shape that 'fits' the institutional goals, culture, and procedures (Kardam, 1991; Young, 1989).

A number of recent developments seem to support the above assertion. In their assessment of efforts by the Netherlands Directorate General for International Co-operation (DGIS) to integrate a gender perspective into its programme assistance, Elson and McGee recommend an analytical framework which draws on several aspects of Palmer's approach (Elson and McGee, 1995). Taking a gender efficiency focus, they argue, 'has the advantage of focusing on the policy process and the design of policy reforms ... facilitating communication with economists' (ibid.:1991).[16] Similar steps are being taken by the German bilateral aid agency, where internal advocates are using efficiency arguments to show the relevance of gender relations to macro-economic analysis and policy options (Palmer, 1995). At a somewhat different level, analyses of structural adjustment policies along the same lines as Ingrid Palmer (and Paul Collier) appeared in a recent World Bank document entitled *Paradigm Postponed: Gender and economic adjustment in Sub-Saharan Africa* (World Bank, 1993c). While the analysis presented in this document has not been adopted as official Bank policy, the arguments are nevertheless being discussed by some of the economists in the organization.[17]

It is nevertheless noteworthy that even within an institution such as the World Bank, where the organizational mandate and culture are strongly economistic, arguments like these have not been winning the macro-economic battle. One alleged reason for this seems to be the lack of rigorous data to support the assertions that are made; they are thus seen as 'feminist advocacy', rather than 'objective/scientific' arguments backed by facts and figures. As feminist economists have argued, stylized facts and formal models can be very useful in fostering better communication with the mainstream of the economics profession (Cagatay et al., 1995). The 'human capital' arguments for investing in women, as we will see below, have been more effective tools for internal advocacy because they were backed by relatively robust evidence. This is not to deny the well-known resistance of economics to the challenges raised by feminism (Beneria, 1995), nor is it meant to deny the notorious unreliability of statistics and the fact that the insistence upon measuring is often less an appeal to empirical rigour than the expression of an ideology.[18] Rather, the aim is to highlight one of the more obvious hurdles that feminist macro-economists need to overcome before their arguments can be taken up by mainstream institutions.

Creating fit is, however, only one aspect of what the internal advocate has to do; an equally important component of effective policy advocacy is the ability to communicate with, and gain the confidence and support of, constituents outside the institution. Comparative studies of institutional response to gender have highlighted the need for sustained external pressure from an organized women's movement if institutional change is to come about (Goetz and Sawer, Chapters 3 and 5).[19] While internal advocates frequently resort to efficiency-type arguments in order to be heard (by insiders), in-depth analyses of gender machineries also confirm the need for these advocates to establish direct contact with the women's movement—their natural constituents—to strengthen their position and to reaffirm the reasons why they are in the bureaucracy in the first place.

Speaking to activists in the women's movement, however, requires a language that is different from the one used to exhort policymakers to take gender issues on board, and yet there needs to be some continuity between the different discourses that advocates use. As Sawer (Chapter 5) argues, gender policy advocates have been most effective when they have succeeded in bridging that gap. Will the type of advocacy considered here be attractive to national women's movements? In view of the recent experiences that many African countries have had with economic reform and adjustment, how useful a rallying call is the 'market' for women's movements? More controversially, can women activists seriously support a plantation policy in their struggles for gender equity in the rural context, given the likely problems in terms of food security? The advocacy literature of some women's NGOs and networks highlights the wide gulf that divides these two sets of discourses. Straddling the two camps (of activists and policymakers) is admittedly not an easy task, but it seems to be one of the main conditions for effective policy advocacy. In fact the absence of a common language may have been one of the factors holding back the emergence of an insider–outsider alliance of gender advocacy in the World Bank; a number of positive steps are now being taken to address that problem (Miller, Chapter 6).

More fundamentally though, the choice of discourse reflects one's assessment of how far the given policy agenda is conducive to the goals of gender equity. Here we have looked at one approach that attempts to integrate gender concerns within mainstream economic thinking because it sees no 'intrinsic design faults' (Elson, 1993) in the market framework that is being promoted through adjustment programmes. It is an essentially 'integrationist' strategy (Jahan, 1995) which attempts to 'add-on' women to the pre-existing policy agenda. There are, however, other strands of feminist economics that are more sceptical of current adjustment policies and the market frameworks that underpin them, because they consider markets to be inherently polarizing institutions (Beneria, 1995; Elson, 1995; Sen and Grown, 1988). And yet, their more critical strand of advocacy is being heard by parts of the development establishment that pursue more transformative strategies. Even though a significant number of policymakers do adhere to the market ideology, it would be erroneous to assume homogeneity of outlook amongst them. Policymaking institutions are not monolithic, either internally or cross-sectionally. Critical feminist advocates who do not adhere to the neo-classical framework are making alliances with parts of the development establishment that pursue mandates which are inherently more conducive to gender equity. In the process they are exerting pressure on other, more resistant parts of the establishment, thereby stretching open the boundaries for those working on the inside. It can be argued that their work is along more 'transformative' lines (Jahan, 1995). Some strands of gender advocacy which have focused on poverty issues have taken this alternative path.

Gender and poverty: transforming the mainstream?

The late 1980s saw an increasing concern with the social costs of adjustment. Highly influential at this juncture were the empirical studies commissioned by UNICEF (Cornia et al., 1987) which documented the negative impacts of adjustment in poverty and equity terms.[20] Even more significant was the internal political opposition to adjustment-related policies which seemed to threaten their implementation in a number of developing countries. By the early 1990s there were signs of a softening of tone in mainstream development discourse: an acknowledgement of the fact that early adjustment packages had paid insufficient attention to the 'social dimensions', a concern with poverty alleviation as an overriding development priority, and the emergence of a more coherent call for an alternative development paradigm that places human well-being and agency at the centre of the development process (UNDP, 1990b, 1995).[21]

According to observers, gender advocacy has played an important part, along with other forces, in bringing about this shift in development discourse (Köhler, 1995). Some of the feminist critique came from mainstream development institutions, such as UNICEF and IFAD, but Southern women's groups and networks were no less vocal in disputing the wisdom of the macro-economic agenda—through their publications and through their active presence at various national and international fora. In this section we will be looking at some of the prominent strands of gender advocacy that have based their critique on the poverty criterion—highlighting the adverse impacts of mainstream development policies on poor women and, more controversially, portraying women as the 'missing link' in an efficient/low-cost poverty alleviation strategy. The analytical weaknesses of these arguments are discussed here, drawing on critical feedback from feminist scholarship. As poverty alleviation gains a more strategic place in policy analysis and formulation, it becomes imperative for internal advocates to ensure that such critical thinking on the linkages between poverty and gender discrimination is reflected in the policy agendas that emerge from their organizations.

One strand of GAD thinking that has become popular in recent years is the so-called 'human capital argument for investing in women'. It has been embraced and developed most enthusiastically by internal advocates in the World Bank, one of the most coherent statements of it being the Bank's recent policy paper on women (World Bank, 1994a).[22] The arguments are by now fairly well known: female education reduces fertility and averts child mortality, and is the highest return investment in the developing world; spending on the healthcare of adult women aged 15–44 offers the biggest return on healthcare spending for any demographic group of adults; women contribute a larger portion of their incomes to family consumption needs than do men, which makes the productivity and incomes of poor women important for alleviating poverty (World Bank, 1993d, 1994a). Thus the argument is made that 'investing in women is critical for poverty reduction, it speeds economic development by raising productivity and promoting the more efficient use of resources; it produces significant social returns, improving child survival and reducing fertility; and it has considerable intergenerational payoffs' (World Bank, 1994a:22).

Another strand of thinking that has become highly visible in debates on poverty is the 'feminization of poverty' discourse; this style of advocacy is more directly needs-based whereas the human capital thesis combines efficiency and poverty criteria. The arguments which constitute the 'feminization of poverty' discourse are voiced by a variety of policymaking institutions, both multilateral and bilateral, as well as NGOs and women's organizations and networks. A number of recurring hypotheses can be identified in their writings: firstly, that women are over-represented amongst the poor; secondly, that the incidence of poverty amongst women has been rising at a faster rate than that amongst men. A third related feature is the combined argument that an increasing number of households have become female-headed (over time) and that the poorest households are more likely to be headed by a woman than a man.[23]

Some of the most influential and transformative feminist advocacy that has emerged in response to the neo-liberal onslaught—with a focus on poverty and to some extent overlapping with the feminization of poverty discourse—has been voiced by the DAWN network of women activists in the South. In the late 1980s, in what was to become one of the most oft-cited feminist advocacy documents, Gita Sen and Caren Grown (1988), laid out the main contours of an alternative policy agenda that was human-centred and conducive to the needs of the poor in general, and of poor women in particular. The document provided a general critique of open export-oriented development strategies which place the 'drive for profits before the needs of people', highlighting their polarizing outcomes in both class and gender terms, and arguing for a re-orientation of macro-economic and sectoral policies so that meeting the basic needs of the poor, and poor women in particular, becomes the principal focus of planning (Sen and Grown, 1988:83). The call for alternatives to the current model of development has been reiterated in other DAWN documents as well (e.g. DAWN, 1994), and stems from the view that there are intrinsic gender (and class) biases in the current models of development, i.e. that the process of capital accumulation, as currently practised, is neither neutral nor benign; it is inherently hierarchical and polarizing.

Both strands of gender poverty discourse have been extensively analysed by feminist scholars, who have exposed their empirical, methodological, and analytical weaknesses. The 'human capital' thesis, for example, has been criticized for its reliance on exaggerated claims: regarding the assumed synergies between women's control of income and child welfare, some recent research (Hopkins *et al.*, 1994) suggests that it might be the particular characteristics of women's incomes (e.g. their seasonality and irregular nature) rather than women's altruism *per se* that can explain gender differences in expenditure patterns. Moreover, insofar as the synergy relies on maternal altruism, the benefits to women themselves are highly questionable (Jackson, 1996). Similarly, regarding the oft-cited education/fertility nexus, while female education appears to be significant in explaining fertility differentials in 13 of the 24 countries included in the World Fertility Survey, it has little or no effect in the other 11—not an insignificant proportion of 'perverse' cases (Thomas, 1991 cited in Kabeer, 1996b). Moreover, the synergies between female autonomy and fertility reduction are far from universal (Kabeer, 1996a).

The 'feminization of poverty' discourse likewise falls into serious empirical and methodological traps. As it has been repeatedly pointed out, the fact that a household is female-headed cannot be regarded as if it were synonymous with gender vulnerability and poverty, for which it is very often taken as a proxy (Jackson, 1996; Moore, 1994; Saith, 1996). The IFAD study on the state of world rural poverty, for example, assumes that all women in female-headed households are poor (Jazairy, *et al.*, 1992:274, Table 9.2). But female-headed households (FHHs) constitute a highly differentiated social and economic group, formed through a variety of mechanisms, such as through male out-migration, death, or absenteeism. Not all FHHs are poor. Much depends on the independent rights/access to productive assets and employment that women enjoy, which varies greatly from region to region. Sometimes the characteristics that account for their poverty arise from their unfavourable demographic attributes (e.g. dependency ratios, life-cycle factors) rather than the gender of the head as is often assumed (Saith, 1996). Time-series comparisons, like those undertaken by the IFAD study, are particularly problematic given the tendency for *de facto* FHHs to be included in more recent surveys while they were excluded from earlier ones—a tendency that exaggerates the rate of increase of FHHs and of female poverty that is associated with it (Jackson, 1996).

In addition, the problematic association of female poverty with FHHs has in practice muted any serious consideration of female poverty within male-headed households—an issue that is methodologically and analytically more complex and politically more controversial. For reasons that are well-known (conceptual bias, methodological convenience), the more prominent approaches to measuring poverty, such as the income/consumption method, have in practice been based on household survey data, even though they are in principle measurable on the individual (Kabeer, 1996a). When such data have been used to estimate the incidence of poverty separately for males and females, they have relied on heroic assumptions: either *assuming* perfectly egalitarian sharing of resources within households or *assuming* a given unequal pattern of distribution across all households; in either case they have simply *assumed* what is supposed to be a key dimension for investigation (Agarwal, 1986; Saith, 1996). Many of the extensive surveys of gender-disaggregated poverty—both cross-sectional and time-series—suffer from such defects.[24]

Criticisms like these raise questions about the methodological and analytical rigour of GAD discourses emanating from a variety of policymaking and advocacy institutions, and can be potentially useful to internal advocates who, as Polsby (1985, cited in Kardam, 1991) suggests, need to engage in a '*skilful* mobilization of facts' (our emphasis). In other words, to establish their advocacy on a more secure footing policy, advocates need to be cautious and selective about the type of arguments they draw upon, ensuring their empirical and analytical rigour.[25] However, as has already been noted, there is also an overriding political/advocacy dimension to GAD discourses that should not be ignored. It is important to differentiate between the needs of policy advocacy and those of academic research. There are also considerable institutional/political constraints under which GAD discourses take shape, to which organizational theorists have been drawing attention.

To return to the 'human capital' arguments, for example, it is clear from both internal and external accounts that around 1987 the WID adviser and her colleagues at the World Bank decided to give top priority to investments in the social sectors because of new opportunities that were opening up within the organization (World Bank, 1994c; World Bank 1992b; Palmer, 1993). This was a time when the Bank, under pressure from numerous quarters, was beginning to acknowledge that the early adjustment packages had paid insufficient attention to the social dimensions. At about the same time that interest grew in exploring the impact of adjustment on the poor, calculations made of the economic benefits attributable to a healthy and well-trained workforce helped to generate

34

concern that 'human capital' not be allowed to 'depreciate' during the adjustment period (Vivian, 1995). This provided a strategic entry point for raising the profile of gender issues in the Bank, especially as the arguments for 'investing in women's human capital' could be backed by relatively robust evidence (World Bank, 1992b:5).[26]

The point raised repeatedly by feminist scholars that these arguments are instrumental in tone is of course valid—policy attention to women is premissed on what women can deliver to development. But on the other hand, as those on the inside convincingly argue, internal policy advocacy has to demonstrate positive spinoffs in order to win allies and to press its claims successfully against rival claimants; it also has to make its case in terms that are compatible with the organizational mandate. WID's history at the World Bank strongly confirms this point. The efforts of the first WID adviser (1977–85) to promote gender concerns using an equality discourse had elicited negative response from within the organization. To counter the structural constraints within which she worked, a significant amount of entrpreneurship was needed on the part of the adviser to build internal alliances, to bargain with management, and to present WID in a persuasive manner. The fact that the WID adviser was an institutional outsider and a sociologist not well versed in the institutional language, however, did not facilitate strategies of this sort. Her main allies seem to have been the sociologists in the Bank who were themselves facing a major up-hill battle at the time (Kardam, 1993).

GAD discourses cannot be analysed without taking into account these institutional/political constraints. What is problematic in this case, however, is the fact that the emphasis on 'human capital' has run alongside the Bank's unchanging 'fiscal constraint' and *'laissez faire'* advice to governments: it has been maintained that the social costs must be addressed within the overall constraints of adjustment measures (Ribe *et al.*, 1990, cited in Vivian, 1995). Under such overwhelming financial constraints, human capital arguments for investing in the social sectors in general, and in female human resources in particular, will have a hard time making a real difference to public expenditure patterns. It thus seems more accurate to describe the achievements of internal advocates as being limited to ensuring 'least-worst scenarios' or damage control (Sawer, 1996), rather than the more ambitious agenda set out by feminist activists.

Somewhat similar political considerations apply to the 'feminization of poverty' discourse. Feminists—whether working as internal advocates in multilateral agencies like the ILO and IFAD, or as activists in women's groups and networks in developing countries—have found poverty to be a useful platform on which to raise their demands for gender justice.[27] This strategy is viewed with apprehension by others who are sceptical of the tendency in development organizations to collapse all forms of disadvantage—including gender disadvantage—into poverty (Jackson, 1996). They recommend that gender be rescued from the 'poverty trap' through 'poverty-independent gender analyses and policies which recognize that poverty policies are not necessarily appropriate to

35

tackling gender issues because the subordination of women is not caused by poverty' (ibid.:35).

There are two related questions that need to be addressed here: first, why have gender advocates relied so heavily on the poverty criteria in making their case for gender justice? And following from that, is separation (of poverty and gender), as some observers seem to suggest, an appropriate and viable strategy? Regarding the first question, several factors seem to have been responsible for the poverty focus, of which bureaucratic resistance is only one. While the early observation made by Buvinic (1983)—that the emphasis on poor women and, by implication, poor men makes the feminist agenda less threatening to male bureaucrats—may have been one consideration in the choice of discourse, it could not have been the only one. A far more significant factor has been the detrimental consequences of economic policies pursued by numerous governments under the aegis of international lending agencies over the past decade, which have made poverty a concrete reality for a growing number of men and women, as the 'new poor' have been added to the 'structural poor' of the past. In their opposition to the neo-liberal agenda, international and national NGOs, parts of the United Nations system, researchers, and citizen groups have identified poverty as a key priority. More significantly though, southern feminist networks have drawn attention to the particularly detrimental consequences of these policies for poor women. Poverty has thus been placed firmly on the agenda—not just by donor agencies and mixed-sex organizations, but also by southern women's groups and networks. The alliance between these different groups has provided a powerful critique of the neo-liberal mainstream; the recent shift in development discourse cannot be adequately understood if these external pressures are not taken into account.

Yet gender advocacy that relies on the poverty criterion runs into a number of thorny analytical and political problems. As Jackson (1995) correctly argues, poverty policies are not necessarily responsive to gender inequalities because gender discrimination is not caused by poverty. In other words, the social forces that create poverty are not the same as those that create gender disadvantage: evidence from the Indian sub-continent strongly suggests that opulence does not always translate into gender advantage; it may in some contexts even intensify certain aspects of gender subordination.[28] Likewise, cross-country comparisons of gender disadvantage undertaken by the *Human Development Report* (UNDP, 1995) demonstrate the disjuncture between overall levels of well-being and gender inequality.[29] In other words, gender disadvantage has a different logic from poverty. And yet, in poor women's lived experiences the two axes are inextricably bound up: as Kabeer puts it, the social forces that create scarcity on the one hand, and discrimination on the other, are 'analytically distinct but empirically seamless' (Kabeer, 1996a:13). This is what makes the conceptualization of the gender dimensions of poverty so complex.[30]

If scarcity and discrimination are 'empirically seamless' can it be convincingly argued that they should be separated in policy advocacy and formulation?

How could gender advocacy then come to terms with the fact that poverty is a serious priority for a significant number of women? And how could it ensure that poverty alleviation policies address the specificities of female poverty? As feminist analysis has shown, female poverty is in many ways distinct from male poverty (and not just more intense): the poverty that women experience is mediated through unequal gender relations and 'local patriarchies' that shape allocative behaviour and constrain women's access to their own labour power (Kabeer, 1989, 1996a). Poverty is indeed a gendered experience (Jackson, 1996), and feminist advocates need to ensure that women's specific poverty trajectories are reflected in 'mainstream' poverty agendas, rather than abandoning poverty analysis and policy formulation to others.

The politics of policy advocacy: instrumentalism and its critics

The discussion of gender policy advocacy and discourses may leave one somewhat disillusioned about what can be achieved through a process of engagement with the development establishment. What emerges from the account is a strong sense of the constraints within which gender policy advocates operate—constraints which have led to alliances, compromises, and the inevitable watering down of the feminist agenda. At numerous points in this chapter reference has been made to the need for creating 'fit' between gender issues and the organizational mandate/culture within which the internal advocate operates. To be persuasive, even feminist activists on the outside have found it useful to link feminist objectives to other, more 'legitimate' concerns of development which can benefit a more diverse range of people. What emerges clearly from some of the recent feminist commentaries on gender and adjustment, for example, is an emphasis on the centrality of social reproduction not only to women's lives, but also for creating a sustainable macro-economy that can produce patterns of employment and output that meet *people's* needs (Beneria, 1995; Elson, 1995).[31]

These strategies are all indicative of the position from which gender policy advocates speak: as supplicants trying to persuade those not convinced of the intrinsic value of gender equality, in terms least likely to generate resistance, that gender issues need to become a priority. As we have seen, resorting to these strategies has not gone without reproach: in recent years a distinct scholarly-feminist critique has emerged which queries instrumentalist arguments on methodological, analytical, and most importantly, political grounds. It is the latter dimension which is of interest here: we argue that the feminist critique is at its weakest when it queries instrumentalism on political grounds. In the world of 'real' (as opposed to 'abstract') politics, strategic alliances, compromises, and instrumental arguments are not aberrations; they are part of the everyday reality that constitutes feminist politics worldwide.[32] In other words, instrumentalism—as opposed to advocacy around a staunchly feminist agenda—becomes inevitable when advocates seek to bring a feminist agenda within institutions and

37

bureaucracies that are immured intractably in their own particular procedural and cognitive mind-sets.

First, while it is true that WID/GAD discourses have tended to use instrumental arguments, it is worth bearing in mind that this tactic is not confined to gender advocacy within the development context. Instrumental arguments have been made by feminists in both North and South long before WID/GAD appeared on the scene. An outstanding and uniform feature of early feminist advocacy in the Middle East, for example, is not merely that it tried to accommodate Islam, 'but that the concern with women coincided with the search for a new family form which would produce a "healthier" and more viable nation' (Kandiyoti, 1991:9).

> A nationalist/feminist alliance of progressive men and women produced a new discourse on women and the family which was predominantly instrumental in tone. Women's illiteracy, seclusion, and the practice of polygyny were not denounced merely because they so blatantly curtailed the individual human rights of one half of the population, but because they created ignorant mothers, shallow and scheming partners, unstable marital unions, and lazy and unproductive members of society. Women were increasingly presented as a wasted national resource (ibid.).

Naciri (Chapter 4) describes the instrumental arguments that were used by nationalist forces in Morocco to promote female education. Similar tendencies can be found in the 'maternal feminist' discourses that gained prominence on both sides of the Atlantic around the turn of the century. Where nationalism and the 'woman question' intersected, there was a 'heightened insistence by women's rights advocates on what the state should do to ameliorate the situation of women as mothers, whose contribution to the strength, welfare and future of the national state was politically arguable'; arguments for women's citizenship were made on the grounds of their 'distinctive functional role as mother-educators and arbitrators of moral behaviour' (Bell and Offen, 1983:11).

Even in retrospect it would be difficult to reach any definitive conclusions as to whether these arguments paid off or worked against women. Naciri (Chapter 4) argues that Moroccan women have seized the opportunities offered to them through formal education in ways that have truly transformed their lives: gaining access to paid employment, postponing marriage, and reducing fertility. Thus even though Moroccan nationalists may have promoted female education for instrumental reasons, the women who have had access to education have pursued their own agenda in ways that were not necessarily expected or desired by policymakers. In other words, women are not instruments.

The other point that emerges quite clearly from the historical accounts is the political agility of feminist advocates: in the face of severe constraints they had to exploit the slightest openings to push forward their agenda, even if it meant having to make an abrupt change in discourse which left them open to new counter-arguments. For example, focusing on women as mothers has always given anti-feminists ample scope to make arguments for limiting women's participation in the public sphere. As we will argue later, no matter what criterion feminists have adopted, anti-feminists have been quick to use it against women; and conversely, feminist advocates have dexterously used anti-feminist discourses to promote items on their own agenda.

Second, critics of instrumentalism maintain that equality should be argued on its own merit: it is dangerous to justify gender equality in efficiency or poverty terms because new evidence may show that women are not as productive as men (thereby questioning the presumed high pay-offs of 'investing in women'), or not necessarily poorer than men (thereby questioning their greater neediness). There are two points worth noting here: first, the dangers of relying on dubious arguments, and second, the dangers of abandoning the equality discourse; the two, we argue, do not necessarily coincide. Regarding the first point, as it has been noted already in this chapter, it is important that feminist advocates engage in a *skilful* mobilization of facts; in other words, that they use arguments that are analytically and empirically robust—an area where collaboration between feminist scholars and advocates has turned out to be very fruitful.[33] As noted above, some of the problems with the gender efficiency discourse stem from its analytical weaknesses and insufficient evidential base; likewise, the 'feminization of poverty discourse' has relied too heavily on dubious data. These are all flaws that will have to be overcome if the arguments are to remain useful tools in the hands of their advocates.

The other point raised by the critique, namely the dangers of abandoning the equality discourse is, in our opinion, more controversial. The underlying assumption seems to be that the equality discourse is somehow invincible, while both the efficiency and the poverty criteria are vulnerable to attack. In fact all three criteria for gender justice—including the equality discourse—are open to counter-claims. Despite its rhetorical appeal and apparent simplicity, equality is a profoundly complex idea because of the basic diversity of human beings (A. Sen, 1989). Feminist debates on the merits of 'equality' versus 'difference' convincingly show the multiple ways in which both discourses have been used for and against women. Equality too is a contested term and much effort has gone into including compensations for 'difference' within definitions of equality as in the case of Swedish 'equality policy' (which includes flexible working hours, maternity leave, childcare facilities, and late evening shopping hours) (Pateman, 1992). In a similar vein, there will always be struggles over the meanings of terms like 'efficiency' and 'poverty' by those who oppose and those who seek to promote policy attention to women; feminist advocates will have to respond to counter-claims no matter what criterion they use in their advocacy for gender justice. Moreover, given the fact that gender advocacy cuts across a wide range of institutional contexts—from those specializing in legal/human rights to financial establishments and technical agencies—one can only expect a multiplicity of discourses. As we noted at the begining of this chapter, the equality discourse continues to be used within a diverse range of national and international agencies; but in the process of engaging with other parts of the development establishment, the relevance and usefulness of other languages (efficiency and poverty) has become increasingly obvious.

Conclusions

This chapter has looked at some strands of feminist advocacy which have engaged with the development establishment over the past decade when a rigid market-oriented policy agenda set the terms of the debate. The discursive strategies of internal feminist advocates reflect, in part at least, the particular organizational contexts within which they have found themselves.

One strategy has been to justify feminist objectives in terms that are compatible with the dominant economistic discourse: gender inequalities have been portrayed as 'market distortions' which cause economic waste, hoping that it would appeal to mainstream policymakers and economists who are diligently searching for 'rigidities' that are allegedly raising production costs and undermining international competitiveness. As a political strategy this strand of advocacy relies entirely on exhortations to policymakers to take gender issues on board—assuming that the 'policymaking establishment' is a neo-liberal monolith, and underestimating the importance of external pressure in bringing about institutional change. While the attempt to re-define 'efficiency' along feminist lines has been an astute political move, the policy recommendations do not sufficiently reflect the problems (especially for women) that are intrinsic to a market-oriented growth strategy, nor is there sufficient recognition of the need for 'public action' (by feminist activists and others) to regulate markets. While this style of advocacy would prove useful to internal advocates working within market-oriented development establishments, it represents what has been called a 'least-worst scenario' or damage-control strategy. If the view is taken that there are 'intrinsic design faults' in the market framework, as we have done, then it becomes imperative to search for more conducive policy frameworks.

A more complex and dynamic view of the policy *process* would not only acknowledge the diversity of the policymaking establishment and attempt to identify and use its 'strategic points of leverage' (Sen and Grown, 1988:85), but would also attach more significance to NGOs, citizen groups, and networks that attempt to change the policy agenda set by the more powerful parts of the development establishment. It is then not only desirable, but also feasible, to try to change the policy agenda along lines that are more conducive to feminist goals. Inevitably the more transformative discourses can be employed by those who are on the 'outside' (activists, scholars) and those working within institutions that pursue mandates which are more open to the social dimensions of development.

As we have seen, poverty issues have provided a point of convergence and a rallying call for a variety of forces—both feminist and non-feminist—to question the wisdom and the long-term viability of development strategies that attempt to subordinate more and more activities and people to the vagaries of market forces.

The strategic alliances between these diverse forces have provided a powerful critique of the mainstream agenda without which it would be difficult to explain the recent shifts in development discourse.

Knowing full well the tendency for mainstream policy agendas to leave out the specificities of gender disadvantage, feminist scholarship/advocacy will have to continue its sustained scrutiny of emerging policy agendas. Neither past experience (basic needs approach of the 1970s) nor more recent developments ('New Poverty Agenda') provide much scope for complacency. It has taken more than a decade for social forces lobbying against the dominant development paradigm to get parts of the development establishment to respond with more socially sensitive alternatives. It remains to be seen whether feminist concerns will occupy a more central place in these new policy agendas than they have done in the past.

3

Mainstreaming gender equity to national development planning

ANNE MARIE GOETZ

State-based institutions for gender equity

Since the United Nations Decade for Women (1976–85), the demand for policy to address women's needs in development has often been framed in terms of a project of access, or 'integration' into a range of development policymaking and project-implementing institutions. The most important of these institutions has been the state, which, in contexts of scarcity and poverty, has been a central player in the distribution of development resources. Although this is a role which has been seriously problematized over the last decade by processes of economic stabilization and structural adjustment, the state is still a critical arena for the promotion of women's interests. This is because of a growing understanding amongst gender policy advocates of the role of public authority in underwriting the asymmetrical distribution of resources and values between women and men, and hence the importance of improving the accountability of public institutions to their female constituencies.

This chapter examines processes of institutionalizing GAD concerns in the state, and finds that efforts to integrate gender in development through national 'women's machinery' have produced many important strategic gains. Above all, they have legitimized a place for gender issues in development. WID/GAD government units have innovated policy analysis and monitoring tools such as gender checklists and guidelines for cross-government use. Other new instruments for co-ordinating gender-sensitive planning across the government have been WID/GAD 'Focal Points' in line ministries, and synoptic gender-sensitive national development plans. The WID/GAD issue has had pockets of success in gaining allies and has made critically important gains in revising databases used for development planning to include aspects of women's lives.

At the same time, WID/GAD national 'machineries' have encountered a range of constraints which undermine their ability to pursue their agenda effectively. These include the marginalization of WID/GAD units through under-resourcing in staff, skills, and funding, and through patterns of institutional location and role assignment which stigmatize and condemn in advance their ambitions for gender-transformative policy change. Beyond the problem of bureaucratic resistance, there seem to be two main constraints on the effectiveness of WID/GAD policy efforts. One is that gender-sensitive policy proposals tend rarely to be traced through to actual budgetary implications, and therefore fail to make a direct impact on the main instrument for national development planning: the public expenditure planning process. The second serious shortcoming is in the nature of connections between WID/GAD units in the public administration and the women's constituency in civil society. Ideally a strong constituency base amongst women's organizations and gender-sensitive NGOs would strengthen the position of the WID/GAD agenda in government, while at the same time sensitizing it to the needs of the national female citizenship. But it has proven difficult to build up or to exploit this iterative relationship.

The international development community has played an important role in supporting national WID/GAD efforts, through the UN Decade for Women, and through the aid programmes of local constituencies mobilized in support of the WID/GAD issue. The overwhelming predominance of donor pressure in some contexts as the impetus for adopting WID/GAD concerns, however, has exacerbated problems of ambivalence in development administrations towards the issue. As a foreign import, the legitimacy of the WID/GAD issue can be undermined and genuine local 'internalization' or 'ownership' of the issue postponed.

This chapter provides a comparative analysis based on seven country case studies: Bangladesh, Chile, Jamaica, Mali, Morocco, Uganda, and Vietnam.[1] These countries are each at different stages of integrating gender into development processes. They also differ vastly in their degree of economic development, their political histories, and the nature of their main economic constraints. What they have in common is a reasonable degree of civil stability and democratic governance, though the specific characteristics of civil society and democracy in each country differs. The singling out of these countries is not intended to give the impression that they are either particularly remiss or progressive in their approach to institutionalizing women's interests in development—when it comes to institutionalizing women's interests in policy processes, no country in the world can be considered 'developed'.

Before proceeding to an analysis of individual country efforts to improve public accountability to women in the development process, a range of issues need to be clarified. We need to develop a gendered perspective on the state and public administration in development, and to understand the meaning of institutionalization, the concept of women's interests from a political and policy perspective, and the distinction between WID approaches and GAD approaches.

A feminist perspective on development, the state and public administration

The injustices worked in women's lives by the power asymmetries attached to gender differences across most social institutions have historically commanded a very weak response from public authority in Third World states, as elsewhere. Nevertheless, the state has been a focus of feminist efforts to redress these injustices on the grounds that it is assumed to have a degree of autonomy from patriarchy, and hence, to the degree that the state assumes responsibility for women's interests, it can provide a resort of appeal against the power of men in more intimate institutions such as the family.

Gender, the state, and development policy

The growing body of feminist literature theorizing the state[2] has put paid to assumptions of state neutrality or 'autonomy' when it comes to gender. Part of the definition of the state and the delimitation of the state's proper sphere involves the active codification and policing of the boundaries between the 'public' and the 'private'. In many states these boundaries also delineate gendered spheres of activity, where the paradigmatic subject of the public and economic arena is male, and the private and domestic arena is female. By confirming and institutionalizing the arrangements that distinguish the public from the private, states are involved in the social and political institutionalization of gendered power differences. For example, states can set the parameters for women's structurally unequal position in families and markets by condoning gender-differential terms in inheritance rights and legal adulthood, by tacitly condoning domestic and sexual violence, or by sanctioning differential wages for equal or comparable work.

This has practical implications for women and men's experience of state development policy. Typically, states have both assumed and construed women's identity for public policy as being conditioned by their social relationships as dependants of men, and have made them the objects of family welfare policy—sometimes almost exclusively so, as in family planning. Even in efforts to integrate women into economic policy sectors, striking gender differentials persist in the design and implementation of policy. Sometimes labelled a problem of policy 'misbehaviour' (Buvinic, 1986), policies for women tend not to provide women with institutional survival bases—such as employment or asset ownership rights—which might be alternatives to dependence on men.

Socialist states have shown a different pattern in this respect, in that the position of women has often been improved as part of a general process of social transformation. For example, frequently socialist land reforms have been of necessity accompanied by liberalization of marriage and inheritance laws in order to rupture patriarchal lineage-based landholding systems by giving women independent rights to land. As will be seen in the case of Vietnam, however, the concern with gender equity in socialist states is often somewhat equivocal, based on instrumental concerns to harness women's productive and reproductive energies for state projects of economic development or population growth.

A pattern is discernible in both capitalist and socialist states, to varying degrees, of a persistent mis-routing of feminist policy ambitions towards either traditional 'welfare' concerns (Buvinic, 1986), or the 'instrumental' use of women's subsistence and family maintenance work to serve efficiency goals (Kandiyoti, 1988; Moser, 1989). This process directs attention to the relationship of public authority to patterns of gender inequality in society, and requires an exploration of gender politics in the institutional contexts in which WID/GAD knowledge and policy are produced. This is the prime concern of this chapter, which concentrates on efforts to integrate women's interests into state institutions.

Gendered institutions

Feminist theories of the state suggest that the state is gendered, largely oriented to male interests, but that it is also a complex set of institutions with conflicting interests offering differing prospects for feminist incursions (Connell, 1990). Because men dominate public institutions, feminists have been concerned to increase the number of women participating in public institutions and in decision-making processes. Recently, growing awareness of how deeply men's interests are embedded in the everyday rules and structures of institutions has focused feminist analysis on gendered features of institutions and organizations (Staudt, 1985; Acker, 1990; Cockburn, 1991). Historically, the purpose of establishing institutions has been to reduce uncertainty by routinizing certain preferred forms of social interaction, thereby limiting choice. The project of institutionalizing gender-sensitive policy, therefore, should be oriented to routinizing gender-equitable forms of social interaction and limiting the possibilities for choosing discriminatory forms of social organization.

The extent to which state institutions are gendered—in other words, promote men's or women's interests—will vary according to the gendered history and politics embedded in institutional rules and processes. The form of state response to women's needs will also depend on the gender construction of the family and the degree of gender polarization in civil society and the economy. Other factors affecting the state's response to women's gender interests are the nature of state–civil society relations, the nature of women's activism in civil society, the degree of state autonomy, and the basis of state legitimacy. These conditions add up to distinctively gendered political and policy opportunity structures.

Women's gendered interests

So far here, the terms 'feminist' and 'women's interests' have been used uncritically to imply a notion of transformation based on a concept of women's interests as gendered individuals. They are both deeply contested concepts, however. In the West alone, there are many different forms of feminism, and in the South, 'feminism' often carries negative associations of being anti-male and anti-family, as well as sometimes being associated with promiscuity and social dislocation. It is often characterized as a Western import. In this chapter, the concept is used to describe analytical and practical approaches based on the premiss that women are oppressed, and a commitment to end that oppression.

With regard to the term 'women's interests', awareness of women's and men's divergent opportunities in the same social institutions—the family, the class structure, the market, the state—has led to the assertion in feminist politics that the sex/gender relationship generates specific social, economic, and political interests. But the concept of 'women's interests' is difficult to define, given that the multiple causes of women's subordination, and the variability of its forms across class, race, age, ethnicity, nation, and culture, have undermined attempts to speak of a unitary category of 'women' with common needs and interests.

Following Molyneux, concepts of 'women's interests' have been replaced by 'gender interests', understood as interests which women and men may develop by virtue of their social positioning through gender attributes. This allows for the fact that differently positioned women will have different social, economic, and political interests (Molyneux, 1985:232). Molyneux makes a further distinction between 'practical gender interests', as those which respond to immediate, situation-specific needs, and which may not challenge prevailing forms of gender subordination, and 'strategic gender interests', which entail transformative goals such as women's emancipation and gender equality (ibid.:232–3).

Molyneux stresses, however, that strategic gender interests cannot be *assumed* in advance or out of context for particular groups of women. This makes it difficult for feminist policy analysis to establish a set of values for evaluating policy measures. Jonasdottir (1988:39) argues that a feminist notion of interests which is respectful of difference yet attentive to transformative projects can begin by reviving the original content of the concept of interest: as a matter of 'being among' (from the Latin: *inter-esse*) the members of a political community (ibid.:39). This stresses the positive 'agency' aspect of interests, where 'interest' refers to conditions of control over choice, and returns us to concepts of institutionalization, where patterns of choice and their limits are determined, and where it is in the interests of women to build up a concrete 'controlling presence' over the conditions of choice. But it is difficult to establish whether women, even once they have access to decision-making, are acting in women's strategic gender interests. For example, conservative women, such as women's wings of Islamic parties, or groups such as 'REAL Women' in North America or 'Women Who Want to be Women' in Australia, are making political gains and have non-feminist claims to represent women's needs and interests. What we are looking for is the establishment of a 'strategic presence' for women's gender interests in policymaking, where there is legitimacy for the expression of the interests of women as a gendered social category endowed unequally with values and resources, and with potentially different ambitions for the way policy is pursued. In the end, value judgements are inescapable in policy analysis. And in the absence of conditions for establishing women's control over policy choices, policy outcomes must be assessed according to the degree to which they promote women's freedom to make their own choices.

In the politics of institutionalizing gendered perspectives on development policy, different experiences of policy according to gender are taken to represent a challenge, not of political interest revolving around the question of *inclusion*, but rather of involving divergent meanings of social and economic change. In this sense, efforts to 'integrate' women into development policy are not necessarily transformative, so the concept of 'institutionalizing' women's interests in policy processes is used here to indicate a more transformative process. Sometimes the term 'mainstreaming' is used to indicate this process, but 'institutionalizing' will be preferred here because it puts the accent on institutional change.

This distinction is embedded in the ways WID policy and GAD policy are used in this paper. The term 'Women in Development' itself implies an integrative project, and it is taken here to imply a discourse preoccupied with issues of access. In contrast, the term GAD policy describes the political project intended by feminist analyses of gender relations in development. Here, the technical project of access, as numerical inclusion, is seen as insufficient to challenge the unequal allocation of values which sustain oppressive gender relations. The stress on gender is also a reminder that men must also be the target of attempts to redress gender inequities, that their interests are also socially constructed, and amenable to change.

Situating interpretations of WID or GAD in the context of economic and social change

Changes over time in the conceptualization of WID and GAD

Before exploring formal processes of institutionalizing gender-redistributive policy goals, it is important to consider the ways the content of WID or GAD agendas have varied over time in the case countries. The interpretations of WID or GAD vary according to the institutional contexts and political circumstances in which these concepts are employed. Significant actors influencing the meaning of these concepts include state bureaucracies, political parties, religious institutions, women's organizations, and NGOs, as well as international organizations and the international feminist community.

Any consideration of the evolving meaning of WID or GAD policy discourses must be situated in the context of economic and social change over the last two decades within both the national and international policy environment. Four of the countries, Chile, Mali, Bangladesh, and Uganda, have seen profound changes in their political systems, from authoritarianism to democracy. All seven countries have been in deep economic crisis. But these shared political and economic conditions are experienced very differently in each country, according to their degree of economic development, cultural stability, and the nature of their international linkages. Stabilization and neo-liberal economic policies have had gender-differential impacts across a range of sectors. In the social sectors this has included spending cuts and a move towards privatization, or at the least community provision, with implications for women's time and income. Liberalization policies more generally have provided formal and informal employment opportunities for women. In combination with growing poverty in some contexts this has meant that more women are moving into the workforce, but the unstable and transient nature of employment in many new forms of manufacturing and service industries, as well as the informal sector, may undermine any employment gains. This is shifting conventions around the gender division of labour, though not necessarily changing perceptions of the value of women's work, since these forms of employment tend to involve low-skill, part-time, and under-valued work.

Half of the case countries—Bangladesh, Mali, and Uganda—are amongst the very poorest nations of the world, with very high levels of absolute poverty and alarmingly poor human development indicators. In contrast, Chile, Jamaica, and Morocco are middle-income countries with reasonably healthy human development indicators, although they vary: Chile's social indicators are close to those of higher-income countries, Jamaica's are reasonably good but have deteriorated since the 1970s, whereas Morocco, with a similar level of GNP per capita as Jamaica, has much poorer social indicators. Between these two sets of countries is Vietnam, whose GNP per capita ranks it as one of the world's poorest countries, yet its achievements in social development means that the UNDP's Human Development Index ranks it in the same category as Chile, Jamaica, and Morocco (UNDP, 1995:156).

In the official rhetoric, and to some degree the actual policies of most of the case countries, WID discourses have shifted from an initial primary association with social and family welfare issues to a growing association with labour market and productivity issues. 'Welfare' has taken on a pejorative meaning in the discourses of gender policy advocates. Gender-transformative welfare policies, however, are socially and economically critical to the effective transformation of the terms of gender inequality, and it is crucial that these policies are reformed in women's interests. In practice, however, they have often been the most visible vehicle for paternalistic interpretations of women's identities and needs as subsumed to traditional forms of the family and the community. In what follows, 'social welfare' is not used pejoratively, but is qualified by adjectives such as 'paternalistic' or 'traditional' where it refers to policies which do not challenge conventional interpretations of women and men's reproductive or productive roles.

In most of the case countries WID has long been associated with the traditional social sector programmes managed by the administrative units within which the WID mandate first found a home. Thus in Chile and Mali, it was associated with a traditional interpretation of women's mothering and wifely roles, as promulgated by military governments, and in Bangladesh it was associated initially with the social 'rehabilitation' of women who had fallen out of the traditional family safety net. Many of the WID programmes of the 1970s in both social and productive sectors continued in this vein, but often with more blatantly instrumental intentions. Thus in Bangladesh, investment in women's education was justified because:

[t]he level of schooling of women determines the efficiency of household management. Educated mothers pay greater attention to nutrition, health, and childcare than the uneducated one (sic). (GOB, First Five Year Plan, 1973:479)

In the productive sectors, new development inputs such as credit or technology were made available to women for the purpose of improving their traditional roles, while at the same time servicing national concerns about issues such as population control, improved family nutrition, or improved primary healthcare. None of these programmes targeted men for the purpose of challenging gender-ascriptive reproductive or productive roles, nor opened women's access to non-traditional and sustainable employment opportunities.

Over the last twenty years, fundamental forms of social and economic restructuring have contributed to changes in the view of gender roles in social sectors, and increasingly in productive sectors. These include: the appearance of new social movements organized around gender, democratization, and human rights; the increased visibility of women in formal and informal labour markets, especially in contexts where economic crises have undermined the male productive base in the formal economy and the public sector. Chile, Jamaica, and Morocco have seen an enormous increase in women's participation in the formal labour force. Poverty in Bangladesh, Mali, and Uganda has prompted a focus on women's contribution to family survival. Neo-liberal economic policies and the need to attract foreign investment in contexts such as Vietnam have involved, in contrast, an erosion of the legitimacy of gender equity concerns in government. In all of these countries, these economic changes have had an impact on the economic viability of traditional family forms. On the one hand, this has prompted changes in social sector discourses towards a consideration of women's—as opposed to the family's or men's—social and welfare needs. On the other hand, changes in the family form are prompting a simultaneous policy backlash aimed at reinforcing its crumbling boundaries.

Examples of a reorientation of social policy discourses to include women's interests as whole subjects include new health and education programmes in Jamaica. The Maternal and Child Health programme there now looks beyond women's physical reproductive functions to the full gamut of their well-being, where the concept of the well-woman includes not just her good health but the acceptability of her social circumstances. A new programme in the Ministry of Education is reviewing gender biases in the curriculum of young adolescents. These kinds of programmes indicate ways forward for a radical and gender-sensitive interpretation of social welfare. In Morocco, vocational training programmes have shifted their target clients from married to unmarried women, and from training in homecraft skills to skills needed in modern formal-sector employment, such as computer literacy, carpentry, and metalwork, although more sex-typed training persists—such as skills for nursery school teaching or food preservation. In most of the case countries, however, social sector policies targeting women do so from an increasingly instrumental perspective. The view is to reap benefits from the social externalities expected to flow from women's better education or health, with less attention paid to gendered issues of power or control upon which improved social welfare is contingent.

In all the case countries, the productive sectors have remained the most highly resistant to the gender issue. In Chile, in recognition of women's employment needs, new women-targeted productive programmes have been launched in the agricultural, financial, and industrial sectors. These have remained relatively small and isolated, however, while 'mainstream' programmes still fail to integrate women—only 9.25 per cent of beneficiaries of the Chilean Ministry of Agriculture's rural credit programme, for instance, are women. In Morocco, women have been 'discovered' as new sources of productivity, particularly in agriculture and rural credit systems. The legacy of separate policy approaches for women is very deeply embedded, however, and the credit and agricultural extension resources which do reach them remain negligible compared to those targeted to men.

In Uganda, policy imperatives of promoting economic growth through structural adjustment, and of reducing poverty, have prompted official attention to women's productivity, in a context where women produce 80 per cent of the country's food and provide 70 per cent of agricultural labour. The core of the leadership's support for women centres on a project of improving their agricultural productivity. Thus, according to President Museveni:

> Our policy aims at strengthening the position of women in the economy by raising the value and productivity of their labour and giving them access and control over productive resources (Museveni, cited in Mugyenyi, 1994:1).

In spite of this, the agricultural sector has been slow to address women's production needs. The lack of gender-sensitive agricultural policies is particularly striking given the critical importance of efforts to generate a supply response in agriculture to new production incentives. If, as is the case, women are effectively excluded from membership in existing agricultural co-operatives, and lack access to market information, they will be unlikely to respond to, or benefit from, market liberalization measures. That this obvious and important opportunity to integrate a gender perspective on agricultural policies has not been taken up again demonstrates the intensity of resistance to notions of women as key producers.

This resistance, or indifference, to women's needs as producers, is even greater in the private sector, which, in the context of market reforms in Mali, Vietnam, and Uganda in particular, is slated to take on a central role as the state withdraws from the productive sector through policies of 'public choice for private initiative' (GOU, 1993:75). Very little is being done to guarantee gender equity in the private sector in any of the case countries, with the exceptions of Chile's draft Equal Opportunities policy, and the labour rights which women still enjoy in Vietnam. In both countries, however, resistance is expressed by private employers to the 'higher costs of the female workforce' (Pollack, 1994a:25). The result in Vietnam has been higher unemployment rates for women, and the state's willingness to turn a blind eye to poor and deteriorating conditions in the private sector in the interest of retaining private investment (Moghadam, 1994:19). This resistance to defend women's employment rights in periods of economic austerity reveals one of the greatest obstacles to the development of a gender-transformative conceptualization of the WID/GAD issue, namely, the profound taboos surrounding policy efforts which in any way appear to cause or worsen male unemployment. This problem is no less salient in Western industrialized countries, where concern with rising male unemployment consistently leads to under-implementation of strategies for gender equity in equal opportunities or re-skilling programmes. That concerns over male unemployment are permitted to overshadow measures to enhance women's productivity reveals the deeply gendered sub-text of economic planning. Its continued orientation to men's productive needs has the effect of stigmatizing women's employment support programmes—such as labour-saving domestic technologies, childcare, vocational training, and equal opportunities—as traditional welfare measures, rather than productive sector policies.

The phenomenon of rising male unemployment in urban areas consequent on adjustment and public sector reform policies (particularly salient in Uganda and Mali), or sudden terms of trade shocks in primary commodity exports (Chile, Morocco, Jamaica), or the demobilization and repatriation of refugees and overseas workers (Vietnam), has undermined the viability of the traditional male bread-winner model of the family. Increasing poverty in rural areas consequent on a range of factors such as landlessness (Bangladesh), or drought (Mali and Morocco), similarly undermines traditional forms of male provision. At the same time, community survival strategies and traditional social safety nets have been worn thin by civil conflict (Uganda) or growing population pressure on scant resources (Bangladesh). The result has been the break-up, to some extent, of traditional familial and social coping mechanisms. This has spawned new forms of social organization, where women are playing more visible community roles, as in Chile, and in other contexts, such as Bangladesh, Uganda, Jamaica, Vietnam, and Morocco, there are higher divorce rates and more female-headed households. These threats to the traditional family form have prompted policy reactions with implications for the conceptualization of WID/GAD, in particular where women become the scapegoats for all social ills. In Vietnam, for example, women are being blamed for the negative effects of the market economy, such as increases in prostitution, drug abuse, and child neglect.

One expression of state concern over changing family structures is the recent appearance in official rhetoric of cautionary polemics regarding conflict between the sexes. Thus in a gender policy statement emanating from the agricultural extension service in Morocco, the foundation of society in the future is described as 'the self-fulfilment of the family as an entity and the avoidance of all risk of conflict between its members' (Bennis, 1994:5). Details of the ideal form of this family are left open, but this otherwise progressive document does not address the problem of the gender conflict likely to be provoked by its proposals to orient more agricultural resources to women. In Bangladesh, concern over gender conflict and family disintegration is addressed through an official discourse of gender complementarity and a view of family relations as essentially consensual,

51

rather than based on power and latent conflict. A clear exposition of this view is made in the introduction to the *Fourth Five Year Plan:*

> ... there are two main ways of increasing the contribution of women in development process and for improving their condition. One process tends to highlight the gender differences and brings men and women into greater competition for existing job opportunities. The second process emphasises more the complementary relationship between men and women and tends to develop them as a whole with focus on the integrative aspects of the family. The first approach can improve the economic position of the women but may also increase the incidence of disharmony in the family. (...) Because the majority of the people are poor, therefore, it is necessary that both the husband and the wife should complement each others' income for the benefit of education and maintenance of the children (GOB, Fourth Five Year Plan, 1990:1-8, cited as in the original).

The barely veiled reproach to women's organizations, the evocation of emotive anti-feminist bogeys regarding the destruction of the family and the hijacking of men's jobs, hardly need pointing out.

Backlash politics targeting women and equity policies have emerged from Islamic fundamentalist interests in Bangladesh, and to some degree in Morocco. In both countries, Islam is the state religion, but both have prided themselves on their secular national character. Domestic and international Islamic interests have, however, gained increasing political prominence. These have been embraced by the state in Bangladesh, but they have had much less political success in Morocco. In Bangladesh, Islam has served as a means of backing the right-wing interests of military leaders and of army-supported governments. Since the mid-1970s Bangladesh has benefited from substantial aid from Islamic countries such as Saudi Arabia, and has permitted the spread of Islamic NGOs in rural areas. These NGOs have been recruited to state development programmes to provide education through religious schools, and to provide agricultural extension services and basic healthcare—activities in which women are involved, but in which their participation is generally framed in paternalistic terms (Kabeer, 1991).

In Morocco, throughout the 1980s, militant Islamic groups have been associated with efforts to overthrow the monarchy and have been the target of official persecution. Since 1991 Islamic groups have raised their public profile, and with a view to averting the development of the kind of conflict now raging in neighbouring Algeria, the monarchy and the government have permitted the limited expression of Islamic political interests and the emergence of an Islamic movement. This movement has attracted support from the urban working class, disaffected by the inability of other political parties to respond to the long-term deterioration in living standards. Despite the moderate stance of the palace and the government, an Islamic interpretation has often figured in legal and policy positions in relation to women. Thus, as described below, the recent amendments to the country's personal law retain a conservative Islamic interpretation. Statements are made in the *National Strategy for the Promotion of Moroccan Women to the Year 2000* which imply that a 'liberated' expression of female identity is anti-Islamic. One policy objective in the education sector, for instance, is to '[c]hange the foreign and imported image of women and treat this image according to a modernist Islamic vision ...', and another is to '... reinforce awareness that it is not necessary to adopt ways of life and comportment known in other societies where the values and aspirations differ from those of an arab-muslim society like Morocco ...' (GOM, 1989:50 and 56). These statements suggest that the women's issue provides useful territory on which the state can give ground to placate Islamic interests which it otherwise does not wish to entertain. Concessions on the women's issue neither impinge significantly on 'mainstream' national policy, nor is the women's constituency powerful enough to register an effective protest.

Conceptualizations of gender

In official rhetoric, Chile, Bangladesh, Jamaica, and Uganda have shifted to the use of the term 'gender in development'. Policymakers in Vietnam do not use the rhetoric of either WID or GAD, Mali still focuses on 'the promotion of women', and in Morocco, attention to gender relations as opposed to women alone has appeared in the NGO sector and amongst women's organizations, but largely not in official documents. All too often, unfortunately, the term has been interpreted as a synonym for 'women', or simply as a reinforcement of earlier concerns to shift the WID issue out of welfare and into economic sectors and non-traditional public roles. In any discussion of understandings of the term 'gender', it must be remembered that this English term does not translate well into other languages, and in addition, its use in the development context expresses a particularly Anglo-American feminist understanding of the social construction of gender difference. Given the relative linguistic and cultural inflexibility of the term, it is not surprising that it does not always translate well either conceptually or practically.

In all of the interview reports upon which this chapter is based, respondents either expressed confusion over the meaning of GAD, or charged that it has been misinterpreted by state institutions as, in effect, a means of side-stepping the more radical emancipatory implications of responding to women-specific disprivilege. In some countries, it is taken as an invitation to direct public attention to men's social problems. In Jamaica, for example, 'men at risk' is the most notable new policy target to appear consequent on the shift to 'gender' (Mariott, 1994:8). Kabeer provides a good example from Bangladesh of the way the new GAD discourse can be mis-translated across cultural and institutional contexts. In a workshop on gender-aware planning one woman participant asked: 'Do you think we are ready for gender and development in Bangladesh, when we have not yet addressed the problems of women in development?' (Kabeer, 1994:xii).

Kabeer goes on to explain: 'it transpired that the new vocabulary of gender was being used in her organization to deny the existence of women-specific disadvantage, and hence the need for specific measures which might address this disadvantage' (ibid).

Policymakers interviewed for this study felt that GAD has lost credibility as a policy concept, given policymakers' difficulties in understanding the significance of the discursive shift in the WID/GAD field. The problems with the policy conceptualization of gender signalled in all the interview documents centre on the fact that the shift from 'women' to 'gender' by gender policy advocates is a political, feminist one, implying a transformative vision for gender relations in which men are directly implicated. Bureaucrats charged with the GAD agenda are often themselves unconvinced or even hostile to gender-transformative goals. Where they are convinced and committed, the politics of personal bureaucratic survival dictate that the political project of the GAD agenda be underplayed, as this is seen as an unprofessional, non-technical personal bias.

In bureaucratic contexts, a political goal like this translates badly into technocratic planning languages. In development bureaucracies, these languages are almost always iterated to a primary concern with growth, rather than justice or equity, and hence have little space for gender-transformative concerns. The natural temptation, experienced by many gender policy advocates, to achieve policy legitimacy by re-framing the gender equity concern as a matter which will produce social and economic efficiency gains, has the effect of de-politicizing the issue. It results in the well-documented 'instrumental' perspective on investing in women for the positive social externalities their well-being is expected to produce, and runs the risk that women will simply become more perfectly exploitable for development. A genuine commitment to gender equity in development requires a re-conceptualization of the meaning and measurement of growth, and of equality. But this remains rather distant from current economic planning agendas, although socialism in Vietnam did permit this for a time.

Institutionalizing WID/GAD

The institutional inheritance

In most of the cases in this study, state measures to institutionalize WID/GAD machinery in the state bureaucracy have been in response to pressures exerted either by foreign donors or the international feminist movement through the UN system. In these cases, the main impetus came from the requirement of the 1975 UN Conference on Women in Mexico City to generate data on the national status of women, and to set up national machinery to promote women's integration into development. This is not to suggest that women's organizations had not been actively pushing for the state to take responsibility for gender equity. In some of the cases (Mali, Bangladesh, Uganda, Vietnam), however, the energy of the women's movement in the 1960s and 1970s was co-opted by political

54

parties in an effort to harness additional political support from the country's female constituency. In other cases, such as Morocco, the efforts of women's organizations were oriented towards more conventional women's welfare projects. In only two of the case countries—Chile and to a lesser extent, Jamaica—did a national concern with WID/GAD and the establishment of government machinery emerge in direct response to coherent internal pressure from the women's movement. In another case—Uganda—the integration of women to national *political* structures has been the result of an unusually strong commitment by the country's top leadership. Initial efforts by the state to institutionalize gender equity concerns in development policy often, however, assumed a natural convergence between national social welfare concerns and women's needs in development. This section examines the evolving institutional manifestations of WID efforts.

The case countries fall into two distinct groups with regard to the periodization of the WID agenda. In one group, Bangladesh, Jamaica, and Morocco, the WID agenda was aired in development policy discourses from the mid-1970s onwards, and made an institutional foothold, albeit a shifting one, in a range of development sectors, thereby enabling WID/GAD advocates to develop new policy instruments to make some incursions into the national planning process. This early and constantly evolving process owes more than a little to the influence of foreign donors on development in the country, and to some degree in the cases of Jamaica and Bangladesh, to the activism of the women's movement. In the second group, Mali, Chile, and Uganda, the protracted dominance of military governments during the 1970s to the late 1980s (and until 1991, in the case of Moussa Traore's regime in Mali) effectively postponed serious consideration of the WID agenda. In these cases, the potential influence of domestic women's organizations was either contained through repression, or oriented to oppositional politics focused primarily on political liberation. The influence of the international feminist movement and the UN system was limited either through disengagement by the countries concerned, or by the strength of military ideologies which, in the cases of Mali and Uganda, often framed WID as a liberal feminist issue of concern to professional women, and hence not of relevance to the predominantly rural populations. Vietnam fits into neither category. There, women's specific needs as producers and reproducers have been taken into account in national economic and social planning for decades, with the Vietnamese Women's Union providing a monitoring and mobilizing role. Cut off for so long from the international development establishment, WID/GAD policy discourses were not a part of planning until the early 1990s, and have been seen as superfluous by policymakers, given the extent of existing state investment in women's productive capacities. Indeed, international development agencies, as midwives to economic reform and improved rates of growth in the country, are in effect, though unintentionally, part of a process of the erosion of women's economic and social gains attendant on the shrinking of the socialist social security and welfare system.

Structural and sectoral location

Unlike many other development concerns, the WID/GAD agenda does not fall neatly into a single development sector which might then dictate its institutional location (Staudt, 1985:59–63). Gender policy challenges the purpose and practice of development across all development arenas: from each specific development sector, to overarching systems of law, property ownership, political representation, and labour force organization. There are two current responses to the question of finding an institutional location for the WID/GAD agenda. One is to set up an advocacy unit at a central level with a mandate to influence planning processes across all development sectors. Staudt's detailed analysis of this kind of response in USAID shows how this can be a method for placating troublesome constituencies while at the same time ensuring that the issue is contained because of the inherent difficulties of pursuing cross-sectoral change, especially where the advocacy unit is desperately under-resourced, as tends to be the case (ibid.:19). The other response is to set up a WID/GAD desk in a sector which is seen as most closely identified with the issue, or indeed to create a new WID/GAD sector. Typically this enclaves the WID/GAD issue in a social welfare sector, where it may share in a general derogation of social welfare issues as being marginal to main development concerns such as growth. Alternatively it may be lumped in as a new quasi-sector with a range of residual and marginalized concerns—such as culture, youth, and sports. This section traces the institutional location of the WID/GAD concerns in the case countries from the point of view of their proximity to power in the central state directorate (vertical location), and their thematic or sectoral location (horizontal location).

The different formal roles that WID/GAD units have been assigned fall into the following typology:

○ 'Advocacy' or 'advisory' units, located either in a central political unit, such as the office of the Prime Minister or President, or in a central economic planning unit, such as the Ministry of Planning. In this role, the WID/GAD unit is responsible for promoting attention to gender issues and giving advice to various government units. Very often, however, it is under-equipped in terms of staff numbers and technical skills, and becomes essentially the representative of a 'special issue' in an unfortunate and often resented or easily dismissed policy-pleading role.

○ Policy 'oversight' or 'monitoring' units, which may have rather more robust powers to the degree that they may be granted automatic rights to review projects before approval by central economic planning units, or to review submissions for Cabinet decisions.

○ Units with implementation responsibilities. This allows WID/GAD units to create programmes which may have a demonstration effect on other government activities, and also to respond to policy needs not well catered for elsewhere—for example, by setting up shelters for victims of domestic violence.

But the typically low level of resources for policy implementation means that these efforts are isolated, and cannot produce broad-based policy changes across the public administration.

In practice, WID/GAD units play a combination of most of these roles. A combination of policy oversight, monitoring, and advocacy roles is likely to be most successful in producing cross-governmental change, on condition that the oversight role is backed by clear powers to reject inappropriate policies, and the monitoring and advocacy roles are grounded in strong technical skills for policy analysis and the proposing of alternatives, followed through in terms of direct budgetary implications. As the following review suggests, no one WID/GAD unit has achieved this. The current WID/GAD unit in Uganda seems to have the basic elements in place, but still lacks direct access to central planning decisions and to the technical skills necessary to make an input to them.

Central advocacy or 'oversight' WID/GAD bureaux within the central state directorate have been set up in Chile, Mali, and Vietnam. Chile's SERNAM (National Service for Women) has a curious statutory basis: it is a unit within the Ministry of Planning yet it is headed by a State Minister. Neither a full Ministry with an input to Cabinet decisions, nor an established boundary-bridging body, it straddles two administrative identities in a way which diminishes its potential impact. In principle its institutional location provides it with access to the 'technical core' of policymaking, and indeed rhetoric about gender equity now figures in the Ministry of Planning's work. But it lacks clear mechanisms for ensuring concrete changes in government decisions—such as an automatic review of all new investment decisions, or a clear means of ensuring cross-ministerial compliance with the WID/GAD policy mandate. Women's desks and gender-sensitive programmes do exist in some other Ministries, and SERNAM supports these. Its formal mandate explicitly excludes project implementation functions, except for demonstration and experimentation purposes. Its limited impact on cross-ministerial decision-making, however, has obliged it to retreat to a focus on public awareness-building, and on implementing pilot projects which are donor-funded and often executed by NGOs, prompting the observation that SERNAM behaves more like an NGO than a part of the public administration (Pollack, 1994a:20). In these activities it focuses, importantly, on concerns which are neglected in other areas of government, such as sexual violence, adolescent pregnancy, and female-headed households.

In Mali, following the coup of March 1991, the transitional government under Colonel Traore moved rapidly to involve women formally in the new administrative and political processes, making an official commitment to the promotion of women's interests, nominating women to higher civil service positions, and repealing several statutes which discriminated against women's commercial activities, including their important role in cross-border trade. After the elections of 1992 and the ministerial reorganization of 1993, a Commission for the Promotion of Women was established in the office of the Prime Minister. This

Commission's role is primarily an advisory and advocacy one. It chairs an Inter-Ministerial Committee to monitor WID/GAD policies across the government administration, co-ordinates the work of delegates to various sectoral ministries charged with monitoring WID/GAD policy implementation, manages regional representatives of the Commission, and chairs a Co-ordinating Commission with government, NGO, and women's organization representatives to monitor WID/GAD policies in the NGO sector.

Although it has the status of a state ministry, the Commission does not parti-cipate in the Council of Ministers, and hence is limited in its impact on formal government decision-making. The Commission also suffers from competing roles within the public administration for pursuing the WID/GAD agenda. In 1992 a Ministry of Health, Solidarity, and the Promotion of Women was created and charged with organizing a forum for interested parties to list priorities for WID/GAD actions and to plan a national strategy. A State Secretariat for the Promotion of Women was also set up and has organized a seminar to define sec-toral WID/GAD policies and to co-ordinate funding for a five-year Action Plan to implement these policies. In these circumstances it is becoming clear to some observers that, like its predecessor, the *Commission Nationale pour la Promotion de la Femme* which was set up in 1976 and vanished in 1988, the Commission had been set up purely to comply with UN requirements and to ensure an appro-priate form of representation for Mali at the Beijing Conference (Ben Barka, 1994:26).

In Vietnam, the Vietnamese Women's Union (VWU) is one of several import-ant mass organizations which make up the 'Fatherland Front of Vietnam'—or the ruling communist party. Although by official statute it is a non-governmental organization, it has strong links to government and has been influential since the 1950s in promoting progressive legislation for women, in particular, labour legis-lation protecting women's conditions of employment and rights to maternity leave. During the war years, however, its main function was the mobilization of women as combatants, suppliers, and supporters of the war effort, and as a result, its main skills are in 'agit prop' (Tran Thi, 1994:29), rather than in structured pol-icy advocacy. One feature of its wartime organization was the development of an extensive grassroots network in villages, as well as representation in trade unions, giving it a valuable structure for co-ordinating gender and development efforts nationally. However, with just 150 staff members, the VWU is grossly under-resourced, and apparently its level of influence in villages and trade unions is highly uneven (Olin, 1988:16). Its commune-level chapters must func-tion on the derisory funds of 200 US dollars per year, most of which is used to pay the salary of the head of the chapter, making the chapter reliant on the funds of local authorities for any activities (Tran Thi, 1994).

Although the VWU gained the formal right, in a 1988 decision by the Vietnamese Council of Ministers, to be consulted and involved in any decision regarding women in the country, its lack of resources and the failure to specify specific measures to facilitate consultation, as well as the apparent lack of measures to veto unsatisfactory government policy, mean that the VWU has to rely primarily upon the uncertain mechanism of the goodwill of government members to include it in decision-making. Whilst its formal mandate as an arm of the Party is to focus on issues of national concern to women, since 1990 it has increasingly turned to the implementation of gender and development projects— such as income-generation—in response to the new availability of funds from international donors. There are two other small government units with responsibility for women's issues. The Board for Women's Affairs in the Vietnam Confederation of Labour, also a part of the Fatherland Front, monitors labour standards for women. It is tiny (six staff), but it ensures that all trade unions have a full-time women's representative. The Vietnam National Women's Committee was set up in 1993 to prepare for the Fourth UN Conference on Women in Beijing. In effect, it is a sub-component of the VWU, chaired by the VWU Chairwoman, with a mandate to monitor international treaties such as the Convention on the Elimination of all forms of Discrimination Against Women (CEDAW).

In Bangladesh and Uganda the WID/GAD agenda has been institutionalized in distinct Ministries, but in both cases they share space with marginalized public concerns: children, in the case of Bangladesh, and youth and culture in Uganda. Both Ministries suffer from under-resourcing, significant power distance from the central state directorate, association with residualist welfare or community issues, and overlapping roles with ruling party-linked women's units.

In Bangladesh the central WID/GAD unit has had a long but very administratively discontinuous history. It has been entirely hostage to shifting political currents, having been promoted to Ministerial status under the Bangladesh National Party (BNP) regime of President Zia ul-Rahman in the 1970s, demoted to a Department of the Social Affairs Ministry under President Ershad in the 1980s, and reinstated as a Ministry under the BNP regime of Zia's widow, Begum Khaleda Zia. These changes owe less to any significant variation in the official commitment to the WID/GAD agenda than to its utility at various times in generating international political capital in demonstrating a progressive national position. What has remained a constant in these opportunistic administrative *tergiversations* has been an unclear mandate, and deficiencies in staff, financial resources, and administrative privileges.

The current Department of Women's Affairs is part of the Ministry of Women and Children's Affairs. The Ministry's formal mandate combines an advocacy role with a programme implementation role. It is, however, under-equipped to carry out either role. Since 1990 it has been granted right of oversight and appraisal over projects of other Ministries and agencies, where it is given 10 days to review new projects before they are forwarded to the Planning Commission. Just two staff members are available for this, however, and they are constrained by the tight time limit and by a lack of gender analysis skills. On the operational side, its tiny budget for implementing programmes (just 0.22% of the national development budget) restricts it to small projects which are largely urban-centred, although it uses these to promote issues neglected by other Ministries, such as working women's need for hostels and childcare, shelters for domestic violence, legal education and legal aid, and vocational training. Many of its top-level posts are vacant, and have been for years, and it is quite unable to fulfil its functions as a line Ministry, with staff in less than a quarter of sub-districts. In this, its role conflicts with the better-resourced BNP-linked *Bangladesh Jatiyo Mahila Sangstha* (National Women's Association), which is located within the Ministry and which has staff in all districts.

In Uganda the central WID unit has also suffered from a certain amount of administrative precarity, where the 1988 WID Ministry was demoted to one of the three sections of the Ministry of WID, Youth, and Culture as a result of adjustment-inspired civil service reforms in 1991. Unlike the situation in Bangladesh, it has focused on its advocacy and policy co-ordination role, concentrating on provoking sustainable attitudinal and procedural changes across other Ministries, and has made some strategic gains in consequence. Its main activity since 1991 has been a cross-sectoral review of development policy with a view to formulating a National Gender-Oriented Policy Statement whose implementation will be the responsibility of the government's chief economic planning unit, the Ministry of Finance and Economic Planning. It has supported this process with gender-awareness training for senior civil servants and by instituting WID Focal Point Officers in each Ministry. It has also embarked on a unique process designed to enhance women's participation in civil society and their impact on national politics as an active electorate, through a civic education programme and through a nationwide consultative process which elicited women's views on the country's new Constitution.

Every one of these activities relied on donor funding. Many, also, are governed by what one WID official calls a 'contingency approach ... when something is happening, we focus on it and develop a programme to address a specific issue at a certain time, for a specific need' (cited in Kwesiga, 1994:18). Whilst this illustrates a laudable capacity for flexibility, the near total reliance on outside funding undermines the sustainability of these efforts, and at the same time illustrates a lack of long-term strategy and institutionalized mechanisms for promoting the WID agenda. For example, the UNDP-funded 'Umbrella Project' through which gender-awareness training was provided to senior civil servants, at the same time served as a mechanism for communication between WID and Focal Points in Ministries. The project is now over, but in consequence the important point of entry and communication it provided has been severed.

Another threat to sustainability, paradoxically, is the extent to which the WID agenda relies upon the strong support of President Museveni, who has been institutionalizing a positive role for women in his National Resistance Movement (NRM) government. But aside from the obvious precarity inherent in having support for the WID agenda reside so prominently in one individual, the association of the WID concern with the NRM—which, for all its genuine cross-party democratic inclusiveness is still a single ruling party—poses problems. There is a

Directorate of Women's Affairs within the NRM Secretariat, which has been headed by women who were active combatants in the civil war. The Director of Women's Affairs is responsible to the National Political Commissar, and the Directorate's role is the political education and mobilization of the country's female constituency. It has played a very important role in ensuring a politically institutionalized place for women in local government. But its role sometimes overlaps with that of the WID unit in the public administration system, with both units working on political and legal awareness issues. In addition, the importance of the Directorate of Women's Affairs within the NRM may mean that the WID agenda will be associated with that party, and hence vulnerable to its political fortunes, rather than institutionalized as a fundament of the public administration. The risk of a political blurring of the WID issue became apparent in 1994, when the Ministry of WID, Youth and Culture, as a non-priority administrative unit, was yet again under threat of being dismantled by IMF/World Bank pressures to down-size the civil service further. Though it fought this off, there was talk at one stage of absorbing some of its functions into the NRM's Directorate of Women's Affairs.

In Jamaica the Bureau of Women's Affairs has had an uneasy history on the administrative peripheries of the state, shunted back and forth between the Ministry of Youth and Community Development, and the Ministry of Social Affairs. Only once, in response to heightened awareness of the issue provoked by the UN Women's Conference in Mexico City, was it located in the Office of the Prime Minster, from 1975 to 1978. Since 1989, however, it has been located in the Ministry of Labour, Welfare, and Sport. This is significant and appropriate, given women's very high participation in the country's formal labour force. This latest institutional placement, however, may have owed less to women's strong history of labour force attachment than to the fact that at the time that Ministry was headed by the only female Cabinet Minster, prompting a sex-typed association between her person and her appropriate functions.

The Bureau has had a combined mandate of advocacy and project implementation, and has been highly dependent on outside funds to carry out these functions. In the late 1980s these funds were withdrawn in reaction to the government's persistent failure to provide counterpart funding, forcing the Bureau to withdraw from project activities, most of which had an income-generating focus, and to focus on efforts to influence the national planning process. Though this shift in focus is regretted by Bureau members (Mariott, 1994), it is a mixed blessing, as the Bureau was never properly equipped to implement projects. Also, curiously, the majority of these projects were conventional small-scale and informal-sector income-generating ventures. In a country which has one of the highest rates of female participation in formal employment in the world, this conventional WID focus seems unjustifiable. It perhaps best reflects the Bureau's intellectual and financial dependence on outside donors and their externally-derived WID perspectives.

Of all the case countries, Morocco has invested the least in setting up a coherent WID/GAD administrative entity. Instead, women's desks have been set up in an *ad hoc* manner across a range of Ministries, in response, primarily, to new funding opportunities available through the international community. The Women's desk in the Ministry of Employment and Social Affairs has had nominal responsibility for responding to international pressures for WID policy statements, but has no policy oversight role, no advocacy role, and no policy co-ordination role. Otherwise, there are women's units in the Ministry of Youth and Sports, of Public Health, of Agriculture, of Planning, of Foreign Affairs, and in the National Agricultural Credit Service. It is impossible to speak of a coherent WID strategy emerging from any of these units. Each responds to Ministerial priorities, and usually each is focused around women-specific and foreign-funded project activities which make few encroachments into broader Ministerial activities.

Overall, then, in no country except Vietnam has the WID/GAD concern found a secure and sustainable institutional expression. When located in advocacy units close to central state decision-making units, they tend to be inadequately resourced to fulfil their functions. When set up as separate Ministries they can become isolated as a peripheral enclave and associated with marginal concerns. There are cases where the WID/GAD issue has been seen by the dominant political party as a useful political resource, as a means either of demonstrating national progressive attitudes to the international community, as in Bangladesh, or as a source of political support from a hitherto neglected constituency, as in Uganda. This kind of politicization of the WID/GAD agenda may undercut its legitimacy and may cut it off from its natural constituency, where autonomous women's groups may shun association with party-linked WID units. A serious problem the WID/GAD issue faces is its association with an external concern. This means that WID/GAD units may be established in response to international pressures, but a mandate which is seen to have an external origin lacks national credibility and hence fails to generate commitment. The overwhelming degree to which WID/GAD advocacy and project activities in every one of these case countries depends on outside funding underlines the shallowness of national commitment to the issue and fundamentally undermines the sustainability of efforts to institutionalize the WID/GAD mandate.

Mechanisms for influencing other ministries: mainstreaming

Most of the WID/GAD units in question here have a mandate to pursue their agenda across other government departments, a project sometimes called 'mainstreaming'. For this they have devised a range of policy instruments, such as gender monitoring checklists, guidelines, inter-ministerial committees, gender-awareness training, and WID Focal Points. Gender-specific national policy statements or plans have also been formulated; these will be reviewed in the next section. Mainstreaming measures are intended to provoke gender-sensitive institutional, policy, and operational changes across the public sector in order to make responsiveness to women's interests a routine part of each sector's activities. At the very least, it is hoped that they will tap the technical and administrative resources of other departments to make up for resource deficiencies in the WID/GAD sector in research, advocacy, and implementation. Vietnam and Morocco will not be discussed in this section as the state units charged with gender equity in both countries do not appear to be equipped with mainstreaming mechanisms.

Jamaica is the only case country to have elaborated detailed gendered project guidelines and checklists, although Uganda is in the process of elaborating these kinds of tools, as well as gendered indicators to monitor project implementation. Jamaica's Project Profile format for all new projects incorporates a procedural step for assessing potential gender-differential impact issues. Linked to this, methods for assessing gender-differential impact have been incorporated into the training for civil servants at the Administrative Staff College. To ensure adherence to this measure, the Bureau of Women's Affairs has a seat on the project Pre-Selection Committee of the Planning Institute. For projects in process, a Gender Monitoring Checklist specifies five benchmarks against which development actions are assessed: whether sex-disaggregated data are used or collected; whether the project coheres with national policy commitments; whether mechanisms exist to consult with women and men on gender issues; whether the project takes action on equity issues; and whether the context for the project is gender-sensitive, in the sense of incorporating women's specific needs.

These measures are all well-designed, but have not been applied, owing to a lack of commitment and conviction—even, it seems, from the Bureau itself. According to interviews with civil servants, training associated with the gender component in the Project Profile format is 'vacuous', and the Bureau has failed to turn up on occasions to represent women's interests on the project Pre-Selection Committee. The Gender Monitoring Checklist was to have been piloted in two Ministries, but no results of this experiment have been circulated (Mariott, 1994:5).

Chile, Bangladesh, and Uganda have experimented with designating WID Focal Point officers in other Ministries. In Chile, this has been an informal process. SERNAM lacks institutional measures for communication and co-ordination with other Ministries, and hence requested that each Ministry designate a contact person for SERNAM to communicate with. There are no institutional rewards associated with the Focal Point position, and unsurprisingly it has not been awarded to high-ranking officials. In most cases, the informal Focal Point position has been occupied by individuals uninterested in the issue and hence unwilling to commit time to it. Without exception, where gender-sensitive changes are occurring in sectoral policy, it is in response to pressure from independently committed individuals, not to SERNAM's influence. The Ministries of Labour and Education are notable in that there has been committed top-level support for the gender issue from male Ministers. This, however, is not enough, as the strongest resistance comes from mid-level male staff. Training is only a partial solution, as it reaches only a few individuals, and often, as in the case of the highly resistant Ministry of Agriculture, the majority of staff reject training opportunities by failing to attend seminars on gender awareness (Pollack, 1994a:17).

In Bangladesh, a formal Focal Point system has been introduced recently, where designated contact individuals in 27 Ministries constitute an inter-ministerial co-ordination committee which meets every three months. Again, these positions have often been given to lower-ranking individuals who lack commitment to gender issues. WID planning cells in Ministries are understaffed and lack technical skills, and hence are unable to arm their Focal Points with relevant information or policy analyses. Ideally, the Bangladesh Department of WID would provide this technical support, but it is equally under-resourced in this area.

In Uganda, each Ministry has been responsible for designating a Focal Point Officer since 1991, with the WID Department advising that this should be a high-ranking official, such as a Commissioner or Assistant Commissioner. Considerable energy has been invested in providing gender-awareness training to these individuals and in encouraging them to initiate and chair the Ministerial policy reviews which are part of WID's cross-governmental effort to generate a national gender policy. The strategy has not been very effective, however, and in some Ministries staff are unaware of the existence of a Focal Point (Kwesiga, 1994:32). Outside of particular policy initiatives, or the opportunities afforded by the availability of funds for training, there are no clear mechanisms for routine communication and collaboration between these individuals and the WID Department. The civil service structure militates against this kind of boundary-crossing project. Influential entry-points are needed to Ministries, but high-ranking officials lack the time, and often the commitment, to take on a new and controversial policy agenda. The position is not budgeted for, and in a context where civil servants are desperately underpaid, and hence devote considerable time to outside income-generating activities, it is unrealistic to expect anyone to take on new responsibilities without reward.

By and large, in the cases under review, 'mainstreaming' has been interpreted as a project of simply gaining access to other Ministries; as a means of inserting staff charged with the WID mandate into the administrative structure, and inserting women as a target or client group in every development sector. The difficulties of achieving this alone has postponed a more transformative project of challenging the basic operating assumptions of each sector and their underlying disciplinary biases.

There is a more general problem inherent to projects of seeking cross-ministerial compliance to a new policy mandate. This has to do with the embeddedness of bureaucratic interests and their defence within bureaucratic boundaries. Most public administrations feature a strong propensity to protect ministerial territory and to resist cross-cutting interests. Especially in contexts of resource scarcity, administrative units tend to guard jealously their own territory, because development resources attached to programmes and projects offer opportunities for patronage and sometimes personal profit. This imposes competition between Ministries, who defend privileged access to resources by evolving distinctive mandates and operational processes tied to disciplinary and sectoral concerns. These same kinds of incentives operate on national WID units as well, producing a strong incentive to concentrate on women-specific projects which provide a visible justification for administrative existence.

There are very few precedents of efforts to infiltrate bureaucratic territory of other Ministries, and indeed, boundary-bridging activities are seen as contrary to technocratic norms. WID units have few positive incentives to encourage a positive reception in other bureaucratic units. They lack the technocratic and research capability which might mean that they are providing valuable services to other administrative units. Instead, they are seen as a drain on other Ministerial resources, which is not welcomed in contexts of resource scarcity.

Promoting national ownership of the WID/GAD agenda: integrating gender into national planning processes

National development plans and budgets are important public statements expressing politically chosen priorities for change and progress, and are based on a macro-economic framework designed to create the conditions under which this national vision can be realized. Integrating gender into this process requires both political and economic groundwork by WID/GAD policy advocates. This involves securing a top-level commitment to WID/GAD priorities, agreeing action programmes and earmarked funds for every planning sector, generating gender-disaggregated data, and designing gender-specific quantitative and qualitative achievement targets and progress indicators at the macro and sectoral levels.

In Chile SERNAM is currently formulating a national Equal Opportunity Plan. This is conceived much more broadly than the conventional association of equal opportunities with employment rights to 'promote an equal distribution of resources and social tasks, of civil rights, and participation, and access to power between men and women, and to value women's contribution to economic development' (Pollack, 1994a:3). SERNAM has also been successful in providing a new impetus for collecting gender-disaggregated data both within the Ministry of Planning, where it is located, and in other governmental departments. Within the Ministry of Planning, the annual socio-economic population survey is disaggregated by sex, and all new analytical work related to poverty and labour market issues address the gender dimension. However, no new indicators of relevance to gender difference—such as might touch on issues of physical security, reproductive health, political participation, or legal rights—have been included in statistics or surveys, although as of 1995 households were to be disaggregated by headship in living standards studies.

In Bangladesh since 1973 issues related to women have been raised in each successive five-year development plan. All of these plans have put primary emphasis on enhancing the quality of women's domestic role through, initially, handicraft training and family planning and later, through improved provision of rural credit and better access to education. The second development plan (1980–5) was the first to propose a multi-sectoral approach to women's development. But despite such suggestive rhetoric as: 'to ensure a balanced socio-economic development of the country full participation of women is an absolute necessity' (GOB, Second Five Year Plan 1980), no strategies were formulated, nor funds made available, for specific sectoral responsibilities. In this and subsequent plans, only the social sectors show significant expenditure allocations for women. The Third Five Year Plan (1985–90) raised employment issues for women, but these were almost entirely oriented to informal micro-enterprise opportunities which enable women to raise the productivity of their home-based work. No measures were detailed to increase the number of women participating in the formal labour force, save for a 15 per cent quota for women in public sector employment. Neither resources nor institutional mechanisms have been specified in these Plans to enable the Women's Ministry to discharge its co-ordinating, information generation, and policy design functions.

Somewhat mitigating this poor history of efforts to integrate women to the national planning process has been a gendered definitional coup in the way labour force statistics are now compiled in Bangladesh. In official statistics, women's labour force participation rate has leaped from 9.9 per cent in 1985–6, to 63.4 per cent in 1989 (BBS, 1992:95). This reflects a shift in the definition of the 'economically active' population in Labour Force Surveys. The 1989 Labour Force Survey identified a range of women-dominated forms of labour as 'economic activities'—such as weeding and hoeing, threshing/cleaning/husking/drying/boiling (of paddy), growing homestead vegetables, and processing and preserving food (BBS, 1992:96). This change does not yet entirely represent a gendering of the concept of labour as women's reproductive labour in the home is still not recognized. Nevertheless, it is an improvement.

An alternative approach to the promotion of women's interests in national planning documents has been the formulation of separate gender-focused national perspective plans by WID/GAD units. In Jamaica a National Policy Statement on Women was produced by the Bureau of Women's Affairs and adopted by Cabinet in 1987, and a five-year National Development Plan on Women was produced by the Bureau and the Planning Institute of Jamaica in 1990. The 1987 document is a brief but pointed articulation of a set of gender-egalitarian principles intended as a guide to government policy, although, as pointed out by the All-Island Women's Conference in Jamaica in 1992, it omits a statement on the political empowerment of women (Tomlinson, 1992:5). It details implementation responsibilities only at a very general level: Permanent Secretaries of all Ministries are charged with responsibility for monitoring respect for these principles in their Ministries, while the Permanent Secretary of the Ministry responsible for the Bureau of Women's Affairs (Labour, Welfare, and Sport), was charged with chairing an Inter-Ministerial Committee to monitor implementation, to formulate a detailed Action Plan, and to report annually to the Cabinet on progress. None of these measures were taken seriously, with junior civil servants, rather than Permanent Secretaries, sitting on the Inter-Ministerial Committee (Mariott, 1994:5). In the end, only the Planning Institute of Jamaica contributed significantly to the work of this Inter-Ministerial committee in formulating the National Plan of Action and the 1990 Five-Year Plan on Women, reflecting previous groundwork by the Bureau of Women's Affairs in gaining representation on the Planning Institute's Project Pre-Selection Committee. This Plan details actions to be taken in each major development sector and identifies main agencies responsible for implementation. But its implementation remains the sole responsibility of the Bureau of Women's Affairs. It has neither a budget nor details of budgetary implications for other government departments, and it has not been internalized by other departments since it was elaborated without any effective participation from them. Further, since it was elaborated separately from the Jamaican Five Year Development Plan to 1995, it remains essentially external to the main planning framework.

In Morocco, there is no WID presence in the Ministry of Planning or other central government department, which means that there has been no clear point from which gender-sensitive planning guidance should emerge. The Centre of Demographic Studies in the Department of Statistics in the Ministry of Planning does, however, produce valuable gender-disaggregated data, particularly in relation to the formal workforce. But no women or gender-trained researchers are part of this team, nor is it animated by any concern to illuminate significant information on gender for planners. This restricts the potential impact of gender-disaggregated data on the policymaking process, and it has also meant that a range of important gender issues are not included in national surveys—for example, legal and political aspects of women's lives (Barkallil, 1994:17). This lack of a national perspective on gender issues was sharply highlighted in the context of the 1985 Nairobi conference, and the Division of Aid and Social Protection of the Ministry of Employment and Social Affairs was charged with producing a national plan, the National Strategy for the Promotion of Moroccan Women to the Year 2000. The document was not completed until 1989. Unfortunately it is a desultory effort, reflecting the limited perspective of its urban and formal employment-focused ministerial location. It does not even differentiate between the needs of urban and rural women, in spite of the availability of data. It clings to conventional assumptions about the labour market, disregarding non-waged forms of employment. And as Barkallil points out, it is also absolutely inoperative, failing to detail action plans worked out over time, to quantify targets, or to specify budget implications (ibid.:12).

Sector-specific planning efforts have featured gender issues according to the relative strength of such women's units as may be present in line Ministries. Curiously, in the social sectors, where a WID/GAD perspective might have been expected to take hold because of the association of women with social issues, they have been completely by-passed. A draft strategy statement for social development presented at a seminar at the Ministry of Planning in Rabat in June 1993 completely lacks a WID/GAD perspective, with women and girls only mentioned parenthetically as recipients of healthcare and education (GOM, 1993). In contrast, a very strong gender-focused planning statement was produced in 1994 by the Ministry of Agriculture's extension division. This short draft statement details women's role in agricultural production and their needs from research and extension services, although it lacks specific programme or budgetary details (Bennis, 1994). This reflects the growing legitimacy of the gender issue within this Ministry, much encouraged by significant donor-funded programmes within the agricultural extension service which tie family planning, literacy, and nutrition education to agricultural extension functions (Barkallil, 1994:14). The growing legitimacy of gender issues in the agricultural sector is owing, importantly, to a data 'discovery': a 1986/87 survey of the rural workforce managed through the Statistical Division of the Ministry of Agriculture which revealed for the first time the extent of women's participation in agricultural production. Pressure from donors, in particular the FAO, the UNFPA, and the World Bank, meant that the definition of agricultural employment was expanded to include unwaged family labour, revealing that 50 per cent of the rural population active in agriculture are women (ibid.:20).

Vietnam, like Morocco, has no system for mainstreaming gender equity concerns in national planning. No systematic attention is paid to gender equity in the State Commission on Development Planning or in technical or line Ministries. That vigilance is required is evident in a national employment generation programme launched in 1992 which did not include a component for women until the Vietnamese Women's Union put pressure on the government to allocate some of the funding to a credit programme for women (in the end, just 1.8 per cent of the funding from this national programme was allocated to women) (Tran Thi, 1994:26). Observers feel that gender equity concerns have tended to be addressed in national planning only when features of gender relations impede national production goals (Olin, 1988:16). For example, the concern to free women's labour for employment in public sector services and industries during the war turned attention to the need to replace women's domestic labour through the provision of childcare. The Vietnamese Women's Union, though not a part of the public administration, has nevertheless played an important role in promoting women's rights. It fiercely lobbied the government to retain the provision for six months' maternity leave in the new Labour Code adopted in 1994. In this, it actually clashed with another women's department, the Board for Women's Affairs in the Confederation of Labour, which was promoting a reduction of maternity leave to four months to discourage newly privatized businesses from avoiding hiring women because of the costs of maternity leave. Another motive behind this was popular resentment at women's capacity to moonlight in a second job during paid maternity leave. The Labour Code eventually adopted ambiguous wording guaranteeing six months' maternity leave to state workers and four months for women employees in private business. The absence of a legitimate government unit with responsibilities for mainstreaming gender equity concerns means that it becomes impossible for women to take a concerted stand against the incursions on their labour rights represented by economic liberalization. The VWU's efforts are turning increasingly towards the satisfactions of implementing discrete WID projects rather than the stress of pursuing cross-government policy changes, and it is encouraged in this by the availability of project funding from international donors.

This problem of cross-government ownership of the WID agenda in development planning is currently being approached in a different way by the Department of WID in Uganda. As in the other case countries, gender issues are insufficiently detailed in the national planning document, the 1993–6 Rehabilitation and Development Plan, which is the 'single most comprehensive statement of Government's principal social and economic policies' (GOU, 1993:1). This plan is primarily concerned with co-ordinating macro-economic stabilization measures and structural adjustment in agriculture, industry, and the social sectors. There is an emphasis on encouraging private initiative and a stronger export-orientation in the productive sectors through privatization and market liberalization. The focus in the social sectors is on improving the delivery of primary- and rural-level services in a cost-effective manner. Three paragraphs under a small sub-heading on WID reiterate the government's commitment to integrating gender in development, and acknowledge that women 'are the overwhelming majority of the producers in agriculture which is the mainstay of the economy' (ibid.:58). But in the rest of the document, gender is not integrated into planning assumptions regarding the impact of liberalization on patterns of labour and asset deployment in productive sectors such as agriculture, nor the impact of higher prices for basic commodities on domestic consumption budgets. Gender-specific issues are not detailed in the social sector chapters, nor are the gender-differential impact of new measures in the social sectors such as cost recovery for health and education services assessed. Instead, gender issues are relegated to the attention of the Programme to Alleviate Poverty and the Social Costs of Adjustment (PAPSCA). In this marginalized programme, the relatively undifferentiated category of 'women' is listed as one of six vulnerable groups (children, the urban poor, the disabled, redeployed civil servants, and residents of the twelve poorest districts). In essence, this labels women as a residual group whose poverty, like those of the other groups mentioned, is inadequately mitigated by traditional and other safety nets.

The Department of WID has launched a major cross-Ministerial planning exercise in response to this. In an important alliance with the central economic planning unit, the Ministry of Finance and Economic Planning (MFEP), it elaborated a National Policy Statement on Gender Issues and set up procedures for 'Gender Oriented Policy Development' in every Ministry. For each Ministry, a team of officers from the Department of WID works out an initial policy paper which is presented to Cabinet by the relevant Minister. Once approved, the

Ministry in question forms a top-level committee, mainly of Department Heads, to elaborate policy details. The team of WID officers works with this committee, often providing gender-awareness training as a first step, and a draft statement consisting of a gender analysis of the Ministry's existing work, and recommendations for changes, is formulated. The draft is submitted to a Ministerial workshop, and then presented at a national two-day policy workshop which finalizes a set of policy guidelines. Drafts are under discussion in the Ministries of Education and Health. Once all sectoral Ministries have completed this process, these policy statements will inform the watchdog role the MFEP will perform in using budgetary measures to monitor implementation progress in each Ministry.

As this policy exercise is still in process, it is difficult to assess its impact. It has moved slowly so far, primarily because the team of WID officers trained in gender, planning, and development economics carrying out this exercise for each ministry is small and over-stretched. A gender training project for senior civil servants supported by the UNDP has been helpful in raising gender awareness within the bureaucracy and in supporting the planning exercise. Two of the available draft gender-oriented policy statements show policy analysis work of good quality. The statements for the Ministry of Commerce, Industry and Co-operatives and the Ministry of Education and Sports show strong conceptual clarity in identifying gender differences in labour deployment and resource control, access to markets and social services, and socio-cultural power in public and private institutions. Interestingly, they are also attentive to issues of sexuality, and - identify sexual harassment in the workplace and gender differences in personal physical security in the schoolroom as factors requiring policy responses.

On the other hand, neither the sectoral gender policy statements, nor the draft national policy statement detail budget implications of any of the proposed policies. As suggested in the reviews of national planning experiences in Morocco, Jamaica, and Bangladesh, this failure to follow through recommendations with clear calculations of public expenditure implications has been an important reason why WID/GAD policy commitments tend to stay trapped on paper.

In sum, WID/GAD institutions in many of the case studies have developed a capacity for strategic planning, but what they still lack is a capacity to ensure that national policy commitments to the integration of gender in development are clearly tied to budget allocations. Here, skills are needed in budget analysis, and in the identification of important policy documents—such as public expenditure reviews, or published national budget statements—for analysis and exposure. For this to be effective, however, more gender-disaggregated data are needed about the extent to which government spending actually reaches women, and more generally, about women's income, consumption, and contribution to production. There have been some noteworthy successes in challenging definitional biases in some databases used for planning purposes—most particularly, in labour force statistics. Less success has been achieved with data on expenditure and consumption such as Living Standards Measurement Surveys or Integrated Household Surveys which continue to regard the household as the main unit of

70

analysis. It has also proven difficult to introduce indicators relating to gendered asymmetries of power—such as participation in local and national politics, sexual violence, juridical rights—to official data used in planning. With regard to the latter, the strategy of WID/GAD units has been to focus on raising public awareness of these issues, as a preliminary step in legitimizing them as matters for policy and planning. These efforts, many of which involve liaising with constituencies and amplifying women's 'voice' within the administration, are the focus of the next section.

Developing WID/GAD constituencies in and outside the state

Making space for women in the state

Themes which emerge powerfully from the interview data on which this chapter is based are the chronic short-staffing of WID/GAD administrative units, the general paucity of women in the higher levels of the civil service and in government, the lack of awareness of and commitment to gender issues generally amongst state personnel, and the critical importance of allies in government and in the administration. Some WID/GAD units have been staffed and headed by men who are often not gender-sensitive. As career civil servants, they consider placement in a marginal administrative unit to be a demotion (which indeed it may often be). Women civil servants in the same positions may share these characteristics and attitudes. As a range of studies of women bureaucrats in other contexts show, women bureaucrats and politicians cannot by any means be assumed automatically to be predisposed to work in women's interests (Hirshman, 1991; Hale and Kelly, 1989; Dahlerup, 1988). Their class status distances them from the concerns of poorer women. More importantly, the few women who do gain access to administrative or political positions tend to be isolated from other women and are under powerful pressures to conform to the dominant orientations of their institutions and the work patterns and concerns of their male colleagues. These pressures limit possibilities for developing sensitivity to, and acting in, women's interests.

Association with an under-prioritized agenda like WID/GAD can exacerbate problems of individual marginalization and, ironically, problems of personal disaffection with the issue. High-flying careers in the civil service are not often made on its 'softest' peripheries, and certainly not in stigmatized 'women's' sectors. All of the interview reports detail the great frustration WID/GAD bureaucrats feel at their lack of resources and limited impact, their uncertain mandate, and worst of all, at the lack of legitimacy the issue appears to have. It is worth quoting Barkallil on the perspectives of Moroccan civil servants in WID units:

They (WID bureaucrats) find themselves engaged on an issue for which they often do not feel prepared, all the more so because their mission is in no way defined by written directives coming from higher levels of the administration

71

like the Ministries concerned or the Prime Minister. One has the impression that they are assigned to a delicate question which they have been left to manage as best they can, not with a view to satisfying objectives of effectiveness but in a manner such as to appear to be doing something, from the perspective of national and international opinion, but above all, from the perspective of foreign donors (1994:22).

Where interviewees cited instances of a positive reception of WID/GAD policy goals in line ministries, these almost invariably relied upon the presence of a gender-sensitive civil servant—often, but not always, a woman. This speaks not just to the importance of gender training for state agents, but to the importance of building up what Dahlerup terms a 'critical mass' of women in public administration (Dahlerup, 1988).

The impact of gender training efforts has been mixed. In Jamaica, gender training is given to all new bureaucrats in the administrative staff college to equip them with gender-sensitive project assessment skills, but the training itself is considered 'vacuous' by gender policy advocates. In Chile, gender training opportunities for staff in the Ministry of Agriculture were largely ignored. The evidence from the Chilean interviews suggests that the gender-sensitivity of a bureaucratic unit depends on the number of women at mid- and senior levels, and in particular, on support from the top. Two consecutive male Ministers of Education, for example, have had a strong commitment to gender equity, as does the new Minister of Labour appointed after the March 1994 elections. The new President, Eduardo Frei, has also supported gender equality, having included equal opportunities on his political platform (Pollack, 1994a:4–6). Even this strong top-level support, however, has been insufficient to combat the resistance of mid-level career bureaucrats (ibid). The UNDP-funded gender training project in Uganda appears to have been fairly successful, especially as it is tied to an ongoing sectoral planning effort. There, several male Permanent Secretaries have given the issue strong support (Kwesiga, 1994:21).

Obstacles to the increased representation of women at senior levels in the bureaucracy are considerable the world over. Quite aside from structural problems stemming from sex-typing of women in the education system and labour markets, and from the competing demands of women's private lives, women who do gain access to the bureaucracy eventually bump into glass ceilings maintained by the bureaucratic fraternity. In Morocco, this process is personally managed by the representative of traditional patriarchy—the king—who makes appointments to high administrative office, and has not once conceded this honour to women civil servants.

In Bangladesh, there is a recruitment quota system in the civil service. Since 1972, 10 per cent of gazetted and 15 per cent of non-gazetted posts have been reserved for women. No other special training is provided to enhance their performance in the civil service, let alone their gender-sensitivity. The system has evolved into a maximum ceiling for women recruits, rather than a minimum threshold. Quotas have had the effect of stigmatizing women's presence in the civil service, where they are regarded as having gained access by virtue of their sex, rather than merit. On the other hand, they have without question allowed for a greater presence of women in public service than would have occurred without special measures.

At Independence, Bangladesh also institutionalized a system to compensate for women's political invisibility by reserving Parliamentary seats for them—15 out of 300 seats in the early 1970s, raised to 30 in 1978. Three seats are also reserved for women—to be filled by nomination—at every level of local government. This system of reservations, far from providing an effective channel for the expression of women's interests at policymaking levels, effectively cuts them off from political processes. At the parliamentary level, reservations for women effectively excuses political parties from nominating women candidates to contest seats and cuts women off from a popular base (Chowdhury, 1985:269–70). Since these seats are filled by nomination by the government, they serve merely as a means of providing the ruling party with an extra block of votes. These women have not, however, been entirely inactive as advocates of women's formal rights, occasionally putting pressure on the government for reform of personal and family law, while their concern to prioritize social development and poverty problems contrasts with their male colleagues' concerns with national security (Jahan, 1982). At the local government level, nominated women tend to have the same class interests as their male counterparts, and the women who have successfully run for leadership positions on these councils have tended to be wives or relatives of male politicians, elected as proxies (Alam, 1987).

In Vietnam, quotas for women's employment in the public administration do not appear to have generated the same problems as in Bangladesh. To begin with, quotas were much less a reluctant and tokenistic gesture towards gender equity, than a campaign to ensure adequate staffing levels in the civil service given men's absence on the war front. In 1967 the then Prime Minister suggested an increase in the quota of women civil servants in education and public health offices, as well as trading and light industry establishments, from 50 per cent to 70 per cent (Tran Thi, 1994:9). Though the proportion of women in public administration has not appeared to exceed the high point of 48 per cent in the 1980s, this nevertheless suggests an extremely gender-balanced bureaucracy. The picture is rather different when scrutinized by status levels; women have never held more than 5 per cent of directorships in state-run firms. Nevertheless, the high number of women in the rank and file of the public administration may account for the consistency with which gender-sensitive legislation on such issues as, for example, labour and property rights has, until recently, been promoted and implemented, unlike other contexts in which top-level policies for gender equity encounter bureaucratic resistance at the implementation levels.

Women's high participation in the economy and in public administration, as well as in the war effort, has never been reflected in the number of women represented in politics. Though women war heroes have held prominent public positions and have been role models for women, women's involvement in political decision-making has been low. Indeed, since the mid-1980s, with the beginnings of economic liberalization, there appears to be an accelerating retreat of women from politics, with the proportion of women in local councils from the Commune- to the Province-level falling by half to a 1993 average of 10 per cent. Women's representation in the national assembly has remained fairly constant at 18 per cent (Tran Thi, 1994:18). One can only speculate that women's increased workloads consequent on the loss of public subsidies for childcare, and women's expanding economic opportunities under market reform, are either eroding women's time for politics, or providing them with more lucrative activities.

In Uganda no formal mechanisms exist to enhance women's representation in the administration, although there are a range of measures to enhance women's political participation from the village to Parliament. Within the administration, nevertheless, women have been appointed to important positions, including a number of Commissions reviewing government policy in education, human rights, and public service. A woman university professor, the head of the Department of Women's Studies at Makerere University, was appointed Deputy Chairman (sic) of the Constitutional Commission, a very important post, given the need to incorporate women's views into the country's basic legal framework. In comparison with many other countries, women have achieved a respectable level of representation at the highest position in line Ministries accessible through promotion, where they are 26 per cent of Under Secretaries.

At the village level and upwards, a unique process of improving channels for women's political access to the state is underway. In April the 1993 National Resistance Council (NRC)—in effect the country's Parliament—approved the setting up of a decentralized network of National Women's Councils (NWCs). These parallel a local government system of 'Resistance Councils' (RCs) which were first set up during the civil war by Museveni's National Resistance Army and were retained after the war by the National Resistance Movement government. Each of the country's 32 districts is divided into five administrative zones, with Resistance Councils at each level. Women's participation is already institutionalized as a part of these structures, where there is a mandatory place for at least one woman (usually the Secretary for Women) on the nine elected seats at each of the five RC levels. Each District elects a woman representative to sit in the NRC, which means that since the first nationwide elections took place in 1989, the numbers of women Parliamentarians has increased.

The new National Women's Councils system is designed to enhance women's political participation beyond that provided through the RC system. A parallel elected hierarchy of women's councils at all administrative levels will culminate in a National Women's Council made up of delegates from each District and will elect five representatives to Parliament. A similar Youth Council system has also been set up. Ideally, the NWC system should produce an institutional base for the political expression of women's interests, debated in a democratic

74

manner from the bottom to top levels of government. In the existing RC system, women's electoral and political participation appears to have increased, with women standing for positions other than Secretary for Women's Affairs in the second RC elections which took place in 1992. But the RC system alone was seen as insufficient to promote women's political participation; predictably, lone women representatives on RCs have tended to be dominated by their male counterparts. The NWC system may provide a privileged space for women to develop political voice.

Alternatively, the NWC system may come to provide an excuse for the neglect of women's interests in the RC system. The existence of parallel systems may become strongly gender-typed, with the 'female' NWC system contrasted to a 'male' RC system, and undervalued or marginalized as less legitimate in consequence. The parallel development of Youth Councils might reinforce this process, where women and youth come to be associated with a lesser degree of political citizenship than adult men, by virtue of these special measures. In other words, the system may end up reinforcing the conventions which exclude women from electoral processes and define the political world as male.

Another problem regards ruling party control. The NWC system is managed out of the Directorate of Women's Affairs in the NRM Secretariat. The NRM has been extraordinarily inclusive of oppositional interests as part of Museveni's desire to build a national government of democratic reconciliation without returning to the sectarian multi-party system which proved so destructive in the past. But it is still effectively a one-party system, pending the decisions of the Constituent Assembly on the revision of the Constitution. This means that the National Women's Councils system risks becoming in effect a women's wing for the party. To the degree that it does so, it will be completely unsustainable when there is a change of government.

Several general observations can be made about efforts to gain allies and to increase women's representation in politics and the administration in the case countries. Firstly, most often women who are already in the administration, even if gender-sensitive, are too isolated to risk association with the GAD issue. Efforts to network amongst them, however, as is happening in Uganda and Chile, sometimes through the 'Focal Points' mechanism, can strengthen their resolve and effectiveness. Secondly, quota systems for increasing women's representation in the administration are not necessarily effective in building up an internal GAD constituency. This should not, however, be taken as an argument against minimum quotas for women, as the possibility remains that they may eventually constitute a 'critical mass' with enough mutual support to venture allegiance to the GAD agenda, as may be the case in Vietnam. Thirdly, efforts to gain allies through gender training will inevitably be limited in impact unless supported by positive incentives for changed behaviour, and concrete measures to change institutional rules and structures. Attitudinal barriers amongst the balance of civil servants constrain the effectiveness of gender training. As Barkallil notes for Morocco, 'the problem is not linked to an absence of professional qualifications, but, rather, to the absence of engagement in favour of the question' (1994:25).

A final point regarding the history of efforts to improve women's representation in political decision-making fora. However laudable in theory, many of these efforts appear in practice to have treated women as a captive or at least 'capturable' constituency for the ruling political party. In patrimonial political systems where power revolves around a ruler and his or her family, women have often been brought into politics on extremely paternalistic terms, as a constituency in need of nurturing, directly under the arm of the ruler's party. The not infrequent association of a national leader's wife or female relative with women in politics or national women's associations, reinforces this connection. Inescapably, this seriously compromises the relative autonomy of women in politics from 'men's' politics, and undermines their capacity to raise oppositional perspectives on political decision-making. It also undermines the capacity of these women's units to adapt to significant changes in the economy or the political situation. This may be the case in Vietnam, where the Vietnamese Women's Union's association with the Indochinese Communist Party means that, unfortunately, its feminist concerns are associated with an increasingly discredited socialist system. Active and independent women's organizations in civil society—the subject of the next section—can mitigate this, by providing continuity and legitimacy for women's concerns.

Cultivating a constituency: mechanisms for public advocacy, co-ordination with NGOs and linkages to women's organizations

In the politics of policymaking a critical point of leverage on decision-makers is popular pressure and public opinion—an active constituency. Ideally the best source of constituency pressure in the context of efforts to integrate gender in development planning and to institutionalize gender-sensitive governance is WID/GAD's natural constituency: the organized expression of women's interests from outside of the government administration, with support from male allies. The WID/GAD agenda faces particular obstacles when it comes to finding or cultivating an effective political base amongst its constituency. Women are almost by definition excluded from public political space the world over, and lack histories of organizing on a corporate basis in defence of their own interests, although there are plenty of examples of women organizing along with men to pursue social, economic, and political agendas, though not necessarily on their own terms. Even where women's interests do converge and find organizational expression, women often lack the financial and social resources and political experience to make an effective impact on public decision-making. In some cases their non-conventional forms of protest, as evinced by women's human rights groups in Chile, or protests by market women in some African countries in response to price rises, have had an undeniable impact on politics. As Jacquette argues, however, these 'new social movements', in their preference for relatively weak organizational forms, have not been able to sustain a role in politics, as they lack the structures to aggregate interests, represent constituencies, and produce workable outcomes (1994:338–339).

Important strategies for official WID/GAD units in the context of uncertain constituencies have included raising public awareness of gender issues to challenge the acceptability of gendered asymmetries in resource access and social values, promoting the development of women's organizations, and establishing links with sympathetic NGOs. National umbrella organizations for women's groups have been one means for this. Ideally, these are mechanisms for a two-way flow between the bureaucracy and women's groups. In practice, these have been highly vulnerable to political co-optation and become instead the means for a one-way flow—of government control over women's organizations. This has been the case with the Uganda National Council of Women (formed in 1978 by Amin's government). This institution still exists within the new Ministry of WID, Youth and Culture, and though its functions have been entirely superseded by the autonomous National Association of Women's Organizations in Uganda (registered as an NGO in 1992), its statutory powers have not yet been repealed by Parliament. This situation makes for conflicts of interest and status between bureaucratic WID/GAD units. Other strategies for cultivating constituencies and co-ordinating with NGOs are reviewed below.

In Uganda the explosion of women's activism in associational life in the context of peace after decades of insecurity has been an important resource for the Department of WID. The National Association of Women's Organizations in Uganda has registered 60 NGOs and over 2000 community-based organizations since its inception in 1989. Some of these organizations have collaborated with the Department of WID to conduct research, to promote legal change, and to implement pilot projects. For example, the Department of WID has worked with the Uganda Women's Finance and Credit Trust (UWFCT) and the Ugandan Association of Women Lawyers (FIDA-U) to implement a credit and legal education pilot project in rural areas. Action for Development (ACFODE), a feminist advocacy group set up in 1985, and FIDA-U collaborated with WID to propose legal reform of family law to the Ministry of Justice. The Women's Studies Department at Makerere University has been involved in gender training of civil servants.

By far the most exciting of the Department of WID's efforts to build connections to its constituency have been related to the political reform processes underway in the country. It has embarked on a series of efforts to provide political education to women and to solicit their views on national policymaking. In 1990 the Department of WID launched an unprecedented process: it consulted women all over the country to collect their views on the country's basic legal framework—the Constitution—for submission to the Constitutional Commission. This was probably the first time in history that a nation's female citizenry was so closely involved in framing a constitution. Supported by DANIDA, the Department of WID launched a major training programme and produced a simple illustrated manual outlining the main elements of the Constitution (GOU, 1990). Seminars were held all over the country with a range of women participants—from illiterate farmers to RC officials, lower-level civil servants like teachers and nurses, and members of women's groups and local NGOs. The resulting recommendations report faithfully on women's views on every aspect of the Constitution, including the electoral system, the powers of the executive, judiciary, and the legislature, and detail women's views on marriage, divorce, inheritance, child custody, property rights, employment regulations, and children's rights (GOU, 1991). One outcome of this process was the greater politicization of women on Constitutional issues, with 30 women contesting for seats in the Constituent Assembly elections of 1994 (nine succeeded). The Department of WID's involvement in exercises such as these gives it more direct access to the concerns of its rural constituency than is common in many national WID/GAD units.

In Bangladesh, the Department of Women's Affairs has no institutional mechanisms for communicating with and co-ordinating efforts amongst women's organizations and NGOs. It does maintain an impressive register of women-friendly NGOs. But women's organizations prefer to maintain distance from the DWA, most probably because it is largely staffed by members of the *Bangladesh Jatiyo Mahila Sangstha* (National Women's Association), with links to the Bangladesh National Party. This connection is particularly strong given that the current Prime Minister, Khaleda Zia, had been involved in founding the BJMS in the 1970s, as the wife of the then President Zia. Finally, the DWA's capacity for influencing development processes in rural areas is extremely limited; it has offices in just 22 of the 64 Districts and has staff in just 100 of the 460 sub-districts. By and large, in consequence, it is relatively isolated from the women's movement.

In Jamaica, processes of constituency outreach on the part of the Bureau of Women's Affairs are well institutionalized, but its relationships with NGOs and women's organizations have been uneven, and very much dependent on the economic situation—both of the Bureau itself and the country. Parish Advisory Committees have acted as liaisons between women's organizations in parishes and the Bureau of Women's Affairs since 1985. They also act as a lobbying force locally to ensure that changes are effected in rural women's lives. Over the years, the Bureau has come to work more closely with NGOs as its own capacity to initiate, research, and implement projects withered with the withdrawal of donor funds because of the government's failure to provide counterpart funding (Mariott, 1994:5). Disappointingly, however, its relationship with women's organizations has not been strong over the 1980s. Observers suggest that the women's movement has been decimated by the economic hardships brought by austerity measures in the 1980s, diverting efforts from advocacy to economic survival (ibid.:6).

In Mali, the new Commission for the Promotion of Women is one of the few WID units in the case study countries to have clear institutional means for collaborating with NGOs and women's organizations. One of its main responsibilities is to chair a representative government/NGO co-ordinating body, composed of ten government officials, ten representatives of NGOs, and ten representatives of women's organizations. Amongst women's organizations, a loose form of co-ordination exists already, but has faced several problems likely to affect the Commission as well. These owe something to the character of many women's organizations, which are very new, primarily urban, and as yet less concerned with development issues than with the political transition to democracy (Ben Barka, 1994:26). No coherent perspective on gender and development has yet emerged from this group.

In Morocco, reflecting the uneven institutionalization of WID units across the administration, there is a notable absence of a point of communication or co-ordination between the government and women's groups or NGOs. Some degree of consultation with women's organizations has occurred in women's units in certain Ministries and government units (particularly the Ministry of Youth and Sport, the Ministry of Agriculture, and the National Agricultural Credit Service), but these are about isolated events such as seminars which tend to be sponsored by external donors and focused on particular projects.

With regard to more cross-sectoral and legal issues of critical relevance to gender relations and matters of equity and redistribution, consultation with women's organizations has been almost insultingly cursory, showing an astonishing degree of condescension and disregard for women's perspectives on public policy. For example, in the recent process of reforming the country's Islamic family law code, the *Moudouana,* managed by the king, women's organizations were only peripherally consulted. They were contacted in writing; public debate and the possibility of conflict was avoided. Not a single woman from the women's movement or a woman from within the legal system sat on the commission charged with revising this critical piece of legislation. The resulting legislation reproduced a patriarchal family model, ignoring changes in women's social and economic roles in Morocco.

Chile differs from the above cases in that its National Service for Women (SERNAM) has had no formal mandate to work with women's organizations or NGOs. This may to some degree reflect a desire on the part of the main coalition of feminist organizations (CNMD) to preserve its autonomy and to pursue a more radical agenda outside government. SERNAM has pursued a project of putting gender issues on the public agenda primarily through the creation of Centres of Information on Women's Rights, concentrating on democracy, poverty, and human rights. It has collaborated with NGOs for the purpose of research into employment and domestic violence issues, but only when funded by international agencies. According to some observers, this relative detachment may owe to a reluctance to become embroiled in political differences within the NGO and women's communities (Pollack, 1994b:4). In a context of highly politicized forms of associational life in civil society this reticence is perfectly understandable, and probably healthy. In any case, the dynamism of CNMD and its autonomy from the administration are probably the best guarantors of the continued development of a feminist constituency in the country.

Finally, Vietnam differs radically from the other cases in that women's activism in civil society, independent of the Indochinese Communist Party, was one of the political freedoms absent in socialist Vietnam. There is much interest now, in the current environment of liberalization, to relax controls on civil society, and also, to give formal Party units such as the Vietnamese Women's Union more autonomy from the Party. In the meantime, the Vietnamese Women's Union's contact with its constituency has been primarily through its extensive grassroots network.

Overall, the relationship between national WID/GAD units and the national female constituency as expressed in women's organizations and NGOs has tended to be somewhat uneasy, with Uganda offering a more positive recent experience of collaboration, and Morocco illustrating the problems which arise for collaboration when there is an absence of a legitimate institutional location for this within the administration.[3] One serious obstacle to effective collaboration stems from bureaucratic norms. Too much interaction with outside constituencies can be seen as a violation of professionalism to the extent that it is regarded as politicizing the administration and eroding its integrity. For example, in a relatively open and transparent administration, a WID/GAD unit might rightly illuminate deficiencies in the government's accountability to women, thereby providing outside constituencies with 'ammunition' with which to lobby for change. This means divided loyalties for many WID/GAD bureaucrats, which can undermine their credibility in the bureaucracy. A similar set of constraints operate in the opposite direction. Women's organizations in particular may resist association with an administration linked to a government which is not seen as responsive to their concerns. This appears to be the case in Bangladesh. The transformative potential inherent to an iterative relationship between an active women's constituency and WID/GAD agents in the administration is perhaps best exploited where both retain a degree of autonomy from the other, yet attempt to ensure that their activities on either side of the state/civil society divide are mutually supportive. It is too early to say for certain, but this appears to be the pattern developing in Chile.

Conclusions: constraints, opportunities, missed opportunities

This review of efforts to integrate gender to the development process demonstrates above all the deep obstacles to what has been called 'de-institutionalizing male preference'. These obstacles are embedded in the everyday functioning and the overall structure of government bureaucracies, which give little space and no legitimacy to a political project of gender equity. This final section reviews the constraints faced by WID/GAD units and looks at the opportunities for change.

A primordial constraint on the WID/GAD agenda is the hierarchical and undemocratic nature of bureaucracies, and their hostility to agendas which challenge accustomed organizational patterns. In national public administrations, this hostility is deeply compounded by the high boundaries erected between different sectoral Ministries and by the patronage politics preserved by Ministerial boundaries. The most important constraint, however, is inherent in the deeply embedded gendered conventions in public bureaucracies, where women's needs are largely seen as a matter for private provision, not public administration. Challenging these conventions, which the WID/GAD agenda does, arouses profound resistance and fairly efficient subversion.

In effect, subversion inheres in the under-resourcing and stigmatization of which members of WID/GAD units interviewed for this study universally complained. The structural location and the nature of the operational powers assigned to WID/GAD units have exacerbated these problems. WID/GAD units tend to have had unstable histories as organizational entities. Shifted between different administrative units, they have been unable to establish themselves institutionally as part of the basic structure of the administration. Their roles and mandate vary from 'advisory', 'oversight', and 'monitoring', to 'implementation', but what remains a constant is that they lack sufficient personnel, financial, and technical resources to fulfil any combination of these functions effectively.

There is no clearly preferable combination of roles for WID/GAD. The Ugandan, Chilean, and Bangladeshi women's units in government combine policy oversight, monitoring, and advocacy roles, as does Chile's SERNAM, but the Ugandan and Chilean cases appear more successful. The significant difference is a more positive institutional environment for the WID/GAD issue, reflecting the current support it has from the national leadership in Uganda and Chile. It also seems clear that responsibility for actually implementing WID/GAD programmes is best left to line Ministries, given the lack of resources in WID/GAD units to implement programmes which might have a national-level impact, and the tendency by other government units to assume that gender issues are spoken for when programmes are implemented by WID/GAD units.

Ideally, WID/GAD units ought to perform a policy advisory role and provide technical inputs. A strong theme emerging from the interviews regards the lack of technical skills of WID/GAD personnel, both in terms of skills in policy and project analysis, design, implementation, and evaluation, and in terms of skills in gender analysis. With regard to the former set of skills, the most serious shortcoming has been a failure to follow the implications of new policy and planning proposals through to budgetary implications. This means that many national gender planning statements produced by WID/GAD units have a curiously detached and abstract nature. They gain top-level endorsement yet are inoperable, lacking indications for budget allocations or clear instructions for line Ministries to implement.

With regard to skills in gender analysis, an important constraint has been the lack of conceptual clarity in the use of the term 'gender', and the tendency to assume it refers to 'women' alone. This has sometimes had the effect of narrowing the focus of policy scrutiny to 'women-only' policies and programmes, diverting attention from the broader sweep of development policies. One result is that the analyses of new policy agendas—such as poverty reduction initiatives or the introduction of environmental sustainability concerns—may not be 'tracked' through to their implications for women and men in all sectors. Instead, 'gender' issues will be 'noticed' only where these policies impinge on sectors traditionally associated with women, on social development and welfare matters, for example, or in fuel-gathering and domestic sanitation. To improve the quality of gender analyses there has been a notable increase in the amount of gender training now available, usually through outside funding, to WID/GAD personnel and to other members of the development administration. Gender training is ultimately constrained by an attitudinal barrier; the interview reports suggest predictable differences between the receptivity of women and men bureaucrats to this training. Another fundamental constraint on the effectiveness of gender training, as with efforts to promote gender-sensitive policy and planning, is the absence of rewards attached to re-orienting individual and institutional approaches towards gender-sensitivity. WID/GAD units still lack the resources for institutional change beyond their own bureaucratic boundaries. They are not equipped to alter the incentive structures governing individual bureaucrats and bureaucratic units; they usually cannot offer material or status rewards, nor offer useful technical support, and they lack powers of ultimate sanction over policy and programme proposals that fail to incorporate gender-sensitive perspectives.

The critical role that outside constituencies might play in supporting institutional change is muted for political reasons: divisions within the women's movement, the weak organizational forms often adopted by women's organizations, and the distrust with which they may regard the national administration, especially given the tendency for patrimonial states to exploit women's presence in the state for political support purposes. On the civil service side, WID/GAD units, when staffed with personnel with a clear commitment to gender equity, will have divided loyalties, which will undermine their credibility within the rest of the bureaucracy. Advocates for gender equity working in the public administration have to manage a complex form of politics, identified by a UK feminist collective as working both 'in and against the state' (London–Edinburgh Weekend Return Group, 1979).

According to all the interview reports, the support which international aid donors give the WID/GAD issue has been an important temporary substitute for the lack of concerted domestic pressure and the lack of national resources to pursue the WID/GAD agenda in development planning. But many of the interviewees were ambivalent about its long-term impact. The availability of foreign funds absolves governments from mobilizing their own resources for gender-sensitive development practice. It also sharply undermines the sustainability of

WID/GAD policy efforts, which can evaporate once funds are spent. Where projects and institutions are set up primarily in response to an external initiative, there is little incentive to actively internalize and 'own' a policy initiative. Instead, its legitimacy is suspect, and even though the funds are welcomed, the imposition of 'alien' cultural notions regarding gender is deeply resented. The reports from Mali and Morocco were most explicit about this problem. Cultural imperialism in the projection of Western notions of gender equity to other contexts is an undeniable problem, and the resentment this arouses can have the unfortunate effect of stigmatizing indigenous feminisms as Western derivatives, thereby undermining their local legitimacy. Further, national-level bureaucrats are hardly impervious to the ambivalences in the support which the WID/GAD issue receives within multilateral and bilateral institutions. This too can inhibit the degree to which the issue is internalized locally. It can also contribute to a cynical exploitation of the issue for the purpose of accessing new development funds and burnishing the nation's image in external eyes. This cynical tendency is exacerbated by the typical donor preoccupation with the rapid disbursal of funds on projects, to the detriment of investing in costly and slow processes of attitudinal change.

A final and important constraint on the WID/GAD agenda has been the depressed economic environments in which most of the countries examined here currently find themselves. Governments have been less willing and indeed less able to accommodate demands for distributional equity in periods of severe economic crisis. When the accent in economic planning is on stabilization and growth, equity-focused concerns, which imply new resource commitments, tend to be postponed. In more urbanized countries, the problem of male unemployment during economic downturns is seen as a serious political problem. This will mean under-implementation of WID/GAD policies to the extent that they are seen to challenge men's employment privileges.

Political and policy opportunities

Opportunities for furthering the WID/GAD agenda have come from strategic allies, from moments of political systems change, and from changes in the international development policy environment. In Chile and Uganda, the WID/GAD agenda has recently benefited from strong support from the top state executive, and across the other case countries, there are many examples of individual Ministers or top-level civil servants who have given the issue support at critical moments, enabling, for example, gender-sensitive personnel and policy tools to be introduced to a particular department. Though welcome, it is nevertheless a disturbing signal of the fragility of the institutional status of WID/GAD efforts that successes are so often contingent on the support of individual powerful men. The incidence of this form of support is entirely arbitrary and unpredictable, and it speaks to the need to develop stronger support bases across the administration.

Similarly, there are cases where the WID/GAD agenda has been furthered in moments of political systems change, as in the transitions from military dictatorships to democracies in Uganda and Chile. Two dynamics are at work. One represents a strategic gain for women, where they seek to represent their interests amongst a new configuration of political interests, and may be less obstructed than at other times because some traditional power-holders have been unseated. The other is less of a direct strategic gain. It involves the concerns of new leaders to demonstrate legitimacy both at home and abroad. Extending opportunities for political participation to women is an effective symbol of progressive national attitudes. It can also be, as seen earlier, a mechanism for co-opting women as a valuable supportive political constituency. The challenge for women is to exploit these kinds of opportunities by seeking effective forms of institutional presence in the state. The process of soliciting women's views on the new Constitution in Uganda is a striking example of an effort to exploit this kind of opportunity.

These sorts of efforts essentially involve holding states accountable for policy promises. Seeking to enforce state accountability to women requires an understanding of state policies and an assessment of their implications for gender relations. It is also contingent on the degree of effective democracy in a country, and the shift to democratic governments in the case study countries in recent years has provided an important opportunity for women to demand legitimacy and representation for their needs and interests. The important exception to this are socialist economies in economic and political transition. Here, the introduction of capitalist relations of production has tended to erode women's labour rights, increase their work burden, undermine their capacity to influence political decisions, and discredit state feminism as an unwelcome legacy of socialism.

New international development policy agendas also provide special opportunities for furthering the WID/GAD agenda, if the individual country in question has subscribed to these policies. The most important of these of course is the WID/GAD agenda itself as promoted through the international feminist movement and the commitment agreed at conferences of the UN Decade for Women. Each of these, and the Platform for Action agreed at the 1995 conference in Beijing, has provided important opportunities for coalition-building between women's organizations and for establishing constructive linkages with national WID/GAD machinery.

Other recent international policy agendas have included support for human rights observance and for good government, a renewed commitment to poverty reduction, a concern with environmental sustainability, and a focus on human and social development. Each of these represents important new opportunities for furthering gender-equity agendas, though they are rarely presented as such. To avoid them becoming missed opportunities, WID/GAD advocates need to take active ownership of these agendas, assessing them for any obstacles they may impose on women, and exploiting them as points of leverage on the state and international donors. For example, the governance agenda, as currently put into practice by multilateral and bilateral donor agencies, largely centres on concerns with civil service reform and with improving the efficiency of public sector management with a view to enhancing the security of private sector investments. But the actual content of the governance agenda as expressed in policy documents is much broader, embracing notions of enhancing the participation of excluded groups in policymaking, strengthening civil society, and improving respect for human rights (World Bank, 1992a; 1993a; ADB, 1993). In this broader reading, there is important space for inserting concerns to enhance public accountability to women. Though this involves a degree and form of institutional change not foreseen in these documents, commitment to good government provides a point of leverage to demand it.

By and large, WID/GAD units have failed to exhibit this kind of strategic analysis and planning to exploit new policy agendas. They tend instead to be reactive, missing opportunities for challenging and changing new policy initiatives so as to engineer a gender-equitable impact. The phenomenon of 'globalization' or of the greater permeability of international boundaries can also work as an opportunity for local WID/GAD efforts. The participation of individual countries in international development conferences and agreements means that nations expose themselves for comparison with other nations. Many of the new international policy agendas make this comparison explicit—an example is the way the UNDP's Human Development initiative uses the Human Development Index for country rankings. Transparency at the international level means that abuses at the national level are more visible, and more embarrassing to governments. Again, this can be exploited by women's organizations to expose injustices and provoke responses.

Since the mid-1970s, many governments have made formal or rhetorical commitments to women's rights and gender equity in development without necessarily having any strong intention to implement or enforce these measures. At the international level, this has allowed them to burnish an image as progressive modernizers. At the domestic level, the relative weakness of many national women's movements, and the masculinist interests entrenched in state bureaucracies, has meant that governments have rarely been held to account, either by outside constituencies or by state agents, for their generosity at the rhetorical level. That situation is changing fundamentally. Women's movements the world over have gained enormously in strength and credibility as viable political forces. Within the state, women are gradually, but surely, making their way into state bureaucracies and into political society, slowly taking their places amongst decision-makers. Both within and outside of the state, amongst women activists, civil servants, politicians, and their male allies, a momentum is building for institutional tranformation towards more socially just processes and outcomes in development decision-making. There is a recognition that constraints faced by national WID/GAD units are at root political; that is what is meant by the repeated lament in the interview documents about a 'lack of will' or a 'lack of commitment'. Effective strategies for institutionalizing women's interests in the state must therefore be attuned to political opportunities and backed up by the mobilized political energies of advocates of gender justice in civil society and the state.

4

Engaging the state: the women's movement and political discourse in Morocco*

RABÉA NACIRI

This paper aims to contextualize debates over the status of women in Morocco in relation to the contemporary political history of that country. As in many other countries, the claims of the women's movement have been marginalized in conventional political debates. In Morocco, the status of women has been constructed as a 'taboo' subject, and consequently any discussion of the issue elicits deep-rooted passions, particularly with regard to the country's national identity. Nowadays this tendency is particularly pronounced because Morocco, like other Muslim and Arab countries, has seen the development of Islamic fundamentalist movements which intensify both the national identity crisis and the contradictions inherent in the progressive image of the state and the political élites by focusing attention on the status of women. Indeed, debates over the status of women must be viewed against the backdrop of efforts by the state to contain the forces unleashed by democratization and the threat of political Islam.

From the mid-1980's onward, the women's movement, although resembling liberal feminism in terms of demands, has rarely identified its activities as 'political'. While its energy and skill in using unconventional means of engagement have greatly helped to widen the political field in Morocco by making the status of women a subject for political debate, ironically, its discursive strategies have tended to uphold the attitude that 'politics' is exclusively limited to the formal, political sphere (political institutions and parties), largely dominated by men. This paradox must be ascribed to the political and historical context of Morocco. The strong emphasis on the country's Muslim and Arab identity and its focus on ethnic, linguistic, and cultural unity are some of the factors that contribute to the ambivalence of the state and political bodies with regard to women's claims, and this also explains the varied strategies adopted by the women's associations in order to achieve their goals.

*This chapter has been translated from the original French by Erika Drucker, with editing by Jenifer Freedman and Carol Miller.

On the pretext of religious and cultural sensitivity, conventional political actors have attempted to keep women's issues off the political agenda, and to limit women's visibility and impact on public life. In response, women's associations, which have emerged since the mid-1980's, have adopted a twofold "strategy"[1] aimed, first, at integration into civil society and, secondly, at a rapprochement with institutionalized political bodies, particularly the most progressive social and political elements. A further tactic has been to exploit the contradictions between the progressive claims of the state and its need to ensure the loyalties of the old patriarchal structures. The latter were destabilized by the social and economic changes which followed independence but have grown in force since the early 1980's. This study will assess the extent to which the strategies of the women's movement have contributed to and succeeded in redefining social and political gender identities. It will aim to show that, despite its claims to eschew conventional 'politics', the women's movement has none the less established itself as a partner in political discussions on women's issues and in reformulating the terms of the debate. Indeed, the greatest success of the movement has been the 'politization' of women's issues.

Redefining politics and political participation

The question of the political participation of women was initially taken up in Morocco as a claim for political rights by a generation of educated women who were active in the process of national policy development in the post-independence years. In the euphoria of this period, a number of these women, who had ideological and family links with the formal political arena, claimed the right to political representation as a public recognition of their abilities and patriotism at a moment when the country greatly needed national administrators and political leaders. They emphasized the right of women to participate in the management of national matters on the basis of their skills and their socio-economic roles. In other words, their claims were not linked to the need for representation of women in terms of specific gender interests or a female political consciousness ('women's voices'), but upon the provision of political 'space' for women on the same terms as those required for men. In this optimistic view, it was sufficient for a woman to have a militant or academic background, or both—which was often the case in this social class—to benefit from the same opportunities as men and to be recognized as political actors.

This view gradually eroded with the emergence, in a context of economic liberalization and democratization, of a new generation of women's associations and with the interest of researchers in these new structures. The appearance of new forms of social organization helped to give direction to analysis and discussion on broader socio-economic and political developments, rather than confining debates to questions of political participation.

According to a narrow definition of 'politics', which deems as political those activities in which political actors engage with conventional political institutions (political parties, government, parliament, trade unions, etc.), it is possible to conclude that the women's movement in Morocco has remained at the margins of the formal political sphere and has had a limited impact on the contemporary political agenda. In classical political theory, the question of women's participation in the political sphere and their role in democracy are characterized in two ways: first, by the division between the public and the private spheres, which are artificially separated and gender-specific; and second, by a very narrow, male-centric, view of democratic participation, which is essentially restricted to formal political institutions and procedures.

In critiques of classical political theory, various analysts—including feminist scholars—have attempted to extend the concept of participation by deconstructing the assumptions underlying the dualistic understanding of the public and the private spheres. Feminist political theorists have challenged the characterization of the public sphere as a masculine world of reason and rationality and the private sphere as a feminine world of familial love and duty, and, in particular, the attendant notion that the family and the private sphere were somehow excluded from conceptions such as equality and justice central to liberal political theory. 'The real contribution of a feminist critique of liberal political theory to democracy is in transforming this conceptualization of the private sphere to achieve a wider notion of political participation and representative democracy' (Phillips, quoted in Siddiqui, 1995:6).

Further, feminist scholars have attempted to oppose the public/private duality by demonstrating the degree of interdependence between the two spheres and the extent to which social justice for women depends upon equality within the private sphere as well as outside it. From this perspective 'whatever influences or affects women's identity and their roles in either sphere has to be considered "political"' (Phillips, quoted in Siddiqui, 1995:7). In sum, '... the recognition of this reality redefines our understanding of public concerns, democracy and politics' (Rowbotham, quoted in Siddiqui, 1995:8). It would be incorrect, therefore, to consider the experiences of women's movements as being at the margin of political activity since their claims—women's rights, legal and social entitlements, political participation—are fundamentally political, even if their methods of public action are not always conventional in the narrow political sense.

Fraser's (1989:166) distinction between the use of the term 'political' in a narrow institutional sense and in a broader discursive sense is useful for the present study. According to Fraser, an issue is deemed political in the institutional sense 'if it is handled directly in the institutions of the official governmental system, including parliaments, administrative apparatuses, and the like'. A distinction is often made between activities carried out through formal political institutions ('official political') and those carried out in institutions like 'the family' and 'the economy', both of which are seen as being outside the official political system even though, as Fraser points out, 'they are in actuality underpinned and regulated by it' (ibid.:167). In the discourse sense of the term, she continues, 'something is "political" if it is contested across a range of different discursive arenas and among a range of different publics'. The crucial point here is the understanding of 'politics' in the discursive sense: an issue can be construed as political if it is discussed and debated by 'different discourse publics'. Using this definition of politics, it is possible to see how the boundaries between the political, the economic and the domestic change constantly in accordance with places, societies and history; the line of demarcation between the spheres is always a contested matter. Consequently, for the purposes of the present study, not only must the forces traditionally recognized by the Moroccan constitution as 'political' in the institutional sense be identified, but also broader discursive terrains on which the status of women is debated must be analysed.

Democratization and the emergence of civil society

Democratization of Moroccan political institutions began in the 1980s, largely as part of a process of consensus building over the country's claims to the Western Sahara. Moroccan claims on the Sahara necessitated a unified political front internally in order to reinforce the country's position internationally. Political democratization has gone hand-in-hand with economic liberalization. The economic disengagement of the state in favour of the private sector began with the structural adjustment programme initiated at the beginning of the 1980's, following a serious financial crisis and increased foreign debt (DIS, USAID, 1996). Economic reforms followed 'the new orthodoxy of development which imposes three axioms: priority to exports, liberalization of trade, and privatization of public enterprises' (Camau, 1989). The omnipresent state, which for decades shaped social and economic life and was a significant provider of employment, social services, and goods, could no longer meet the increasing needs of a growing, young, urban population. The state has thus gradually allowed an opening for new economic actors. Despite the dynamic nature of a new generation of entrepreneurs who are better educated, and demand more independence from the state and more transparency in the rules which govern the economic sphere, the economy is still dominated by political élites (Leaveau and Bennani-Chraibi, 1996).

At the same time, there has been greater freedom of speech and association that offers an opportunity to the institutionalized political forces as well as to new social, economic and political actors to make known and defend their interests publicly. An indication of this greater openness was the recent closing of the files of political prisoners and arbitrary detainees. Although the present Moroccan political system can be characterized as pluralist, it is also true that it has been largely controlled by the monarchy. With increased democratization, however, a certain number of demands made by political opposition groups—which four years ago formed a democratic bloc[2] (Koutla)—have been met. These include constitutional reforms, the organization of two legislative elections, the appointment of a Minister of Human Rights, the establishment of an Advisory

Council for Human Rights and of channels for dialogue and social mediation, and reform of the Trade Code.

These changes reflect the consensus achieved in recent years between the King and traditional parliamentary opposition parties. In the post-independence years these parties refused any 'compromise' with the *Makhzen*[3] (central authority). Following the constitutional reform of 1993, however, consultations and negotiations took place with a view to the participation by the opposition parties in the government for the first time in Morocco. Political observers have spoken of the emergence of a new political culture based on dialogue and consensus that aims to provide constructive solutions to the political and economic problems confronting the country, an important departure from the culture of confrontation/co-optation between the King and political actors which has prevailed since independence. Indeed, the economic crisis, the globalization of the economy, the political crisis in Algeria, and the progress of the Islamist movement in Morocco—especially in the universities—have led to a sense of urgency among political actors in closing ranks and presenting a united front.

The opposition parties of the Koutla represent the only legally constituted and authorized political force enjoying legitimacy among the urban middle and upper classes. This legitimacy derives from participation in the independence movement and from the fact that the Koutla has distanced itself from responsibility for the present social and economic crisis. The political and ideological approaches of the Koutla coalition cover a wide spectrum, though subsumed under the headings of 'the opposition' and 'the left'; the latter range from the nationalist and pan-Arabic left to the socialist and communist left. The ideological convictions of the political actors are, however, divergent, and dialogue on women's issues in some cases represents a threat to the already fragile political consensus.

The two most important members of the Koutla, the Socialist Union and the Istiqlal (Independence) Party, have been unsuccessful thus far in widening their social base, especially among women, youth, and the poorest groups. Their support has gradually eroded in a country where more than half of the population was born after independence and is faced with unemployment, inadequate educational and health facilities, and poverty. Because of the élitism of these parties and their inability to present a credible political alternative, their legitimacy is now being questioned. Periodic popular revolt is considered by political analysts as an indication of the exclusion of large population groups who do not identify with any political structure (Bennani-Chraibi, 1994).

This trend coincides with the reform of economic and political institutions which has favoured the proliferation of new civil society groups;[4] these groups have seized the opportunity to participate actively in the process of political democratization. The variety of elements of what is now commonly called civil society, and its consolidation around associations for women's rights, human rights, civic development, environmental and children's rights, the disabled, consumers, etc., make it into a powerful potential actor on the public scene.

Although the associations are highly varied, many have in common a new vision of politics and the role of public opinion. The emergent social actors agree on the need to establish a legally constituted state in which the rights of individuals and citizens, both male and female, will be recognized and respected; this represents a transformation of, and even a break with, the practices and mentalities that have prevailed in the country until now.

The disaffected youth, in particular, represent a formidable challenge to the Koutla coalition parties. The universities, which until the mid-1980s were centres for the recruitment of new members of the leftist parties, have since the beginning of the 1990s been controlled by the Islamists. Partly as a result of the crisis of the educational system and the extent of unemployment among graduates,[5] the university is seen to contribute to the creation of a social class of frustrated youth who tend to reject outright the traditional political institutions.[6] Educated Moroccan youth thus attempt to organize their political claims and formulate them outside the traditional circuits. Unemployed graduates have discovered an original way of formulating their claims through the creation of associations of young graduates, which are perceived as an alternative framework independent of all partisan or political influences and count a high proportion of young women members.[7] At the same time, the state has recognized the importance of these bodies in community development. They are interpreted as a response to the state's inability to respond to the desire of the population for social and economic well-being. The state's recognition of these groups can, at one level, be interpreted as an attempt to limit the influence of the Islamists, who use charitable associations for political propaganda purposes. These new associations are seen to constitute a rampart against the Islamist movement, aiming to compete with it on its own ground.

The emergence of new groups active in a range of non-conventional issues, outside of formal politics, does not leave the institutionalized political élite indifferent; the élite attempt to take over these movements by appropriating their discourse, co-opting some of the best-known members, and encouraging like-minded organizations. But the capacity of the new civil society organizations to present social and political alternatives and to exert a positive influence depends on the strength of their position in the urban population as well as in the rural population, and on their ability to remain independent from formal political institutions. One example is the women's movement. As demonstrated below, it can be considered a 'pioneer', with a special strategy and approach linked to its efforts to achieve autonomy from the the groups of the Koutla.

In view of the instrumental use of religion which takes place in a Muslim country as soon as women's interests are involved, and by way of background to the discussion below, further mention must be made here of the fundamentalist movement—a force not usually included in discussions of 'civil society', the latter being implicitly seen as both independent of any partisan affiliation and as the carrier of civic, democratic, and modern values.[8] Like the monarchy, and the territorial unity of the country, Islam is an integral feature of the political system in Morocco. The ancestral religious legitimacy of the king as a descendant of the prophet and at the same time the temporal and spiritual leader (*Amir al moumi-nine*) is reinforced by the recent history of the monarchy, which symbolized resistance to foreign occupation, and is reflected in the Constitution, which states that Islam is the state religion.[9]

The monarchy's management of religion has shaped the political culture of the country since independence. Religion has been called upon to legitimize the monarchy (Leaveau, 1989). Marxist ideologies and those of the nationalist left, both of which opposed the legitimacy of the monarchy, were thwarted and the Moroccan communist party was prohibited. In this context, Islam was called upon as a means to exclude political opposition parties, which were accused of being imported, secular, and thus illegitimate. In reaction, the parties of the Koutla have taken cognizance of these facts in order to avoid being excluded from a political arena in which 'the dominant symbolism is of religious origin and where the ... symbolic capital ... determines simultaneously the place occupied by the party on the political fringe and, particularly, its strategy for obtaining power' (Tozy, 1979). This situation, which is fairly common in non-secular Muslim countries, has prepared the terrain for Islamist and extremist ideologies. The discourse of Islamic groups is socially accepted because it is seen to embody a historical continuity.

The political management of Islamist forces in Morocco is unique, however, in so far as the monarchy monopolizes the symbolic religious production and maintains a religious pluralism—represented by currents such as the Oulámas and religious brotherhoods and certain political parties such as Istiqlal—mediated by the monarch himself.[10] The Islamist groups, organized into legal or otherwise tolerated associations, may be active on condition that they respect the rules which govern the politico-religious field. This is the case in particular for the members of the association *Islah wa tajdid* (reform and renewal), who have formed a political party. It has also been possible for well-known Islamists to present themselves at legislative or community elections. The Moroccan government tends to encourage the integration of Islamist groups into the system and acts so as not to radicalize them by an overly repressive attitude. Indeed, the fact that the state religion is Islam is often described as one of the main defences of Morocco against the surging waves of political Islam.

This paper therefore attempts to contextualize the political discourse on women's issues within the context of two interrelated trends: the efforts by the political élites to maintain the *status quo* against processes unleashed by democratization, and the containment of political Islam. The strong bipolarity of the political system, occupied since independence exclusively by the king and the opposition parties, has resisted or sought to contain the emergence of new social or political forces. A system based on co-option of élites and on clientelism has not easily accommodated the expression of other groups organized outside of these circles. However, economic liberalization has forced the state to make

93

some changes and yield a certain number of its privileges to the private sector and to new civil society groups in general. Despite the alterations which have taken place in the relationship between the state and the citizens, allowing the emergence of the women's movement, the resistance of the old political élite remains very strong, especially when women's groups present themselves as political interlocutors.

The women's movement

If the term 'women's movement' is understood to consist of organizations concerned specifically with women's interests, such a movement existed in Morocco long before independence. Then its purpose was to deal with issues such as literacy, social assistance for women and children, etc. But if by this term we understand a current of opinion in favour of women's liberation, we must turn to the middle- and upper-class women who were activists in the women's sections of the political parties before and especially after national independence.

Within the scope of this study we use the term women's movement to refer to those women's associations belonging to the 'second generation' after independence which developed in the mid-1980s. Our purpose is not to make a detailed study of all women's associations but rather to focus on a particular segment which uses a strategy and discourse aimed at re-evaluating women's identity and the status of women in society. It happens that this category is one of the most dynamic; this may be attributed to the skill of its members, acquired within the political parties from which many of its leaders came, although other very active associations provide valuable assistance to women in several fields.

In fact, the contemporary women's movement owes much to the women who, for lack of better options, worked in philanthrophic associations after having contributed actively to the independence movement. It owes even more to the 'first generation' women who continued to work towards integration into the parties of the left in the 1960s and 1970s. The second generation of the women's movement (from the 1980s onwards) is of particular significance because of its qualitative break with the demands, practices, and discourse characterizing the associations and parties of the left during the preceding period. The break occurred at several levels:

○ at the organizational level, by choosing to work solely through women's or independent structures, as distinct from the political parties and trade unions;
○ with regard to its claims and demands, which can be qualified as feminist because they no longer perceived the subordination of women as a function only of class relations but also in terms of gender relations;
○ with regard to new working methods and alliances which contributed to a transformation of the Moroccan political landscape, whereby there has been

an extraordinary opening-up of the structures of civil society and a greater willingness of traditional political parties to work with other groups.

The founders of the first generation (post-independence) women's associations had to face a number of challenges. At some level they accepted certain values of the old colonial system, such as equality and modernity, in a political and ideological context which was hostile to Western values, especially those concerning women and the family. They also questioned the authority and legitimacy of a male élite which, on the pretext of having fought for the liberation of the country, tended to speak on behalf of women and to impose on them a narrow plan for liberation.

Another feature characterizing the first generation of women's associations was that they gradually came to realize that gender equality and gender relations transcend class struggles. The left found in Marxist ideology a rationale allowing them to put off claims for women's equality by making them conditional on, and subordinate to, class liberation. In their desire for acceptance, women of the left long supported this orthodoxy. They also had to overcome the guilt associated with their departure from traditional norms of female behaviour. To be educated, professionally active, and financially independent are privileges that generate some ambivalence for women in Arab societies: not only is their loyalty to their family and children questioned, but their privileged status in a society where the overwhelming majority of women are illiterate and poor becomes a source of culpability. For many years a hierarchy of priorities and loyalties was maintained: inequalities linked to class were perceived as more unacceptable than those related to gender inequalities. For this reason, women of the left were told that 'emphasizing one's woes as a woman is indecent'. As articulated by one Egyptian feminist, 'feminists had to choose between betrayal and betrayal' (cited in Kandiyoti, 1991).

Having been members for years of women's sections created by the centrist/leftist parties, the 'first generation' of the women's movement became increasingly aware of the scale of their marginalization within the 'men's clubs'. The experience prompted a large number of these women to become members of separate associations within which they could easily speak and be heard and where their interests were taken into account. Despite the efforts to 'disengage' themselves to some extent from the main political parties, the strategies adopted by the women's movement in Morocco in the 1980s have been fundamentally influenced by their relationship with the centrist/leftist political groups. Women's associations remain divided between their desire not to cut the umbilical cord from their leftist roots, in their view originating in the political parties—and their desire to affirm their own political identity and their independence from these same groups.

Many women's associations are not yet free of the orthodox political culture that permeated politics in Morocco from the time of independence until the mid-1980s, and which characterized gender claims as a deviation by marginalized women's groups from central political concerns. The women members have been forced to rethink their place in these parties, which they had joined in a reaction to social injustice. Although they challenged the dogma that 'women's liberation is linked to class liberation', this did not lead to a re-examination of the views and policies of the parties to which they belonged. In most cases, political parties assumed that the new women's associations would serve to convey their ideologies and motivate potential sympathizers.

Thus, the women's movement is divided between its desire not to displease the parties of the Koutla or to isolate itself from them, and that of asserting its claims, which are disregarded by these parties and in no way represent a priority concern on their political agenda. Indeed, the fundamental challenge is to be freed from the tutelage of the traditional political parties without becoming isolated. This assumes the ability of the women's movement to extend its base to poor women, to present credible political alternatives, and to make varied alliances.

Overall, then, contemporary (or second generation) women's associations can be differentiated into two broad types. The first group comprises those who see themselves as feminists, originating in most cases from the political parties, but with a more or less real margin of independence in relation to the latter. These include the Association Démocratique des Femmes du Maroc (Democratic Association of Moroccan Women), the Union pour l'Action Féminine (Union for Women's Action), the Collectif 95 Maghreb Egalité (Association 95 Maghreb for Equality)[11], and the Association Marocaine pour les Droits des Femmes (Moroccan Association for Women's Rights). The second group is made up mainly of the women's sections of political parties; these groups are perceived as instruments to reinforce the position of the relevant parties, especially with respect to educated women. This is the case for the Organisation de la Femme Istiqlalienne (Organization of Istiqlal Women) and the Association des Femmes Démocrates (Association of Democratic Women).

In the first type of 'feminist' association, which have dissociated themselves to some extent from the original political groups, priority is given to the most radical claims and actions relating to gender discrimination, such as inequality with regard to civil rights, violence against women, and sexual harassment—all issues on which public discussion is discouraged by the political class as a whole. The associations, which aim primarily at furthering women's rights, find that their struggle is given less political support by the parties to which they are organically near. The second type of association, which has retained or claims organic links with the parties, gives priority to questions of women's 'immediate' or 'practical' interests and to demands for the implementation of rights already established by legislation, and other policy initiatives relating to issues such as female illiteracy, poverty, women and the family, or the political participation of women.

The different types of associations also tend to adopt different discursive strategies. Whereas the 'independent' associations place emphasis on gender

96

equality as an inseparable condition of human rights and democracy, the second category of associations gives greater attention to practical arguments and highlights the contribution that women can make to the national development process. Both types of associations offer educated women from the middle and upper social strata a greater opportunity for greater political visibility than mainstream political parties (Marand-Fouquet, 1995). These new groups compete with the institutionalized political parties, which find it more difficult than in the past to recruit women.

Women's status as a political issue

The status of women has always been a 'political' issue in the sense that it has been the subject of discussion and debate—of contestation—among different groups or 'publics' to use Fraser's (1989) terminology. In order to understand the contemporary debate on the status of women, we must contextualize it within tensions already evident well before national independence. With the development of the independence movement, certain leaders from the urban bourgeoisie who had studied abroad (mainly in Egypt and Europe), and who had been influenced by the reformist current of the Middle East and the West, began to denounce the seclusion of women and their lack of education. This reforming élite attempted to show that Islam could accept certain Western values, such as democracy and the emancipation of women. The Koran was sometimes described as the pioneer in this subject and it was argued that, if read correctly, its tenets would rival the principles of Western modernity. This view was rejected by traditionalist and conservative circles as a threat to Islamic identity, symbolized by and centred on women and the family.

Despite the ideological differences between the two views, they both came to rely on Islam and religious arguments to establish legitimacy. This can be explained in part as a reaction to colonization and by the need to create and reinforce nationalist sentiment in order to stand up to the occupying power. In fact, support from the religious sphere was absolutely essential for the mobilization of nationalist feeling. It is important to emphasize that in both cases the 'woman question' was ideologically very controversial: the education of women symbolized an important political issue for the progressive aspirations of an élite, and simultaneously the aspirations to religious 'authenticity' of the politically marginalized traditionalist circles. In view of the challenges presented by the progressive, Western values of the Spanish and French occupation, efforts were made to differentiate the arguments for modernization from the values and models of the colonizers by taking up the discourse and ideology of the reformist movements of the Middle East, which celebrated women's decisive social role as wives and mothers.[12]

Access to education was recommended on the grounds that women were the educators of future generations. Female ignorance was denounced not as an attack on human dignity but as an obstacle to the education of male citizens,

particularly those who would be called upon to play an important role after independence. At the same time, in view of their functions as mothers and teachers,
women were held up as the protectors of traditional values and 'authenticity',
especially in the face of colonization. The education of women was thus encouraged, but this education was to be limited to branches of knowledge which might
be useful to them in their roles as wives and mothers; their minds were not to be
corrupted by allowing them access to "modern" branches of knowledge, which
conveyed the values of the occupying power and, moreover, were communicated
in the language of the latter.

The predominant aim, therefore, was to ensure that such changes would not
introduce disorder into the familial and natural order, imposed by divine will and
based on the primacy of man over woman. In view of the fear that access to education might become a vehicle for propelling women into the public sphere, they
continued to be kept in seclusion, although the boundaries of the private sphere
were slightly enlarged. These arguments have remained basically unchanged,
while taking other forms more suitable to the requirements of the end of the
twentieth century.

The feeling of national pride that characterized the post-independence years
and the impact of the nationalist movement on political life enabled women to
attain two previously unobtainable goals: education and work. There is no doubt
that the most dramatic changes of the last decade concerned social life; several
social indicators demonstrate the extent of the break with the 'traditional' system of values. Indeed, a 'quiet' revolution has transformed women's lives and
roles in Morocco.[13] As a result of education and employment, as well as
increased urbanization,[14] the average age at marriage has continued to rise gradually (the national average is now more than 24 in rural areas) whereas fertility
has dropped dramatically,[15] particularly in urban areas. Women are increasingly
educated: four university students out of ten are women, and almost every second physician is a woman. Women's employment has greatly increased since
the beginning of the 1970s (though a decrease has been observed in recent
years). Large numbers of women work in industry and services, and half of the
active population working in the agricultural sector are women (Barkallil,
1994).

Another important social change of recent decades, with particular repercus-
sions for women, has been the rise of the nuclear family (paralleling the decline
of the extended family). This transition has been closely linked to the emergence
of 'individual' identity, replacing a social system wherein one's identity was tied
to membership of a tribe or family clan. Such changes have especially favoured
women, since they challenge the image of women as guardians of tradition and
of the honour of the family and tribe. Thus, in contemporary Morocco, women's
roles no longer entirely correspond to the traditional gender division of social
roles.

One of the most characteristic realities of Morocco today is the fact that
women, who were still secluded four or five decades ago, have entered the public

sphere. The strategy used to achieve this transition was that of performance on a professional and familial level. Women endowed with significant social resources, such as education and professional careers, performed several roles simultaneously.[16] Whereas men often identify themselves with a single social role, women use multiple strategies to offset the precariousness of their status and positions. In other words, in order to prove themselves, women tend to fight on several fronts at once, attempting to firmly establish a number of rights which they perceive as uncertain, such as the right to work. The presence of women in the public sphere—such as the workplace, associations, trade unions, art, writing, media, etc.—allows them to acquire new knowledge and experience, and offers a stepping stone for more active engagement in both formal and informal politics.

Many women, therefore, have seized the opportunity structure of the post-independence years to advance their interests. They have not contented themselves with operating solely within the framework of rights granted to them. Instead, education has permitted them not only to 'improve' their functions as wives and mothers, but has also become a means for entering other spheres and for overcoming male resistance. Ultimately, it permits them to challenge the inferiorization of their status in the family and in the public sphere. Indeed, it is this group of educated, career women that has provided the rare women leaders of the formal political institutions of the state and political parties, as well as the founders and leaders of the women's movement. In other words, it is a new élite which competes with the traditional male political élite.

But this remarkable presence of women in the public sphere does not signify that the sphere has been taken over by women, nor that interactions between the two genders is accepted and supported by men. The two sides co-exist in a unpredictable relationship. The implicit rules and the explicit restrictions which govern the relationship fluctuate according to place and time. The degree of tolerance of women in the public sphere varies according to a set of social rules and constraints established by men. It is on the basis of these rules that the political actors continue to legitimatize the exclusion of women.[17]

Islam as a strategy of exclusion and a strategy of resistance

As argued earlier, Islam has been used to maintain the privileges of an official political élite and to exclude the majority of the population, particularly women, from participation in political and democratic initiatives. Until recently, therefore, the main feature of the political debate on the status of women has been the attempt of certain political actors to confine the discourse to the religious sphere. Clearly this has not favoured a frank debate on gender issues. This use of religion to oppose demands for gender equality led members of women's sections of the political parties to opt for independent women's groups. The women's movement helped to re-focus the debate on Islam, but on terms partly defined by them.

Although Islam can be characterized as a strategy of exclusion used by mainstream political actors, the Islamist movement has been used, paradoxically, by women as a strategy of resistance.[18] Women have always used a variety of means and strategies to minimize the effects of oppression and seclusion and, in some cases, these strategies might appear counter to their interests as women. Several studies on Muslim countries have attempted to explain and understand the apparent 'agreement' of women with their subordinate position or their 'conservative nature'. The important adherence of young women, especially students, to the Islamist movement—the ideology of which is clearly opposed to their strategic interests as women—naturally poses a problem for feminist analysts.

One explanation for women's adherence to Islam focuses on the social context. It is young educated women belonging to the less advantaged social strata who are most receptive to the Islamist approach because it values their social roles within the family. The explanation for this paradox may be that 'the gender division of roles has never been envisioned by the Islamists in terms of hierarchy, but as noble tasks which are the responsibility of the Muslim woman (reproduction, education in agreement with the divine law, development of the generations to come ...), and thus contribute to the harmony and coherence of the virtuous Muslim city' (Bessis and Belhassen, 1992). In other words, this approach affirms and exalts gender differences which are seen as natural and God-given.

A related explanation derives from an analysis of the discourse of Islamists in the Maghreb: '... the latter carefully avoid openly advocating the exclusion of women or their seclusion and also avoid developing the theme of women's inferiority. In their opinion women are the best fighters in this new moral order. By a semantic reversal, the most convinced Islamist women affirm that obedience to God frees them from the ascendancy of men (husbands, fathers, tutors, hierarchical superiors)' (ibid.). Islam, therefore, becomes a strategy for some women to resist their oppressive economic and social environments, including confinement to the private sphere, which belies the social visibility their education provides. The immediate social recognition associated with engagement in Islamic movements satisfies needs that the social and economic environment of these women cannot meet.

In relation to this, several authors have studied the meaning of the wearing of the *hijab* (headscarf) by educated women. This practice may be interpreted as the 'use of Islam to conquer the public sphere and an insertion into modern life' (Ferchiou, 1995). These studies have shown that educated women give a multitude of reasons for wearing the veil and do not necessarily see any contradiction between this manner of showing their adherence to a movement which is contrary to their long-term strategic gender interests and their genuine aspirations to emancipation. In her study entitled *Islamist Tunisian Women*, Belhassen (1989) has shown that, for a number of veiled women, the fact that they do not show their body is equivalent to a feminist gesture because, by concealing their body from men, they are no longer perceived as objects, and gender no longer plays a deciding role in the relations between men and women.

The concept of the 'patriarchal bargain' developed by Deniz Kandiyoti provides a useful insight into this dilemma (quoted by Waylen, 1992). Some women in situations of helplessness, whose immediate interests cannot be satisfied, turn to patriarchal protection in order to maximize their security. Recourse to the 'patriarchal bargain' implies a price to be paid in return for which, in the absence of other immediate alternatives, women secure the protection of men. The recourse to religion can thus be seen to represent a strategy of resistance for educated women from modest social backgrounds who have, none the less, higher aspirations; in a situation of very strict social and familial control, these women use the veil as a means of escape. The veil provides the safety and liberty of movement required to enter a male-dominated public sphere.

Overall, the use of Islam as a strategy of resistance can be analysed and interpreted in several ways. It might be seen as a double-edged sword, as it allows immediate social recognition and an opportunity to legitimize women's incursions into the male public sphere at a relatively small price; however, it fits into and is part of the patriarchal ideology which does not allow a woman rights over her own body, since this body belongs exclusively to her husband. In another interpretation, the use of Islam to satisfy immediate needs is interpreted as a tactic which may serve women's struggles in the short term, but might in the long term lead to an opening-up and extension of political debate on the need to secularize Muslim law. In other words, the use of Islam as a means of emancipation runs counter to the idea that women submit to religious fundamentalism as interpreted by men. It may also lead to 'women's active participation in the manner in which Islam might advance gender interests' (Badran, quoted in Kandiyoti, 1991). In fact, by stimulating debate on women's identity, political Islamism has, unintentionally, encouraged the political discussion of the role of Islam in society and has thus opened the way for discussion of secularization. It has also allowed women's discursive strategies to encroach on a sacred area which had until then been completely closed to them.

It is in this sense that the significance of the forms of resistance and reaction mobilized by the women's movement must be analysed. The movement has adopted a dual strategy which is the subject of an as yet unresolved debate. What attitude should be adopted in the face of the instrumental use of religion aimed at denying equality to women in the private sphere of the family? One approach consists of advocating the emancipation of women by examining the Koran and other sacred texts from a historical point of view, so as to be able to contradict the non-historical approach of the Islamist and traditionalist groups. In other words, it is not a matter of challenging the sacred texts as irremediably and definitively anti-egalitarian. Instead, they must be situated in their historical context and interpreted in ways that are more appropriate to modern needs. Some female researchers,[19] for example, have tried to argue that a reopening of the doors of the *Ijtihad*[20] is indispensable, so that Islam might be able to accommodate the recent economic, social, and technological changes in Morocco and throughout the world. The second strategy, often adopted by the 'feminist' associations, calls for a progressive approach, based on the universalist philosophy of the rights of the individual of either sex. The women's movement utilizes one of these two approaches or the two simultaneously, depending on opportunities and the interlocutors. This is not necessarily contradictory, since it represents an adaptation to the ambivalence of the other political actors and more especially to that of the state.

The ambivalence of the state

Since independence, state policy *vis-à-vis* women has simultaneously valued their contributions to national development and their position within the family. The two attitudes have converged to both widen and circumscribe women's participation in the paid economy. On the one hand, women are employed as low-wage labourers in export industries, in social and domestic services, and in the public sector, which also allows the state to project a progressive image of Morocco and to obtain international aid. On the other, traditional familial and gender norms are firmly reinforced in the private sphere and reproduced in the public sphere, including the labour market, leading to bias against women.

Control over women is achieved through the enforcement of the law in certain areas and by the absence of law or its non-application in others. In both cases the state delegates control over women in private and public spheres to their male kin. The state can even replace the husband under some circumstances; for example, it can take on the role of civil party against the unfaithful wife if the husband is absent.

The state thereby secures the allegiance of the male population and reinforces the traditional patriarchal structure, which runs counter to the public image that Morocco attempts to convey in its dealings with the European Union (France in particular), in its international trade relations, and with respect to international aid. The contradictions are reflected in the legal system, which is secularized and very progressive overall, while women simultaneously remain subject to religious law. In other words, the constitutional rights of political and socio-economic equality are negated by discriminatory regulations, such as the duty of obedience to the husband or the need for marital authorization in order to work. None the less, since the International Women's Year in 1975, the international women's lobby has gained strength— and this has had a very important impact on the attitude of the state (which is always sensitive to its international position and image) and on the emergence of the women's movement in Morocco.

Under pressure from the women's movement, in 1993 Morocco ratified the Convention on the Elimination of All Forms of Discrimination Against Women. It stipulated, however, that ratification would not prejudice the rules of succession to the throne, nor the provisions of Islamic law (*Shari'a*) regarding women's rights.[21] The tensions between secular and religious laws help to explain the delay in women's enjoyment of full legal rights and participation in mainstream political institutions, in spite of the enormous changes in their socio-economic position. The Moroccan Code of Personal Status, which governs the status of women and family relations, is based on traditional Islamic law and on the *Malékite* rite,[22] whereas all other legal provisions are secularized and modern (Rachid, 1991). This code places the woman under male tutelage throughout her life—celibacy, marriage, divorce, widowhood—and institutionalizes the strict division of gender roles: the man is the head of the family and is responsible for maintaining the women and children; the woman has duties only towards her spouse (or, rather, master).

Political exclusion also operates through the economic marginalization of women, despite their effective and important economic participation. The precariousness of their employment status and working conditions, mirrored by the high gender gap in wage levels, are such that employment provides a poor conduit for emancipation from family control. Law is used to institutionalize economic marginalization. Women's economic contribution to the household is not recognized. A woman still requires authorization from her husband to go into business, to work, or to obtain a passport.[23] Finally, inheritance laws grant women only one half of the men's part, on the pretext that women do not contribute to the household expenses, although statistics demonstrate the contrary.[24] The result is social devaluation of women's unpaid work in general and marginalization of women's paid employment.

A few years after independence, the state created the Union Nationale des Femmes Marocaines (National Union of Moroccan Women), presided over by a princess. The declared aim of this association is to stimulate women's potential for participation in national development, while protecting women's traditional roles. The real goal, however, is to enable greater official control over the women's movement, especially those members who played an important part in the struggle for independence. The state, therefore, mirrors the approach of political parties, where the provisions made for women's participation have an instrumental purpose. More specifically, tacit prohibitions have long prevented women's access to the high political and administrative posts of the state. The most striking feature of independent Morocco has been the almost total exclusion of women from official bodies, whereas in the other Muslim and Arabic states (with the exception of the Gulf States) women have occupied ministerial posts and seats in parliament—although this is sometimes a result of political expediency rather than a sign of gender equality.

This *de facto* 'veto' was put aside for two women, belonging to the Koutla, elected deputies in 1993 and, more recently, in 1997 by the nomination of four women ministers. Apart from Parliament and the Government, all the other official political institutions remain exclusively male. As regards intermediate administrative posts, a few changes have been made, mainly a result of individual action rather than political will; in any event, they concern posts of responsibility but not of real power. Even if some women achieve a level of responsibility in state structures, they must perform better than their male colleagues to prove that these posts were not granted to them as a political favour or for symbolic reasons related to their gender. Moreover, women must constantly struggle to overcome powerful religious and cultural images that are used as tools to challenge their legitimacy as political actors. Stereotyped images of women still abound in the obligatory school texts (Lemrini, 1993). The role of mother is portrayed as the noblest function for women. The only concessions relate to the professions of teacher and nurse, presented not as professions but rather as vocations 'natural' to women because of their 'caring' nature as mothers. Role models to legitimize more varied social, economic, and political participation of women are absent.

The Janus-faced state allows national leaders to take pride in the attainments of women in the Arab-Muslim context when dealing with Western partners, and simultaneously pride themselves on the fact that the country has been able to retain its traditions. Morocco's identity is based on symbolic constructions that aim to present the country as both Arab-Muslim and open to the West. Everything is accepted from the West except the moral values touching on the Muslim and Arabic identity—the family structure and the situation of women. As a beneficiary of assistance from several donor countries in the West and Middle East, the state thus appears to adhere to different ideologies on gender relations simultaneously, and this leads to the implementation of contradictory policies with regard to women (Kandiyoti, 1991). The policies adopted by multi- and bi-lateral co-operation organizations, particularly the United Nations and the European Union, which include gender issues as an element in lending and aid programmes, force the state to compromise while attempting to maintain the *status quo*.

In recent years some countries providing bi-lateral or multi-lateral development aid have encouraged the government to accept a broader debate on the 'woman question'. Women's rights and status are, however, never seriously taken into account in negotiations between states: no state has as yet been threatened with cancellation of aid or refusal of loans because of the position of its women and female children.[25] In development circles, the status of women is rarely addressed, on the pretext that women's status in the Arab-Muslim sphere is a cultural matter. The manner in which the state administers development programmes involving women demonstrates this very clearly. Instead of responding to the demands of the women's movement which, following recommendations made at various United Nations conferences on women, continues to advocate a women's machinery endowed with financial and political clout, issues concerning the 'advancement' of women are divided up among a division, a service and two bureaux within four of the least prestigious, least politically influential, and poorest ministries (Barkallil, 1994). This represents a deliberate attempt to avoid politicizing women's status.

The attitude of the women's movement with regard to the state has changed appreciably during the last decade. Originating in a '*Makhzen*' culture, the women's movement was essentially hierarchical and exclusive, but has gradually adopted a more democratic approach: the spokespersons and networks are varied, and horizontal relationships with other national and international partners have been established. The movement has broken out of the hierarchical relationship between governing and the governed, thus acquiring a real independence. In this way it has also been the precursor of a new political culture. By choosing to make use of the areas where contradictions in official policy are at their most flagrant, and by adopting a strategy of openness and dialogue with political leaders, the women's movement has put into practice for the benefit of specific gender claims the political skill acquired by women within the traditional political parties.

At the highest level of state institutions, the King has always attempted to maintain, within the framework of pluralism, a balance between the modernist elements of society and the traditionalists and conservatives. In so doing it has been easier to make concessions at the expense of women, since the latter traditionally carry little weight in the formal political sphere. The existence of an independent women's movement has, however, made it possible to put claims forward by directly addressing the King, if necessary, or the Prime Minister or other ministers. It is in this sense that the women's movement has had an important impact; its members come forward to address the state on such diverse political questions as the Code of Personal Status, civil rights in the constitution, violence against women, or discrimination in recruitment of women graduates for public institutions. The political groups of the left, which still see themselves as representative of the population as a whole, have never formulated the problems so sharply, either directly or through their women representatives in Parliament.

The gradual but hesitant recognition of the women's movement by the state has been appreciable at various levels. In recent years, in official speeches and press conferences, the King has recognized that the problems expressed by the various women's groups are fair and their demands relevant. In answer to a question by a journalist on a possible Islamist danger in Morocco, the King insisted that women and intellectuals act as ramparts against this danger. Interestingly, in what can be interpreted as a discursive shift, women are less often praised as the pillars of the family and society, and as protectors of national identity, as was the case in the past, but as ramparts against Islamic fundamentalism which threatens the political stability of the country.

A further aspect of the political recognition of women has been the consultations set up with civil society. Women's associations were invited by the King to give their opinion on the revision of the Code of Personal Status. They were also involved in the formulation of the national report for the Fourth World Conference on Women in Beijing (1995). The women's movement has increased its capacity to diversify alliances and networks for making common claims, and to strengthen solidarity between its various components and other groups of civil society. All these factors ensure the independence of the movement from the state, as well as its effectiveness in formulating and imposing its concerns as subjects of discussion at different social and political levels. The extension of the negotiation capabilities of the women's movement is linked to the strategies for *rapprochement* of the movement with the political groups and its consolidation in civil society. Indeed, leaders of the women's associations are also members (or leaders) of other associations of human rights, professional or civic associations, and members of political parties.

Political parties, the women's movement and the redefinition of political space

The analysis below will attempt to demonstrate the decisive contribution of the women's movement over the past decade to the effective acknowledgement of gender concerns as political questions. Ironically, however, this contribution is not identified as an essentially 'political' one by the members of the women's movement. To understand why we must situate the feminist struggle within the general political context and examine more closely the links of the feminists with the democratic political groups.

The resistance of the main political actors to the demands of the women's movement is mainly based on two concerns: equality of civil rights, with its implications for the division of power and male privileges in the family sphere; and equality in access to political power, which represents a threat to male supremacy in the formal political sphere. It is precisely to these two areas that the women's movement has given priority from the beginning. The other claims, such as education and work, are often perceived as the means to attain these two goals. In this manner the women's movement threatens the strongholds and very foundations of male supremacy and that of the élite groups. Consequently, the traditional political forces have developed several discursive strategies to exclude women.

In addition to the discourse rooted in religious and cultural tradition, already explored above, the male political discourse also uses "naturalist" arguments derived from values and rules associated with the public and private spheres. In contrast to male reason and rationality, supposedly 'natural' feminine emotion and virtue render women unsuited to public life. They are considered uninterested in politics because, as is often stated, 'their nature causes them to tend towards concrete things' (unlike men who easily grasp abstract matters), or because the 'gentleness of women's nature cannot adapt itself to the political jungle'. Overall, the implication of such discourse is that women's character, being closer to nature, is less capable of taking part in the political game, which is defined as an ensemble of implicit and complex rules that only men are able to master. All these ideas come together to form a coherent and powerful mode of thinking which effectively distances and, indeed, excludes women from political power.

In response to a question by a woman journalist on the low representation of women in elected bodies, and measures planned to improve this situation, posed during a press conference in 1996 organized by the Koutla, the leader of the Istiqlal party made use of both discursive strategies (naturalist arguments and social tradition) to explain away the problem. Similarly, the memorandum addressed by the Koutla to the King detailing propositions related to the revision of the Constitution requested recognition of gender equality in civil rights; however, this demand was conditional on the fact that recognition should not counter national religious values. This condition allows the political parties—like the state—to appear to make concessions to the demands of the women's movement, while at the same time disregarding them, since it is agreed that Islam cannot accept equality in civil rights.

Overall, the exclusion of women from the formal political sphere works through an élitist system which, in order to persist, uses a number of symbolic and practical mechanisms of exclusion. Conventional politics follow 'the rules of the game'; these consist of implicit ideas accepted by all and which no one can ignore, at the risk of disgrace and marginalization. Accordingly, it is seen as a strategic error to demand change regarding the status of women on the pretext that the subject is very sensitive on the religious level; instead, the real goal should concern the strengthening of previously established rights and ensuring their implementation. The basis for this argument centres on the situation of rural women, who make up half of the total female population and who are described as having concerns very far from the 'extravagant demands of the feminists'. The demand for the participation of women in the formal political arena is seen as ridiculous in view of the 'physical and moral destitution of the great majority of women'.

This discourse, which is used widely, has two purposes. First, it makes the democratic participation of women conditional on the attainment of a specific level of education and ability. Participation in community affairs is understood to be reserved for educated women. However, the latter are in a minority and are, therefore, seen only to represent themselves, almost as if they form a special interest group. This view is not surprising in a country where formal politics and participation in public affairs in general was until recently limited to a very restricted male political élite. Second, it divests the women's movement of all legitimacy because this discourse implies that the demands made by the movement are not among the preoccupations of the overwhelming majority of women. In this way the women's associations are discredited because of what they represent and particularly because of what they demand. It is a movement seen to be composed of a marginalized, Westernized élite. The same discursive strategies are not employed by the main political actors in order to deny women the right to vote. On the contrary, since women make up a large electoral reservoir—they customarily vote in greater numbers than men—during the electoral campaigns the tendency is to attempt to mobilize women, thereby profiting from their ignorance and destitution.

A recent study on the youth milieu in Morocco suggests that the 'élitist' nature of politics is a general problem (Bennani-Chraibi, 1994). Young people had opinions on all socio-economic problems, but as soon as the issue of 'politics' was raised they asserted that they were not interested or had no opinion. Politics is not seen as dealing with affairs which directly concern the citizen, but as an area of expertise that requires particular abilities: 'people see themselves as lacking the capacity, knowledge or culture'. Not only is there a perception that particular intellectual abilities are required for political participation, but also that the formal political sphere is reserved for powerful individuals: '... politics has its "masters" and "companions"; it is the sphere reserved for the upper class or those who have property and wish to make a profit'. The political parties are thereby discredited in so far as the popular discourse presents the 'political game' as rather unethical and motivated by individual interest. This attitude, aptly described by Bennani-Chraibi as being a way of 'discrediting the very idea that it is individually and collectively legitimate to judge and question political authority', underlines the powerlessness and exclusion of non-élites (ibid.). This relation to politics is therefore not particular to women, but rather a feature of the broader social structure.

In this context it is hardly surprising that only a feminine élite belonging to the middle class and thoroughly familiar with the atmosphere of the political parties could have overcome the various obstacles to political participation and denounced exclusion based on gender. Their social and political proximity to the ruling élites has favoured the emergence of women's associations. At the same time, this situation creates a certain dependency. The women's movement continues to count on political groups belonging to the parliamentary opposition which might, if elected, make a break with the past and agree to women's demands. Women's groups have therefore adopted a non-isolationist strategy vis-à-vis those elements most hostile to their claims, in particular the most conservative social elements within the Koutla. In order to avoid marginalization, they have avoided direct debate on the issue of the secularization of the law.

In recent years, however, there have been developments in this sphere as well. In the preamble to the egalitarian Code of Personal Status as well as concerning family relations in the Maghreb described by the Collectif 95 Maghreb Egalité, the need for secularization of family law is explicitly stated. Similarly, the various articles of this Code undermine the foundations of male authority and supremacy, and of women's exclusion from economic and political power.[26] This marks a shift from the position, long maintained by political parties and even by some parts of the women's movement, that to engage in such questions would be suicidal. Such initiatives became possible owing to the combination of the efforts of several women's groups in Algeria, Morocco, and Tunisia, and indicate the extent of the independence of certain women's associations in Morocco from the political establishment.

Another example concerns the struggles of the women's associations within the framework of national collaboration for revision of the Code of Personal

Status which took place in a loaded political atmosphere coinciding the revision of the Constitution and the national elections. In this context, women's claims could have been profitable electorally, with an ensuing escalation of political manoeuvrings in a national and regional context characterized by Islam. To prevent that possibility the King of Morocco asked the women's associations to refer to him personally when proposing revisions to the Code, in exchange for which they agreed not to turn the question into an electoral issue.

It is to the merit of the women's associations that they have seized favourable political opportunities to place on the agenda questions relating to equality in civic rights and the need to reform electoral laws in order to promote women's participation in elected bodies. The choice made by these associations to collaborate as soon as 'highly political' demands were involved, and to form alliances with other elements of civil society, represents recognition of the need to present a coherent front *vis-à-vis* the actors which are most resistant to their demands, namely, the state and political parties. Similarly, the recourse to forms of struggle and of negotiation which resemble those adopted by the parties, such as sending memoranda to the King, indicates the will of the women's movement to engage directly in the formal political arena.

Overall, this strategy is modelled on that of the traditional political parties. The women's movement follows the methods of the parties while attempting to differentiate itself from them. The limitations of this approach arise from the movement's view of its own struggle, which it rarely describes in terms of instrinsically 'political' actions and initiatives. Politics is still seen as the sphere relating to power and the official political institutions, the rest being perceived as fringe activities. This idea is based on gender segmentation: women are not to be involved in politics, which are a matter for men, nor are their concerns to be acknowledged as political issues. To challenge an established social order and its norms and values in order to change them is an important feature of the women's movement, but it is rarely described or identified as political by its own initiators.

The women's movement has faced difficulties in re-orienting its fighting spirit, support and skill into an institutionalized representation (in government, Parliament, unions, professional associations, etc.) because of its links with the political parties. The instrumental use of women's votes during electoral campaigns provides the best example. The Moroccan electoral system, which discourages candidates in legislative elections from running as independents, forces women candidates to run under a party banner. When candidates were being listed for the election of 1993, however, instead of closing ranks in order to elicit better female participation, the women's movement showed a tendency to fragment, espousing the quarrels of the political cliques. Women thus competed with each other under the respective banners of the various opposition parties. Women became aware of the weakness inherent in this strategy when candidatures were announced: the number of women candidates was ridiculously low—for example, two out of 222 accepted by the opposition coalition (Socialist Union and

Istiqlal Party), which was likely to obtain the greatest number of seats in Parliament. This scenario is likely to be repeated unless women attach greater importance to gender priorities than to partisan loyalties. In the light of past experiences, these loyalties are the most effective instrument for excluding women from representation in official structures.

It seems evident that the strategy adopted by certain leaders of the women's movement, which involves separating the feminist and partisan sides of their activities in order to protect a fragile and continually threatened independence, ultimately increases the ability of other political actors to use the women's vote instrumentally, and is contrary to the declared aims of most of the movement's constituents. Despite the difficulties, however, recent developments with regard to women's co-ordination clearly show that the women's movement is moving slowly but surely towards a true solidarity—the primary condition for making independence *vis-à-vis* the state and other powerful institutions an irreversible reality.

Conclusion

The process of democratization acquired credibility in the Moroccan context mainly through two developments: first, the opening up of the formal political sphere to new actors; and second, the broadening of the subjects discussed by political institutions, as well as the forms and discourses underlying political action. Although still in their initial stages, these changes have nevertheless greatly contributed to a rehabilitation of political action by extending it to questions that touch on the socio-economic interests of large groups of the population, including women.

By becoming aware that the exclusion of women is not unique to the political and sociological context of Muslim societies, the women's movement in Morocco has been able to escape from the trap of double specificity—of situating women in relation to men, and of comparing Arab-Muslim women with Western women—and has cast off its isolation in relation to the theories and discourses of Western feminism. The women's movement has thus helped to promote political debate. It has also focused attention on fundamental questions that challenge the society as a whole, such as modernity, universality, and difference in a country reputed to be deeply traditional.

The women's movement, which was initially marginal and sometimes considered extremist, has progressed since the mid-1980s. Its discourse and claims have become reference points for intellectuals and the political establishment. Its visibility and energy have turned it into a defining element in the structure of civil society. In short, by representing their independent interests, feminists have helped to redefine gender identities and political identities simultaneously. The movement has helped to shift the frontiers of what constitutes the 'political' by encouraging public discussion and debate on issues traditionally associated with the domestic and private sphere, such as divorce, polygamy,

110

matrimonial tutelage, violence, and the political participation of women—all subjects which were previously 'taboo', to be discussed 'among women only' or among specialists in theology or Islamic law. In so doing the women's movement has helped to increase political participation and broaden the 'political' terrain in Morocco.

5

Femocrats and ecorats: women's policy machinery in Australia, Canada and New Zealand[1]

MARIAN SAWER

The idea that governments need specialized policy machinery for the advancement of women to ensure that women receive equal benefit from government activity as a whole is relatively new.[2] It first received widespread acceptance as a result of the priority given to it in the World Plan of Action adopted at the World Conference of the International Women's Year held in Mexico City in 1975. Over two-thirds of the member states of the United Nations adopted some form of policy machinery during the subsequent United Nations Decade for Women (1976–85), although there was great variation in the government agendas involved and in resourcing and effectiveness, particularly in developing countries. None the less, by the end of the Decade there had been a general shift from reliance on advisory bodies to the creation of government units among 137 reporting countries (BAW, 1987).

The new machinery stemmed from the feminist insight that no government activity is likely to be gender neutral, given the different location of women and men in the workforce and in the family, and the predominant role taken by women in social reproduction. It was important, therefore, to go beyond specific 'women's' programmes to ensure that all government policy was monitored and all government activity audited for gender-specific effects. This insight was underpinned by work by Ester Boserup (1970) and others, showing the unintended effects of development policies on women. The practice of feminist interventions in the state outstripped feminist theorizing about the state which was largely generated in the United States and the United Kingdom, the two countries where such interventions were least developed (Wilson, 1977; Ferguson, 1984).

To take a relatively simple example of gender-specific effects of purportedly gender-neutral policy, of the kind the new women's machinery was intended to highlight: a proposal might be made to effect savings in public transport by cutting back on services other than the most profitable peak commuter routes. The relevant women's unit would draw attention to the disparate impact of such a proposal on women, who characteristically have less access to private transport than men and are more likely to need public transport for purposes other than the journey to work. Similarly, a proposal to introduce time-charging for local telephone calls could readily be shown to have a disproportionate impact on women, who make fewer purely instrumental calls and spend more time on the telephone as part of their invisible welfare work in sustaining kinship and other networks.

This paper looks at how such machinery came into existence in Australia, Canada, and New Zealand, three countries which are generally rated highly in terms of gender equity. It raises issues concerning the location of such machinery and the trade-offs involved in the brokering of feminist policy insights within a bureaucratic environment. It also looks at how women's policy machinery relates to other forms of institutionalization of the women's movement—to what extent such machinery assists in resourcing the women's movement and in so doing creates an effective political base for feminist policy (Stetson and Mazur, 1995).

It should be noted that the creation of women's policy machinery in Australia and Canada was assisted by a political opportunity structure which included both reforming governments eager to expand the policy agenda and the economic prosperity of the early 1970s. Greater citizen participation was another watchword of this period, which favoured the entry of new groups into the policy process. Australia and Canada have federal political structures and this helped maintain some momentum even when conservative governments had been re-elected nationally. When the political opportunity came 10 years later, in New Zealand, the economic context was much less favourable. All three countries have Westminster systems of government characterized by majority party rule. The periods of 'conservative' government have been less favourable to women's policy initiatives than the periods of more left-wing government. This paper is also concerned with a more general shift in public agendas in all three countries which have created a difficult environment for women's policy machinery and which have made the old distinction between left and right much more problematic. In both Australia and New Zealand, Labour governments initiated economic reforms in the 1980s which reduced the kind of intervention in the economy practised by their 'conservative' predecessors.

The political tradition of Australia and New Zealand was shaped by the social liberalism of the 1890s with its idea of the state as a vehicle for social justice (Sawer, 1993). This provided the discursive framework within which both the first and second waves of the women's movement placed their claims on the state and within which these demands were accorded legitimacy. Social liberalism has also been important in Canada, but most strongly after the Second World War (Vickers, 1992). In seeming contradiction to this tradition, in all three countries the early days of women's liberation, at the beginning of the 1970s, were strongly marked by anti-state influences from the United States —'women and revolution' not 'women and bureaucracy'.[3] This meant an initial gulf between anarchistic women's organizations and the existing 'polite' women's organizations. As the tradition of social liberalism reasserted itself, so did co-operation to achieve common goals, although second-wave organizational philosophy had a continuing influence in the structuring of women's organizations and women's services.

Historically in the three countries, women had been policy shapers as well as policy takers in relation to the development of the welfare state, and there had been recognition that women had a special interest in the increase of social provision rather than, for example, lower taxes. New Zealand, which in 1893 had become the first country to give women the vote, in 1938 established what was then the most comprehensive welfare state in the world. By the 1980s social liberal traditions were being challenged in all three countries by the increased policy influence of what in Australia and New Zealand are usually referred to as economic rationalists ('ecorats').

It was paradoxical that, as mechanisms for gender audit within government were being developed or strengthened, government policymaking was increasingly coming under the sway of economic views hostile to public provision and based on androcentric paradigms of human behaviour (economically rational man). For the ecorats, the welfare state is basically the problem and greater reliance on market forces is the solution. This conversion to economic rationalism, which was perhaps most striking within the New Zealand Labour governments of the 1980s, was somewhat more restrained by the Australian Labor[4] government's Accord agreement with the union movement, and was less surprising within the Progressive Conservative Canadian governments of 1984–94.

The mandated concern of femocrats for gender equity brings them into an uneasy relationship with economic rationalism. Ecorats believe that public intervention in markets in the name of equity or social citizenship rights is counterproductive and leads to economic inefficiencies. Femocrats had to shift from social justice discourse to market discourse (stressing human resource and efficiency arguments for gender equity) in order to be 'heard'.[5] Even in relation to the basic human rights issue of domestic violence, femocrats increasingly had to stress the economic costs of gender-based violence. At the end of the day, however, femocrats still needed to defend the welfare state on which women were disproportionately dependent but which economic rationalists viewed as standing in the way of international competitiveness.

Another point of conflict in both Australia and New Zealand has been the shift away from historic systems of centralized wage-fixing which provided a greater degree of protection for more feminized sectors of the labour market than is available in decentralized wage-fixing systems. While some safeguards have been secured for women in Australia, such as the legislating of International Labour Organization standards as minimum conditions, the general direction of change is likely to result in wage disparities more like those obtaining in Canada under its decentralized wage-bargaining system.

New Zealander Prue Hyman has described the 'likelihood that general economic policies, including fiscal, monetary, labour, industry, government sector and international trade policies, have far more impact on the economic and social status of most women than specific policies aimed at improving that status' (Hyman, 1994:14). This was recognized in the mid-1980s by large-scale mobilizations by women to oppose the introduction of a broad-based consumption tax in Australia and to oppose free trade agreements in Canada. The disparate impact of free market policies on men and women has been reflected in wide gender gaps in opinion polls on such issues in both Canada and Australia (Bashevkin, 1989:370; Sawer, 1994:55). None the less, it is when women's policy machinery in government attempts to intervene on such economic issues that it meets most resistance—both because of traditional views that these are not 'women's issues' and because of the economic rationalist view that interventions in the name of social equity are invariably 'rent-seeking' in nature and hence illegitimate.

Where not otherwise indicated, material in this chapter derives from interviews conducted by the author over the last 10 years with women who have worked in women's policy machinery in Australia, Canada and New Zealand or have been associated with it in other ways (for example as minister or as community lobbyist).

Australia

Australia has become increasingly well-known for the role of its feminist bureaucrats, or 'femocrats'—a word invented to describe feminists who went into the women's policy positions created in Australia in the 1970s. The word is now in common usage, both by friends and enemies as well as more neutral observers (Yeatman, 1990). In September 1995 the President of the Australian Council of Trade Unions was awarded a prize for the most sexist remark of the year for referring to a group of women unionists as 'hairy-legged femocrats' (*Sydney Morning Herald*, 9 September 1995). Other vocal critics include 'pro-family' organizations which claim that femocrats do not represent the interests of women in the home—despite their efforts on issues such as the inclusion of unpaid work in national accounts.

The origins of Australian femocrats go back to 1972, the year a highly effective non-party organization called the Women's Electoral Lobby (WEL) was created and succeeded in placing the policy demands of women centre-stage during the federal election of that year. WEL was regarded as the 'reformist' wing of the new women's movement but attracted many women who believed, like its founder, that it was time to move on from talk to practical action.

It was the successful intervention by WEL in the 1972 federal election (and the key role in the new Labor administration played by Peter Wilenski, the husband of a WEL Convenor) which was the trigger for the appointment of a women's adviser to the prime minister in 1973. From her very first press conference this adviser[6] articulated what was to be the characteristic Australian emphasis on the need to audit all Cabinet submissions for impact on women.

The election of a federal government bent on reform and eager to take on new areas of social responsibility plus the context of a buoyant economy provided a favourable opportunity structure for experimenting with the machinery of government. The fact that the women's adviser took on a quasi-ministerial status and received more letters than anyone except the prime minister led to the establishment of the forerunner of the Office of the Status of Women (OSW) in the Department of Prime Minister and Cabinet to provide support for her. A separate secretariat, also under the aegis of the Women's Adviser, was set up in another department to administer the large programme undertaken in Australia for the International Women's Year, which funded an enormous amount of consciousness-raising both at community and national levels.

Meanwhile WEL members inside and outside government worked on a model for women's machinery which they presented to the Royal Commission on Australian Government Administration set up by the Labor government. The model consisted of a women's co-ordination unit within the central policy co-ordinating agency of government and linked to a network of departmental women's units responsible for monitoring policy at the point of initiation. Australian feminists decided against a self-standing bureau or ministry on the grounds that it might simply become a 'waste-paper basket for women's problems'.

The emphasis was on policy audit and policy co-ordination rather than on sep-arate women's programmes. In order to have sufficient clout to perform the pol-icy co-ordination role effectively and to have unfettered access to Cabinet submissions and Cabinet processes, Australian feminists believed it necessary to be located within the chief policy co-ordination agency of government (Sawer and Groves, 1994b:chapter 2). In Australia this is the Department of Prime Minister and Cabinet at federal level, departments of Premier and Cabinet at state level, and Chief Ministers' departments at territory level. Experience has also suggested the importance of having at least one adviser with gender expert-ise located in the Prime Minister's office in parliament, which provides policy support of a more 'political' nature to the Prime Minister.

In a speech to an International Women's Year Conference in Canberra, Sara Dowse, an early member of Women's Liberation and the first head of what was to be OSW, spoke of the importance of location.[7] She also suggested that the pro-posed matrix or centre-periphery structure was particularly compatible with women's movement philosophy and the preference for networking over hier-archical arrangements (Dowse, 1975). None the less there was a price to pay for location at the centre of government, most notably the need to conform to exist-ing hierarchical structures and organizational culture which were here at their most rigid. Hence the paradox that it was 'sisters in suits' who acted as the in-ternal advocates for the funding of the quite unconventional models of service delivery developed by the women's movement.

Internal femocrat advocacy was effective in brokering government funding for a very wide range of women's services run by women for women in accordance with collectivist principles. For example, the forerunner of OSW was responsible for finding a bureaucratic home for refuge funding at the federal level to ensure that political opposition at the state level was circumvented. Mediation by femocrats in both co-ordinating and line departments contributed to the ability of women's services to resist pressure to become conventional service deliverers and to persist in modelling feminist organizational forms.

Traditional bureaucrats distrusted, however, the insertion of what was seen as an advocacy body into a department regarded as providing 'objective' advice on cross-portfolio submissions. In the memorable image provided by Anne Summers, femocrats were suspected as 'missionaries' by traditional bureaucrats, while at the same time women in the women's movement often believed they had sold out to become 'mandarins' (Summers, 1986).

In 1977 the bureaucrats had their revenge when it was announced that the Office was to be moved to the newly created Department of Home Affairs, the minister of which ranked 26th in seniority out of the 27 ministries. Sara Dowse went public, resigning her position and making the location of the Office into a political issue. She explained that the Office could not be effective in its policy co-ordinating function from a position of great weakness 'thrown in with war graves and museums' (*Daily Mirror*, 22 December 1977). After leaving the economic security of the public service, she led an at first penurious but then increasingly successful life as a writer. Her first novel, *West Block* (Dowse, 1983), was about her experiences as a femocrat.

The politicization by Dowse of the location of the Office helped make it a priority in the Labor opposition's women's policy. Labor feminists were able, after their party's electoral failure in 1977, to exploit the 'gender gap' they discovered in Labor support to argue the case for a strong women's policy. As we shall see, an apparent historic shortfall in support for Labour among women voters was also exploited by Labour women in New Zealand in the 1970s to make gains in the party.

Meanwhile the Office was able to consolidate its base among traditional women's organizations through the outreach work of the National Women's Advisory Council, in particular the national process of developing a Draft Plan of Action for the United Nations Decade for Women. The Council and its successor body, the National Women's Consultative Council (NWCC), were intended to provide the government with a means of consulting with women in the community. Members were appointed by government from both national women's organizations and other significant bodies such as the Australian Council of Trade Unions. Although serviced from the Office, the Councils were able to speak out on issues in a way that bureaucrats could not—for example, when there was a threat to public health insurance cover for abortions. The Councils also helped protect the Office, broadening its political base and deflecting anti-feminist criticism (this was also true of some state Councils, particularly in Tasmania).

With the return of Labor to government in 1983, OSW returned in triumph to the Department of Prime Minister and Cabinet and was able to reassert its role in co-ordinating a network of departmental women's units. One of its first victories was the requirement for 'impact on women' statements to be attached to Cabinet submissions, a requirement which stayed in place until the 'streamlining' of the submission format in 1987. The Prime Minister resumed portfolio responsibility for the status of women, assisted by a senior woman cabinet minister. Like almost all ministers who have held this portfolio at federal level, the latter had a background in the Women's Electoral Lobby.

The fact that the Minister Assisting the Prime Minister on the Status of Women was a senior Cabinet minister was important in ensuring that debate on the impact on women of major economic decisions was actually carried into Cabinet. This was not the case between 1988 and 1993 when junior ministers held the Minister Assisting the Prime Minister portfolio (attending Cabinet only for 'their' issues). Bureaucratic monitoring of policy for impact on women was also reinforced at the political level by a Caucus (Parliamentary Labor Party) Status of Women Committee, open to all Labor women MPs, which met weekly during sitting weeks to focus the minds of ministerial colleagues on the gender dimensions of their policy proposals.

OSW was still not totally accepted and during the first year its files were kept separate from those of the rest of the department to facilitate an early departure. There was still resentment of the 'feminist eye' being cast over policy proposals, particularly when they were not regarded as women's business: 'Given the role of heading off any proposal that wasn't woman-friendly, we haven't been regarded too kindly by the traditional bureaucrats. We made ourselves very unpopular as we poked around in other people's policies and wrote comments on their Cabinet submissions' (Anne Summers in Sawer and Groves, 1994b:30).

During the 1993 review of OSW, the option of a self-standing Ministry, as in New Zealand, was canvassed. As for the previous 20 years, the conclusion was, however, that a free-standing ministry could easily be marginalized and would lack the access to Cabinet information provided by location in the Prime Minister's Department. The review suggested that stronger support from the Departmental Executive and from the Prime Minister's Office would be a better guarantee of effectiveness.

Under the federal Labor governments of the 1980s and 1990s, OSW and femocrats elsewhere in government were to influence policy over a range of sectors—such as the quintupling of the national childcare programme, increased funding of women's services, legislation requiring private sector companies to develop equal employment opportunity programmes, shifting of family support to primary carers, national programmes on violence against women, programmes to promote equal opportunity for workers with family responsibilities, etc. Many of these new programmes, such as the National Women's Health Policy, were developed through an elaborate and exemplary process of consultation with women in the community. There were also a few successful interventions in what were seen as 'mainstream economic policy issues'. For example, feminist mobilization played an important role in defeating proposals for a broad-based consumption tax and later in ensuring that low income earners (the majority of whom were women) were not excluded from tax cuts (Sawer, 1990:93–6; Sawer and Groves, 1994b:12).

Success on issues was most likely when there was joint work from inside and outside, as on the tax cuts and as with the eventual ratification of ILO Convention 156 on Equal Opportunities for Workers with Family Responsibilities. Labor had been committed to ratification since 1983, but it took a great deal of strategic work by OSW, with the help of its Consultative Council 'voice' and of feminists within the Australian Council of Trade Unions, as well as the exploitation by the Caucus Status of Women Committee of another federal election where Labor needed to woo women's votes, to achieve ratification in 1990. This Convention has not been ratified in either Canada or New Zealand.

Relations between the women's movement and OSW reached a low ebb during the 1980s when the Office was headed by an economist without a background in the women's movement who was blamed for failure to mount internal resistance to a series of cost-cutting decisions detrimental to women, including the means-testing of family allowances. (In New Zealand and Canada more successful resistance, at least for a time, was mounted to the means-testing of what for many women was their only independent income.)

One aspect of Australian women's policy machinery which is not replicated in Canada or New Zealand consists of government funded 'women's information services'. These are located in all capital cities and some regional centres and provide an accessible bridge for women in the community to government or community resources. The policy is to 'take every woman seriously' and the services are usually organized on semi-collectivist principles. They are sometimes used for 'phone-ins' on specific issues of concern to women, and these feed into policy development work. During the 1980s, OSW ran services for a time in two state capitals with conservative governments, but these were later taken over by state-based women's policy machinery. OSW lost its own women's shopfront when the Australian Capital Territory became self-governing and took over the service—which meant that OSW lost this direct link with women in the community.

Inside the bureaucracy OSW was responsible for significant new co-ordination exercises such as the Women's Budget Program (later Women's Budget Statement), which required all departments and agencies to account for the impact of their activities on women in a Budget document. This radical departure was introduced with the assistance of the 'Secretaries' Taskforce on the Status of Women'—a co-ordinating body made up of departmental heads which also oversaw the preparation of Australia's National Agenda for the Advancement of Women to the Year 2000 before lapsing for lack of interest. The Women's Budget Program was a world first in terms of educating bureaucrats to disaggregate the impact of their 'mainstream' programmes rather than simply highlighting programmes for women. It was an initiative subsequently copied at state and territory levels of government and had considerable influence at the international level. For example, in 1994 the Canadian Advisory Council on the Status of Women was recommending to the Finance Minister that it be adopted in Canada (MacDonald, 1995:2008).

OSW continued, however, to have difficulty in influencing macro-economic policy, an area dominated by men schooled in 'gender-blind' neo-classical eco- nomics. While the relationship between the central co-ordinating unit and out- lying units, such as those in economic departments, may be an important source of support for officers marginalized in their own departments, there are limits to this relationship posed by the need for women's units to demonstrate that their primary allegiance is to their department. There were also some frictions between OSW and the long-standing Women's Bureau, with the latter seeing their concerns with industry policy and outworkers (workers working from home, an increasing phenomenon with industry restructuring) as of more rele- vance to working class women than affirmative action programmes.

The increased influence of economic rationalism in the 1980s was one adverse feature of the policy environment. Another was the difficulty displayed by the women's movement in coming to terms with the increased sophistication of pol- icy development processes and the increased professionalization demanded of participants, regardless of their sectoral base. The Australian women's movement was increasingly diverse and fragmented and lacked the kind of national pres- ence which would provide a strong political base for embattled feminists within government. While there was considerable interaction between specialized women's organizations and relevant government agencies, there was no community-based 'peak' body equivalent to, for example, the Australian Council of Social Service or the Federation of Ethnic Communities' Councils of Australia. These are umbrella organizations independent of government but in receipt of government funding to represent constituents in policy development processes. Government advisory bodies, with their limited independence, are no substitute for the professionalized advocacy of peak bodies and neither are the largely volunteer organizations found in the women's movement. As in other countries, issue-based coalitions arose out of the women's movement in response to perceived threats or opportunities, but found it difficult to sustain themselves over time.

A networking structure linking national women's organizations, the Coalition of Actively Participating Organisations of Women (CAPOW), was created in 1992, serving mainly to improve communication flows though some co-ordinat- ing work was undertaken, particularly in preparation for the Fourth World Conference on Women and before ministerial round tables. There was a self- denying ordinance preventing the network structure taking on a representational role as a 'voice for women'. Many national women's organizations were them- selves 'networks', indicating the philosophical preference for non-hierarchical structures. Many of these national networks had been brought into being by gov- ernment grants aimed at building up more coherent policy input from the women's movement and a more effective political base for programmes endan- gered by creeping economic rationalism (Sawer and Groves, 1994a). This gov- ernment role in fostering organization at the national level was particularly important in relation to groups such as women from non-English speaking

120

backgrounds and women with disabilities, who previously had little voice at this level. In 1994–5 the Minister was attempting to push the women's movement along to the creation of a peak body through the funding of a large feasibility study and other pressures.

As we have seen, one impetus to closer co-ordination of women's organizations was the preparation for participation in the Fourth World Conference on Women, held in 1995 in Beijing. Australia has a long tradition of working to promote the status of women through the United Nations, starting with Jessie Street at the San Francisco Conference and including an important role in the preparatory work for all four world conferences on women. The international work of OSW has been of particular importance during periods of frustration at the domestic level, as in the early 1980s. Work towards strengthening international instruments has been seen as an important lever for gains at home and as the other side of work to strengthen the organizational capacity of the women's movement. The Nairobi Forward Looking Strategies provided the justification for the Australian National Agenda for Women of 1988 (updated in 1993), which was in turn preceded by an extensive consultation process including the funding of National Agenda conferences organized by NGOs.

In Australia the ratification of CEDAW was of particular importance as it provided the federal government with the constitutional basis (through its external affairs power) to legislate against sex discrimination. While ratification had taken place in Canada in 1981, before the election of the Conservative government, it had to wait in Australia and New Zealand until after the election of Labour governments in 1983 and 1984 respectively. Australian expert Justice Elizabeth Evatt was to play an important role, as a member and then Chair of the CEDAW Committee, in developing the interpretation of the Convention to cover issues such as violence against women. Together with New Zealand, Australia has promoted CEDAW in the South Pacific and, with the Netherlands, has helped fund an Expert Group to draft an Optional Protocol for the Convention providing right of petition. Australia and Canada were co-sponsors of the United Nations Declaration on the Elimination of Violence against Women and New Zealand worked closely with them in its development.

Australia was the leading regional donor for the Fourth World Conference on Women, funding attendance of one government and one non-government delegate from each Pacific country. OSW also put considerable resources into helping the Australian women's movement prepare for participation. This included resourcing nationwide consultations and co-ordination work in the two years leading up to the Conference and training sessions to enable non-government delegates to participate more effectively in multilateral forums. At Beijing, Australia was regarded as noteworthy for the very close co-operation between government and non-government delegations, which included meetings every evening organized by CAPOW.

The large non-government delegation gave strong support to the official Australian initiative in trying to make it a conference of commitments[8] and was significant in getting the concept accepted (Townsend, 1995:9). According to an NGO perspective prepared by a representative of the Coalition of Activist Lesbians: 'The close co-operation and good working relations between the two groups was noted with envy by NGOs from many other countries' (*CAPOW Bulletin*, November 1995:27).

Sixty-five countries made new domestic commitments. Due to opposition, the United Nations was not given responsibility for documenting and monitoring these commitments. Responsibility was taken up by NGOs, however, and a World Wide Web site was promptly prepared. This close co-operation between official and NGO delegations was not inspired by the Australian government's own commitments which, despite the efforts of OSW, were notably weak on this occasion—too long before an election to be seen as having much domestic pay-off.

As this negative example illustrates, it is the skilful exploitation by feminist insiders of the 'gender gap' in voting intentions which has been largely respons- ible for recent domestic wins. This has counterbalanced the increasingly adverse ideological context and the relatively low level of institutionalization of the Australian women's movement outside government (at least compared to Canada, as we shall see later). While the Labor Party's efforts to attract the female vote appeared to have paid off in the early 1980s, with the closing of the gender gap delivering government to the party, later in the 1980s the gap re- appeared, particularly between elections. Women appeared to have become more 'volatile' voters and were also more likely to be among those making up their minds very late in campaigns. This provided welcome political opportunities, particularly when the femocrats had political as well as bureaucratic credibility and ready access to the Prime Minister and his Office. Dr. Anne Summers was able to gain large childcare commitments before the 1984 and 1993 federal elec- tions in this context, as well as action on other long-standing feminist demands.

Canada

In Canada, the setting up of the historic Royal Commission on the Status of Women in 1967, inspired by President Kennedy's Commission on the Status of Women in the United States, was the first step towards the present national machinery for women (see note 2 on the pre-existing Women's Bureau). A coali- tion of 32 traditional women's organizations, headed by Laura Sabia of the Canadian Federation of University Women, had campaigned forcefully for the Royal Commission together with the newly created umbrella group, the Fédération des Femmes du Québec (Morris, 1980; Bégin, 1992). The process of hearings and submissions, involving thousands of Canadian women all over the country, became a major consciousness-raising exercise for the Commissioners, for the traditional women's organizations and for Canadians more generally. A comparable process did not take place in Australia and New Zealand until the International Women's Year (1975).

Once the Royal Commission had reported in 1970, Sabia again took the lead in lobbying for government action. She persuaded the government to fund the 'Strategy for Change Conference' which brought feminists from all over Canada together for the first time. It led to the setting up of the National Action Committee on the Status of Women to push for the implementation of the 167 recommendations made by the Royal Commission (Heitlinger, 1993:82).

The first step in implementation on the government's part had been the appointment of a Co-ordinator for the Status of Women, reporting to a Minister Responsible for the Status of Women, in accordance with the machinery recommendations of the Royal Commission's report. Initially, the Co-ordinator was located in the government's chief policy co-ordinating body, the Privy Council Office, from where she chaired an Interdepartmental Committee and associated working parties.

The later adding of programme responsibilities to the Co-ordinator's role, in the form of a Secretariat for International Women's Year (IWY), appears to have been partly responsible for the loss of this prime location. The move of Status of Women out of the co-ordinating body and its establishment as a separate agency was not the subject of feminist debate and analysis, as was the case in Australia and New Zealand, and is thus difficult to reconstruct.

Apart from the IWY programme responsibilities, there were other frictions—including uncertainties over the lines of accountability between the Co-ordinator, the Clerk of the Privy Council, and the Minister Responsible for the Status of Women. On the other hand, it was recognized that as a separate agency Status of Women might be more visible but at greater risk of being marginalized or isolated. The 'paper track' is not clear but these points were made in letters and memos by officials in the two-year period leading up to the Order-in-Council of 1 April 1976, which designated the Office of the Co-ordinator as a free-standing department. Ministerial responsibility was rotated among ministers of varying seniority and with varying portfolios. As in Australia, these were initially male ministers.

Despite its brief to monitor all federal policy, and despite the formal requirement for departments to attach 'impact on women' statements to proposals, Status of Women Canada suffered in terms of access to Cabinet submissions and lost policy influence, particularly during the decade of conservative government from 1984. Nor did it have access to Budget processes. It was neither located within the chief co-ordinating agency nor, because of its free-standing character, did it have a powerful department behind it; nor, because a number of functions were located elsewhere (in the Advisory Council and the Women's Program, discussed later), did it have significant community outreach or base in the women's movement. One significant initiative, the Employment Equity Act (mandating affirmative action in federally regulated corporations), was negotiated by the Women's Bureau in Labour Canada, not by Status of Women Canada, unlike the case with comparable legislation in Australia or New Zealand.

The 1976 Cabinet decision also required all federal departments to establish 'integration mechanisms' to ensure that policy relating to the status of women was integrated into general departmental policy development. This was the same year as the network of departmental women's units was established in Australia. There was a similar structural concern in both countries to separate mechanisms concerned with impact on women in the community from those concerned with equal opportunity for government employees. (In both countries departments continued to confuse these functions.)

As in Australia, the largest of the integration mechanisms outside Status of Women Canada was the Women's Bureau in Labour Canada, established in 1954 (now part of Human Resources Development Canada). The interdepartmental committee on integration mechanisms, and departmental units such as the office of the women's adviser in Health and Welfare Canada, were set up in 1976. According to a former head of the Women's Bureau, there was too much resistance to the idea of internal advocacy, within the Westminster model of a neutral bureaucracy, for the 'integration policy' to be generally a success in Canada (Geller-Schwartz, 1995:49). In 1987 the Nielsen Task Force found that the co-ordination function was hampered by the fact that, with the exception of Labour Canada, no federal department systematically reviewed its policies to determine their impact on women (Burt, 1990:200). As in Australia, the women's units tended to be appointed at too junior a level and to be either sidelined in policy development or 'mainstreamed' out of existence.

In Canada, as a federal system, it is important to note the existence of women's policy machinery at the provincial and federal levels and the powerful nature of some of this machinery, for example, in Quebec. There has been greater diversity of machinery in Canada than was true in Australia until very recently. In Australia, WEL lobbied for the replication of the original model at state and territory levels and the quarterly meetings of federal, state and territory women's advisers also helped to ensure that best practice (irrespective of the level it emanated from) was picked up and reproduced. These meetings were off-the-record exchanges of strategic information by feminists and, at least for the first decade, were unlike other intergovernmental meetings.

The Canadian equivalent appears to have been much more like intergovernmental meetings in other policy areas. Canadian femocrats were less likely to be recruited from the women's movement than their Australian equivalents, apart from the early days of the Women's Program, because civil service unions prevented direct recruitment to such positions from outside. (In Australia specialist expertise arguments were mounted to overcome such union objections.) Despite the more bureaucratic style of the Canadian intergovernmental meetings, the 1987 Nielsen Taskforce concluded that the intergovernmental function of Status of Women Canada was its main success—'pulling the provinces together for national awareness of issues relating to women and for consensus building' (quoted in Burt, 1990:200).

Of the women's units in other federal portfolio areas, it is notable that women's policy has had a higher profile in External Affairs in Canada than in Australia or New Zealand, and that the Canadian Women in Development programme within the Canadian International Development Agency (CIDA) served as a model elsewhere, in the 1980s, for integration of gender analysis into the project cycle. Canada has taken a lead role in the United Nations Commission on the Status of Women, in the OECD, and in the British Commonwealth, as an advocate of the integration of adequate gender audits into the forward planning of multilateral bodies.

Despite similarities between the network model of women's policy machinery in Australia and Canada, there have been some significant differences, apart from the location of the central agency. While the staffing of the central policy bodies in Australia, Canada, and New Zealand has been comparable (about 50 in Australia and Canada and about 35 in New Zealand in 1993) Canada put far more resources into two other areas. The first was the large funding programme called the Women's Program, one of the recommendations of the Royal Commission and administered by the Secretary of State from 1973 until 1993. In 1989–90 this had a budget of over Can$13 million, distributed to over 750 women's groups. These included women's services run by voluntary organizations—the refuges and rape crisis centres funded through mainstream programmes in Australia and New Zealand.

When the Women's Program was first set up, the feminists recruited into it tried to model feminist process in terms of collectivity and empowerment, and held themselves responsible to the women's movement rather than to government priorities (Findlay, 1987). The attempt to model feminist process within government, and to work very closely with the women's movement, was similar to that of the New Zealand Ministry of Women's Affairs a decade later. Eventually bureaucratic hierarchy was reimposed through, for example, performance evaluations stressing supervisory skills and warnings against being client-driven (Schreader, 1990:191–192).

There is much more feminist analysis of the Women's Program than of the policy co-ordination function in Canada. Much of it has been inspired by the first director, Sue Findlay, who has described how it was set up strategically by feminists who had decided that the resources of the state could be used to support the development of the women's movement (Findlay, 1987:39–40). Findlay became disillusioned with increased government interference and concluded that the real aim all along had been to shape and control the agenda of the women's movement (Findlay and Randall, 1988).

A different interpretation of the rationale for the Women's Program has been provided by Leslie Pal (1993), who links the relatively generous funding of the Program with the belief of the Liberal government of Pierre Trudeau that the women's movement represented a cross-cutting cleavage that could help ward off Quebec separatism.

Under the Conservatives, the Program came under sustained attack from the anti-feminist organization REAL women, as a result of which REAL itself received funding in 1989 despite its lack of support for CEDAW—usually the threshold for women's group funding in all three countries. At about this time the

Conservative government started to move against the funding of advocacy organizations and to substitute project funding for operational grants (Heitlinger, 1993:90). The Women's Program is now located in Status of Women Canada after a short period in Human Resources Development. Its budget in 1995 was Can$8.5 million, distributed among some 500 organizations.

One significant organization funded under the Women's Program had been the Canadian Research Institute for the Advancement of Women (CRIAW), founded in 1975. CRIAW lost its core funding in 1990, although it continued to attract significant project funding (for example, Can$213,000 in 1995). CRIAW housed the co-ordinating secretariat for NGO participation in the Beijing Conference—which the Canadian government funded 40 NGO delegates to attend.

A second distinctive feature of Canadian national machinery was the importance given to the Canadian Advisory Council on the Status of Women, which was structurally independent and had staffing comparable to Status of Women Canada. Again the creation of the Council flowed from the Royal Commission's machinery recommendations. The significance attached to the Council stemmed from the historic suspicion of political parties on the part of the English Canadian women's movement (Bashevkin, 1993) which resulted in a recommendation that there be an independent Council reporting directly to Parliament. The Council as actually established was an advisory body to the Minister Responsible for the Status of Women and the issue of political independence was to be an ongoing one.

There seems to be general agreement that whereas the Council produced good research (and was also able to use its Ottawa base to monitor government) it had no significant impact on policy and its research was not tied in to policy development. Its independence of government was a negative factor in terms of the policy process, while on the other hand the Council tended to be distrusted by the women's movement for not being sufficiently independent of government. In 1981 Council members supported ministerial intervention to cancel a constitutional conference which had turned out to be politically inconvenient (the President resigned over this issue). In the late 1980s several researchers claimed that their reports were altered by the Council and that it was dominated by patronage appointments (Vickers, personal communication, January 1996). In March 1995 the Liberal government announced the abolition of the Council as a deficit-cutting measure, and there was little in the way of repercussion. Its research and communication functions were to be taken over by Status of Women Canada. Fears were expressed over loss of independence of the research function, although the minister promised that Can$2 million would be reserved for some form of research grants programme.

In Australia the less independent and less well-resourced National Women's Consultative Council had also been disbanded by this time, replaced by periodic Round Table meetings between the Minister and representatives of national women's organizations. As we shall see, the New Zealand machinery created in the 1980s did not include an advisory council at all. It is a matter for debate

126

whether resources put into such councils might more usefully be directed to community-based umbrella (or 'peak') organizations, and depends in part on access of the latter to ministers and capacity to defend or promote feminist initiatives within government.

Canadian feminists have provided a generally negative evaluation of the achievements of Canadian femocrats at the federal level—partly reflecting the increasingly conservative climate of the 1980s, partly the complexities of trying to achieve change within a federal system where provincial governments were successfully challenging the balance of power. This resulted in frustration, for example, of attempts to achieve a national childcare programme. The Canadian accounts are more pessimistic than those provided by ex-femocrats in Australia, who tell stories of battles won as well as lost (e.g. Eisenstein, 1995). Geller-Schwartz (1995) does suggest, however, that Canadian femocrats have been effective when they have been able to exert pressure for compliance with international obligations or when they have fostered pressure from non-government lobbies through resourcing and information, or both, as with equal pay legislation.

It is in the area of its national non-government women's lobby that Canada has a remarkable record. It has sustained an umbrella organization—the National Action Committee on the Status of Women (NAC)—for more than two decades (see Vickers *et al.*, 1993). As noted above, NAC was created to push for the implementation of the Royal Commission's recommendations. By the time of its creation second-wave organizations had also appeared and played a lively role, sometimes startling the long-standing women's organizations. Women's Liberation (Toronto) was one of the groups on the first steering committee—along with the Catholic Women's League, the Canadian Federation of University Women and the YWCA (Bashevkin, 1989:364). This kind of co-operation between the traditional and the more organizationally radical new-wave organizations has been characteristic of Australian and New Zealand women's movements as well—but the latter have not yet institutionalized this co-operation to the same degree as in Canada.

NAC has some 600 groups affilated to it, ranging from national bodies and provincial umbrella organizations to local groups with a minimum of 10 members. This has been achieved despite tensions and conflicts over organizational and other issues. Jill Vickers has argued that the umbrella structure 'can tap the energy and views of women in grassroots collectives largely without requiring them to change their internal norms and modes of operating' (Vickers, 1988:3). None the less, the size and diversity (as well as geographical spread) of NAC meant that it was forced to adopt relatively formal structures which were viewed as antithetical to feminist process by many of the collectives which were affiliated to it. Increased functional specialization was also required in order to develop its political capacity, and this again was often viewed as élitist. As the Executive Co-ordinator said in 1992: 'When we are able to focus on issues there is lots of unity; when we try to talk about structures and philosophy there is lots and lots of division' (Alice de Wolff, personal communication, July 1992).

In order to have credibility with the federal government as a 'parliament of women', it has been important for NAC to try to retain the well-organized Quebec francophone women under its umbrella. There have, however, been fundamental differences between the latter and anglophone feminists on vital constitutional issues. Anglophone feminists have favoured the federal government over provincial governments, as the custodian of women's legal and social rights, while the francophones put more trust in the Quebec government. Because of these internal divisions NAC was unable to take a leadership role in the successful feminist mobilization over relevant clauses in the Charter of Rights and Freedoms.

Subsequently, in the 1980s, groups representing visible minority and immigrant women and disabled women became more active in NAC, increasing its claims to 'representativeness' but making compromises over constitutional matters with the Quebec women more difficult (Vickers, 1988:64). The Quebec women withdrew for a second time at the end of the decade, leaving NAC as the 'nodal point' of the anglophone women's movement (Phillips, 1991). NAC now has a 'three nations' approach to constitutional issues, recognizing the special status of both francophone and indigenous peoples. The current NAC President is a recent immigrant from Tanzania and there is now a policy that 50 per cent of office-bearers be from minorities and that committees have majority/minority co-chairs.

It is interesting that, despite the organizational differences between the Canadian and Australian women's movements, there have been some remarkable parallels in policy evolution—for example, the attempts to move from 'margin to mainstream' of economic policy debate in the mid-1980s. In Canada the lead role taken by NAC in 1985–8 in mobilizing women against the free trade agreements (with the help of the impressive briefs of feminist economist Marjorie Cohen) also brought it into direct confrontation with the government on a cornerstone of government policy (Cohen, 1992). It meant participating in coalitions with the churches and unions and forms of protest such as nationwide rallies and pickets. Tensions between Status of Women Canada and the women's movement were exacerbated by the fact that at least one Minister Responsible for the Status of Women also had portfolio responsibility for privatization.

Subsequently, government ministers boycotted NAC's annual lobby day and NAC's funding was cut in half between 1990 and 1992, causing severe disruption to an organization heavily reliant on government grants. NAC gradually restructured its financial base, raising significant amounts through direct mail appeals (Vickers et al., 1993:293). Relations with the government improved with the appointment of a more sympathetic minister, and government attendance at the lobby day resumed (the Liberal Party and the New Democratic Party attended in force). Today NAC is held up as a model in terms of providing a strong and independent voice for women on public policy issues.[9] It continues, however, to face serious funding problems as well as the structural problem of being a centrally focused organization in an increasingly decentralized federation.

New Zealand

In New Zealand women's policy machinery had not been established by the time of the defeat of the Labour government in 1975 and was delayed until Labour was next elected in 1984, although there had been previous advisory bodies. Labour women had pressed for a separate Ministry of Women's Affairs with its own Minister in Cabinet which would enable the modelling of feminist structures and processes as well as the direct representation of feminist perspectives in Cabinet.

As in Australia and Canada, there had been a turning point in the 1970s when the demands of the women's movement became part of the public agenda in New Zealand, and something to which political parties needed to respond (see Devere, 1990:1; Sawer and Simms, 1993). As in Australia, WEL played a significant role in this process in New Zealand (Preddy, 1985). In New Zealand, however, WEL was fairly quickly displaced as the most prominent women's lobby by the long-standing National Council of Women.

More important in New Zealand, however, was the rapid progress made by feminists in the Labour Party from the point in 1974 when Labour women picketed their own party's annual conference demanding that women's issues be given greater priority. As in Australia, Labour women were able to argue that their party had to do something to attract women voters and to close the 'gender gap' which stood in the way of electoral success. They were aided by the fact that the structures of the New Zealand Labour Party were relatively favourable to women. There was an absence of the Irish Catholic machine politics found in Australia and affiliated unions also had much less power in the party structure. Absent as well was the institutionalized faction system of the Australian Labor Party (intra-party organizations with formal membership), which pitted women against one another. Women in the New Zealand Labour Party were able to act to a much greater extent as their own, gender-based informal faction (Curtin and Sawer, 1996:152–3). All this led to a rapid increase of Labour women in parliament and on the front bench, and to a series of women holding the position of Party President (including an 'out' lesbian).[10] The influence of Labour women ministers and of the Labour Women's Caucus in parliament were to be an important adjunct to the women's policy machinery described below.

By the 1984 election in New Zealand a substantial collection of policies for women had been put together, after extensive consultation with Labour Party members (Curtin and Sawer, 1996:154). The content was similar to that of the women's policy on which the Australian Labour Party campaigned in 1983, although there were differences in detail, particularly in relation to bureaucratic machinery (discussed later). Commitments included CEDAW ratification, affirmative action, and increased funding of childcare, labour market re-entry programmes, women's health, refuges, rape crisis centres and other services.

Approved by Cabinet in November 1984 and officially established in March 1985, the Ministry of Women's Affairs began with a staff of 20 women and a mandate to advise the Minister on the implications of government policies for women. The Ministry would have significant outreach functions with women in the community and the Minister would ensure that women's perspectives were taken directly into Cabinet (Nathan, 1989:30). With its free-standing character it was a radical departure from existing machinery across the Tasman. It was thought that the creation of a new organization, with no institutional baggage, would enable it to model feminist processes for the benefit of the rest of government (O'Regan, 1992:199). All of its initial staff had backgrounds in community organizations and were familiar with non-hierarchical ways of working.

In addition to attempting to incorporate feminist organizational principles, the new ministry was committed to working towards biculturalism 'before any other government department had seriously addressed that issue' (O'Regan, 1991:165). A Maori Women's Secretariat (*Te Ohu Whakatupu*) was established, responsible for seeing that the specific needs of Maori women were included in all areas of the Ministry's work. All non-Maori staff of the Ministry were required to undertake anti-racism training.

The biculturalism of the Ministry makes it significantly different from its Australian counterpart. OSW helped achieve the creation of an Office of Indigenous Women elsewhere in government through the painstaking organization of the first nationwide consultation with Aboriginal women in 1983–4, but has had little further specific responsibility in this area. OSW shares responsibility for issues relating to women of non-English speaking backgrounds with the Office of Multicultural Affairs, but this too has had relatively little impact on its operating style. Status of Women Canada is bicultural and bilingual, but again in the mainstream fashion of Canadian government rather than in this more radical early style of the New Zealand ministry.

The first head of the Ministry of the Women's Affairs, Mary O'Regan, tried to minimize hierarchy to encourage collective decision-making and open government. Decisions were talked through until consensus was reached and at the weekly staff meeting time was allocated for staff to mention issues in their private lives, such as teething children, which were impinging on their public role (Nelson, 1989:21). The Ministry was to be accessible to all women and so included a playpen at the entrance and greeted callers with '*kia ora*'. Initially O'Regan contemplated all staff having the same status and the same salary. This idea was quashed, however, since it was likely to harm the future career prospects of the women involved (O'Regan, 1992:200).[11]

Considerable effort was put into consultation with women in the community, including a massive programme of open forums or *hui* around New Zealand in 1984 to establish priorities for the Ministry within the framework of the Labour government's women's policy. These consultation processes continued, both with special interest groups, such as lesbian women or Pacific Islanders, and on specific policy issues. A monthly Newsletter/*Panui* was distributed along with updates published in the *New Zealand Women's Weekly* (parallel to the zip-out Status of Women Reports placed by OSW in the *Australian Women's Weekly* at this time). Women with diverse experience and expertise were included in Ministerial working parties, such as the Ministerial Committee of Inquiry into Pornography, and they undertook wide-ranging community consultation.

New advisory bodies were created in other portfolios, such as a Women's Advisory Committee on Education, in addition to the long-standing National Advisory Council on the Employment of Women. As we have noted, the new machinery differed from that in Australia and Canada, however, in that it did not include any generalist Advisory or Consultative Council to provide public advice to government on the status of women.

Within the bureaucracy the Ministry initiated measures to ensure women's interests were accounted for by other government departments—being wary of becoming the dumping ground for women's issues. Each department was asked to appoint a senior liaison person to act as a link with the Ministry of Women's Affairs. As in Australia and Canada, departments often initially confused this function with equal employment opportunity functions and appointed people from personnel areas. Training workshops were held and examples were provided from each department of policies which had failed to take the impact on women into account. A checklist was later provided to help with better policy analysis and consultation procedures (Washington, 1988:11). In 1996 this was substantially upgraded and published as *The Full Picture: Guidelines for Gender Analysis.*

No formal women's units or women's adviser positions were set up in other departments, and there was no direct equivalent of the Australian and Canadian Women's Bureaux, although there was a National Advisory Committee on the Employment of Women serviced by bureaucrats with specialized knowledge. There was an absence of the kind of high-level co-ordinating mechanisms represented by the Australian Secretaries' Taskforce on the Status of Women of the 1980s. Because the Ministry was not a control department, there was no formal obligation on the part of other ministers and their departments to consult it. Formal obligation did not come until 1991, when departments were required to certify that they had consulted with the Ministry of Women's Affairs over all Cabinet or Cabinet Committee submissions 'which relate to the economic or social status of women, especially Maori women' (according to a Cabinet Office manual). Prior to the introduction of this formal requirement, the political clout of the Minister was of utmost importance. The first Minister of Women's Affairs had high political credibility and was able to push her agenda effectively in Cabinet. Her successor, although having impeccable feminist credentials, had less political weight.

Meanwhile, the 1988 New Zealand State Sector Act signalled an end to the Ministry's attempt to create an alternative feminist model of government machinery. Mary O'Regan threatened to go on strike over this, an unusual step for a permanent head, and by June 1988 had resigned (Nelson, 1989:47). The

Ministry was restructured in accordance with the new precepts of cost-effectiveness and economic efficiency, no longer emphasizing the kind of flexible, non-hierarchical modes of operation of the early days. Judith Aitken, a recent convert to economic rationalism, was appointed Chief Executive. Under the new State Sector Act this was a performance-based contract position and Aitken replaced feminist collectivism with a more managerialist style of decision-making—although decision-making still remained much more open and less hierarchical than in other government departments.

The Ministry was now formally accountable only to the Minister (through the Chief Executive) rather than acknowledging a more diffuse accountability to women in the community. The Ministry was refocused on its policy advisory function and the need to achieve definable outcomes (Curtin and Sawer, 1996:159). It had become conventional wisdom in the Labour Party and in the bureaucracy that the Ministry had been too preoccupied with process. There were some parallels with the review of the Australian OSW which took place in 1993 and also resulted in a cutting back of community outreach functions and a refocusing on strategic policy advice. In both cases the restructuring was accompanied by an increase in resources (to 35 staff in the Ministry and to about 50 in OSW).

In addition to its monitoring function and its attempt to model alternative feminist processes, the Ministry, like OSW, had been involved in the initiation and support of policies specifically designed to increase women's equality. In New Zealand, as in Australia, there was a marked increase in funded childcare places under Labour in the 1980s, as well as increases for a range of women's services, despite the constant pressure for reductions in public expenditure. Discursive strategies were required to demonstrate the economic rationality of increased expenditures in these areas.

The Employment Equity Act of 1990 was also achieved in the face of the Labour government's conversion to labour market deregulation. Compulsory arbitration had been abolished in 1984 and the Labour Relations Act of 1987 had paved the way for industry—or enterprise—based awards. The lack of concern for equity issues meant 'women had to develop their own strategies to reinstate equitable incomes as part of the labour market policy' (Wilson, 1992:120). One strategy was to seek separate legislation to cover equal pay for work of equal value and equal employment opportunities (EEOs).

The preparation of New Zealand's employment equity legislation (requiring organizations with more than 50 employees to prepare EEO programmes and making provision for pay equity assessments) was a protracted process, opposed at every step by the Ministers of Finance and of Labour who believed that pay equity should be left to the market. The Ministry of Women's Affairs, strategically placed women MPs and Ministers were crucial to the eventual passage of the legislation in 1990 (Wilson, 1992). The repeal of this landmark Act was one of the first steps of the new National Party Government.

Another Ministry initiative related to the measurement of unpaid work through time-use surveys. Time-use surveys and campaigns based on their findings had a number of strategic objectives: to increase awareness of the 'double load' being carried by women as they increased their participation in the paid workforce; to alert employers to the impact of family responsibilities on employees and the need for these to be accommodated in the design of paid work; to strengthen the argument for parental and family leave, as well as workplace flexibility, to enable men to take up a greater share of family responsibilities; and to increase awareness of the contribution of unpaid work to the economy and hence to strengthen the case for increased expenditure on infrastructure to support it.

It is a former New Zealand National Party MP, Marilyn Waring, who has done most to promote the inclusion of unpaid work in national accounts whether in Australia, New Zealand, or at the international level. Her tireless advocacy has been important both in mobilizing the large traditional women's organizations on the issue and in achieving its inclusion in international instruments such as the Nairobi Forward Looking Strategies which could be used by femocrats at home. In addition, the second New Zealand Minister of Women's Affairs, Margaret Shields, was also Minister of Statistics. Shields had worked in the Department of Statistics as a statistician in the mid-1970s and had then pushed for time-use surveys. Holding both portfolios provided the perfect opportunity to achieve this goal (Curtin, 1992:101).

In both Australia and New Zealand, Labour governments undertook pilot time-use surveys to measure the extent and distribution of unpaid work, and this was followed in Australia by the first regular national survey in 1992. In Canada questions on unpaid work were included in the 1996 census, thanks to pressure from women's groups and from Status of Women Canada and the Canadian Advisory Council on the Status of Women. The Australian Bureau of Statistics survey of 1992 found the value of unpaid work to be 58 per cent of GDP, using the replacement cost method (ABS, 1994:88). Information generated by the time-use surveys was used extensively in Australia in programmes related to the implementation of ILO Convention No. 156. As noted above, New Zealand has not ratified this Convention and the current National Party Government has informed the ILO that 'no formal consideration had been given to developing a national policy committed to the delivery of effective equality of opportunity for women and men with family responsibilities' (ILO, 1993c:91).

The National Government elected in 1990 also cut state spending on childcare, abolished the universal family benefit successfully defended under Labour, cut the Domestic Purposes Benefit, undid initiatives in women's housing policy, repealed the Employment Equity Act, and introduced the Employment Contracts Act (for criticism of the effects of these policies on women see, National Council of Women, 1992 and Hyman, 1994). Instead of the Employment Equity Commission, an Equal Employment Opportunities Trust was set up as a joint venture between employers and government, to promote equal employment opportunity on a voluntary basis. The first head of the Ministry commented: 'My experience with the Ministry is another very stark reminder of just how easily any gains can be swept away ... every single thing that we achieved is now either gone or going' (O'Regan, 1992:166).

The new National government did not, however, refocus the Ministry into a Ministry of Family Affairs as had been mooted—perhaps because of the active constituency the Ministry had created within the women's movement during its early years. Within the new set of constraints the Ministry undertook some significant initiatives such as those relating to the promotion of Maori women's enterprise. (Maori women are now increasing their involvement in business at a faster rate than either Maori men or any non-Maori New Zealanders, although starting from a low base.) In 1993 a new Human Rights Act extended the grounds on which discrimination is prohibited in New Zealand and resources were increased for the Human Rights Commission as a consequence. The grounds now cover sex (including pregnancy, childbirth, and sexual harassment), marital and family status, sexual orientation, disability, age, race, religion, employment status, and political opinion. In the same year controls over the circulation of violent and pornographic material were tightened, in response to widespread campaigning by women's groups. The National Government has also continued the community-based approach to HIV-AIDS education, including the funding of the New Zealand Prostitutes' Collective for this purpose.

Throughout 1993, events were held to commemorate the centennial of women's suffrage in New Zealand and many significant projects of either a practical, symbolic, or historical nature were funded through a semi-independent Trust housed in the Ministry of Women's Affairs. Feminists participated enthusiastically in these government-sponsored events—even though the women's movement was in other respects, as we have seen, extremely critical of continued cuts to social provision and of the effects on women of labour market deregulation. Under the National Government there were two Ministers of Women's Affairs, the senior minister being noted for her 'dry' agenda in her other portfolio of Social Welfare. In 1997 the same minister, Jennifer Shipley, resumed the portfolio shortly before becoming Prime Minister.

As in Australia and Canada, there has been a significant level of co-operation between traditional and second-wave women's organizations. For example, it was a combination of work by women from inside and outside government that saved the universal family benefit from the economic rationalists in New Zealand in 1987 and 1990. The Labour Minister for Women's Affairs played an important strategic role in asking her Ministry to consult with women's groups on the issue, the *New Zealand Women's Weekly* canvassed women's views and the National Council of Women, active in New Zealand for 100 years, played a major part in mobilizing resistance (Curtin and Sawer, 1996:164). In Australia, by contrast, the economic rationalists were able to move with much greater stealth on the issue.[12]

Other issues which have brought traditional and newer organizations together have included pornography, the treatment of cervical cancer patients at an Auckland hospital, and the attempt to save the pay equity legislation: 'It was

134

wonderful to see the president of the National Council of Women and a radical feminist trade unionist standing together in parliament grounds leading the "pots and pans" protest rally against the impending repeal of the pay equity legislation' (O'Regan, 1992:168).[13] As in Australia and Canada, women working in government were very aware of the importance of organized pressure from outside in achieving feminist agendas in government: 'I don't feel threatened by those women outside who say we aren't doing enough' (McKinlay, 1990:84). Again, getting information and resources out to women in the community was important in fostering this pressure. McKinlay says of one of her interviewees: 'Part of her strategy is to raise the awareness of women in the community on a particular issue she is working on through seminars and workshops, to stimulate a demand for change' (ibid.:84).

New Zealanders have voted for the introduction of a new electoral system which will mean that governments are much less likely to have a clear majority of seats or to be able to push through the kind of radical changes witnessed in the last 10 years. A mixed member proportional system (similar to that in Germany) was introduced in 1996 and increased the amount of bargaining needed over policy changes as well as further increasing the number of women in parliament (from 20 to 29 per cent).

There have been close links between Australia and New Zealand on women's policy matters, with the head of the New Zealand Ministry attending the regular Commonwealth/State Women's Advisers meetings, and the New Zealand Minister attending the more recently established Commonwealth/State Ministers' Conference on the Status of Women. As we have seen, New Zealand is also to be found co-operating with Australia and Canada on status of women initiatives in the United Nations and in other international forums. New Zealand is currently represented on CEDAW by Dame Silvia Cartwright, a respected feminist High Court Judge, who rapped Australia over the knuckles in 1997 for its recent retreat on international gender equity issues and inadequate CEDAW report.

Conclusion

As we have seen, the political traditions of Australia, Canada, and New Zealand encouraged women to look to the state to meet their claims, and significant gains were made by feminist interventions in the 1970s and 1980s. Unfortunately the very traditions of social liberalism which enabled women to make these gains were at the same time being eroded by a loss of faith in the state as a vehicle of social justice. There was increasing hostility, regardless of the political complexion of the government in power, to the kind of social provision and regulation needed if women were to have equal opportunity. This makes the achievements all the more remarkable. In all three countries women's policy machinery has survived conservative governments and there has been cross-party support for its continued existence. It is an institutionalized acknowledgement that governments should be accountable for their specific impact on women. This institutionalized agenda has often caused friction with those parts of government more bent on deregulatory and market-driven agendas, rather than serving as a mask for such agendas. The achievements of women's policy machinery may be limited to ensuring 'least worst outcomes' or damage control, but even in unfavourable environments progress can usually be made on issues such as women and small business or violence against women.

Feminists who have worked in such machinery readily acknowledge the constraints and compromises involved, the kind of bilingualism required in dominant and oppositional discourses, and the need for strong pressure from outside to be effective. Femocrats have tried to foster such external pressure through making resources available to community organizations, including funding, information, and access. Attempts to make community organizations more effective have ranged from financial assistance to create national structures, advice on the pressure points in the budget cycle, and training in international meeting procedures.

There has often been tension between femocrats and women in community organizations because of the constraints of government agendas on the former including, more recently, a managerialist preoccupation with quantifiable outcomes. One New Zealand study cautions us, however, against simplistic attempts to explain these differences in terms of labels such as 'liberal feminist', 'radical feminist', 'socialist feminist' and so forth. The differences may be not so much between different groups of women or between liberal and radical feminists, but between the ways the same women operate when in their official roles as contrasted to when they are working through community groups (McKinlay, 1990:78; see also Washington, 1988).

A number of other variables have been discussed in this paper, such as the location of machinery and the strength of its bureaucratic clout. Gender expertise must be backed by routinized access to policy development and Cabinet processes, and institutionalized forms of accountability for gender outcomes. While the policy-brokering skills of individual femocrats and ministers may be important, bureaucratic entrenchment gives lasting returns.

The intersection of international and domestic pressure and networking, both at the multilateral and intergovernmental levels, has also been important to progress on feminist agendas. The three countries reviewed here have all been active on human rights issues at the international level and have jealously guarded their reputations as good international citizens. Femocrats have been able to use this sensitivity both in promoting work on gender equity at the international level and in pressing for implementation of relevant international obligations.

Political variables, such as the ability to exploit a gender gap in voting patterns, have also been important. In both Australia and New Zealand the deficit in women's votes, discovered in the 1970s, became a lever to push the labour parties towards more pro-woman policies. Volatility and delayed decision-making among women voters, and the way this was constructed, was later of particular importance in Australia in generating strong electoral competition on childcare policy.

In all three countries women, both inside and outside the state, have played an important role in resisting the retreat from the welfare state and preserving equity agendas within the unfavourable environment provided by economic rationalism. When ecorats dominate government policymaking and femocrats are on the defensive, the policy capacity and organizational strength of the community-based women's movement is of particular importance. It falls to the women's movement, working through separate organizations and through caucuses within political parties, trade unions, and other community organizations, to challenge economic assumptions which ignore the social economy and to promise political pain if priority is given to market forces over gender equity.

6

Gender advocates and multilateral development organizations: promoting change from within

CAROL MILLER

This chapter explores the project of integrating gender concerns in three multi-lateral organizations: the United Nations Development Programme (UNDP), the World Bank and the International Labour Organization (ILO).* The chapter draws loosely on the conceptual framework for understanding 'organizational reponse' to WID/gender elaborated by Kardam (1991; 1993). According to Kardam, three main sets of factors influence organizational response to WID/gender. The first concerns the extent to which an organization is vulnerable to external pressures for change in its ways of thinking about and carrying out development assistance. The second involves the degree of 'fit' between WID/gender concerns and the organization's mandate, ideology, and procedures. The third relates to the existence and capacity of internal WID/gender policy advocates. Kardam's framework, based on organizational theory, provides an interesting entry point for understanding responses to WID/gender in the UNDP, the World Bank, and the ILO. By focusing on the dynamics of organizational change, the framework illuminates certain aspects of the process of feminist engagement with international development institutions that may otherwise be overlooked or misunderstood.

Two main criticisms are often levelled at the way in which internal advocates have sought to promote WID/gender concerns within development organiza-tions. One is that they have tended to promote WID/gender concerns using 'instrumental' arguments. In other words, instead of basing their case for atten-tion to women primarily on the grounds of 'gender equality', they have tended to make 'synergistic' arguments about the linkages between gender concerns and other development goals, such as efficiency, poverty alleviation, social develop-ment, and environmental sustainability. Accusations of 'instrumentalism', while important for drawing attention to cases where synergies simply do not exist, fail

*This chapter draws on three main sources of information; primary material produced by the agencies themselves; analyses of agencies by external researchers and reports on inter-views with agency staff carried out by Rhadika Jha, Carol Miller, Ingrid Palmer and Shahra Razavi between 1993 and 1995. The chapter is a revised and updated version of *Gender Mainstreaming: A study of Efforts by the UNDP, the World Bank and the ILO to Institutionalize Gender Issues* (Razavi and Miller, 1995b) to grasp the constraints faced by internal advocates. If we examine more closely the organizational contexts in which internal advocates are working, we gain some insight into the political nature of their advocacy work. What we discover is that their arguments change between organizational contexts and even within organizations, reflecting their strategies for building internal alliances with other (male) colleagues. Furthermore, there are subtle and sometimes abrupt changes in discursive strategies in response to perceived paradigmatic shifts in thinking about development policy, again an indication of the extent of political manoeuvring by internal advocates. Razavi (Chapter 2) provides a detailed analysis of the gender policy discourses used in the development context.

Another criticism of the way WID/gender concerns have been promoted in development organizations is that procedural issues have taken priority over more substantive concerns. The aim of WID/gender policy advocacy is to see concrete change in the activities of an organization—its projects, programmes, and policies—and, ultimately, to see improvements in the situation of the subjects of policy intervention (Jahan, 1995). A critical step in this direction is to ensure that gender considerations are routinely included in the way an organization operates—what Jahan refers to as the 'means' (process). As we see later, over the past two decades WID/gender policy advocates both within and outside development organizations have devoted considerable attention to 'means', so much so that Jahan has recently argued that, within development organizations, the concerns over means have often taken precedence over ends (outcomes) of gender justice (1995:113). In our view, an organizational approach to understanding response to WID/gender, justifies concern with procedural issues. Engagement with public institutions and, in particular, efforts to take WID/gender issues into the very core of their policymaking processes—often referred to as 'mainstreaming'—requires an astute understanding of the organizational context into which gender is to be inserted and, following from this, an awareness of the kinds of internal strategies and procedural changes that will be necessary to institutionalize WID/gender concerns.

Such insights do not sideline the issue of 'male resistance' raised in other studies of feminist engagement with bureaucracies (Ferguson, 1984). Instead, they help us to concretize the forms that such resistance takes and the strategies that are used, in turn, by internal advocates to challenge it. For WID/gender advocates, engagement with institutions necessarily involves compromises and trade offs and, as Staudt puts it, 'troubling ethical questions about where they invest their energies and the ends they thereby serve' (1990:7). Nowhere has this been clearer than in efforts to gender the activities of the World Bank. Yet the alternative—'disengagement'—proposed by some feminists is untenable as long as multilateral development institutions continue to exercise influence over the development policy process. In other words, if alternative development strategies, like those proposed by some women's NGOs (Sen and Grown, 1987; Wee and Heyzer, 1995), are to play a role in transforming development into a more gender-equitable process, their impact may depend upon how far they can infiltrate the thinking and practices of mainstream development institutions.

This chapter begins with an overview of the kinds of external pressures and influences that have conditioned response to WID/gender concerns in each of the three multilateral organizations. It then considers the organizational context into which advocates have sought to insert WID/gender, exploring in particular the ways the 'WID/gender policy machinery' set up in each of the organizations has been shaped by the organizational context. The final section explores in more detail the discursive strategies that have been used by internal advocates in each of the organizations in their efforts to promote WID/gender concerns, and focuses in particular on the political and policy opportunities provided by shifts over the past two decades in the dominant development discourse.

External pressures and influences

This section considers how external pressures for change in WID/gender policy have succeeded in permeating the UNDP, the World Bank, and the ILO. It is almost commonplace to assume that the extent to which multilateral organizations have taken up WID/gender issues has been in direct response to pressure from the international women's movement.[1] In fact, there has been little investigation into the processes by which such influence is exercised. This section suggests that while the international women's movement has played a crucial role in getting WID/gender issues on the development agenda, other mechanisms have been important in translating external pressure for change into concrete action by the multilateral organizations considered here.

WINGOs and the international women's movement

Women's international NGOs (WINGOs) have provided the impetus for many of the changes that have taken place within the UN system over the past two decades, if not before, to promote the WID/gender agenda. There have been few attempts, however, to provide a sustained analysis of the processes by which they have attempted to influence the activities of the UN system as a whole, or of specific UN agencies. There is nothing comparable to the analysis provided by Sawer (Chapter 5) of the relations between femocrats in state institutions and women's movements. Where literature does exist, it focuses mainly on NGO activities surrounding the UN conferences over the past two decades (Alter Chen, 1996; Davis, 1996; Jain, 1996).

What the literature suggests is that only a small group of WINGOs has been in a position to exercise direct influence through their consultative status with the Economic and Social Council (ECOSOC) of the United Nations. This status provides the right to attend meetings, suggest agenda items, speak, and submit written statements, although it does not provide the right to vote. It was partly through this mechanism that women's organizations were able to have a United Nations

Decade for Women (1976–85) declared and the various UN conferences on women held. At these conferences, where increasingly greater numbers of NGOs have been given 'accredited' status,[2] they lobbied government representatives to ensure that their priorities were reflected in the action plans that emerged. In some cases, NGO representatives have been invited to serve on government delegations to world conferences in recognition of their crucial role in feminist policy advocacy.

Apart from the direct channels of pressure noted above, the mechanisms by which the international women's movement exerts influence on international organizations appear to be largely indirect. National and international women's organizations, for example, play an important role in mobilizing and making visible women's constitutencies that legitimize action by international organizations on WID/gender issues. Public awareness and advocacy work serve to stimulate public support for policy change. Similarly, the impact on multilateral organizations of the explosion of research on WID/gender issues since the early 1970s, while difficult to measure directly, should not be underestimated. Often it has been women's NGOs which have provided the channel of communication and information exchange between researchers and international organizations. Women's national and international NGOs can also exert indirect pressure by lobbying government delegates to pay attention to gender issues in the international fora. Alter Chen (1996) describes how many of these strategies have been used by the international women's movement to put gender issues on the agendas of the Earth Summit in Rio (1992), the World Conference on Human Rights in Vienna (1993), and the International Conference on Population and Development in Cairo (1994). One important dimension of each of these conferences was the 'Women's Caucus' which included representatives of government, NGOs, and UN agencies. These caucuses enabled a sharing of information and strategies between 'insiders' and 'outsiders' during the conferences and, as Davis (1996:21) puts it, helped to 'unleash the power of civil society at the United Nations'.

Apart from activities related to the world conferences, networking between external advocates in the women's movement and internal advocates within the UNDP, the World Bank, and the ILO appears to be relatively limited. This is in marked constrast to the alliances forged between national women's movements and 'femocrats' in government, described by Sawer and, to some extent, Goetz (Chapters 3 and 5), which have in some cases taken an institutionalized form. As we see later, this may relate to the political and financial accountability structures of these multilateral institutions which tend to operate primarily, though not exclusively, at the level of states. It should also be noted that as far as the UNDP and World Bank are concerned, WINGOs have only recently begun to target these organizations directly in their lobbying activities. Two recent initiatives reflect a new departure for the international women's movement and are perhaps illustrative of the increasing skills of economic analysis and advocacy amongst its members. The first is the 'Women's Eyes on the World Bank' campaign organized by DAWN 'to transform World Bank policies and practices' and 'to hold the Bank accountable to the Beijing Platform for Action' (DAWN, 1995). Another is the World Bank's External Gender Consultative Group comprised of Bank staff and representatives of NGOs, women's organizations and research institutions, which seeks to facilitate communication between the Bank and its development partners on gender-related issues.[3]

Only tentative efforts have been made by international relations theorists to understand how the international women's movement has influenced the norms, rules, and regulations of international decision-making (Stienstra, 1994). Kardam (1997) assesses how far the body of international legal instruments on the status of women, the international agencies and commissions dedicated to promoting and monitoring the advancement of women (CSW, CEDAW, DAW, INSTRAW and UNIFEM), and the multitude of policy pronouncements of a wide range of international organizations and governments, can be seen to constitute an 'international womens' regime'.[4] From her discussion, it is possible to conclude that, at the very least, these structures provide a normative framework within which international (and state-level) decision-making takes place. Within this framework, the discourse is firmly rooted in the language of equal rights and social justice for women. None the less, as we see later, the institutions examined here appear to have been unevenly affected by this overall framework.

Political and financial accountability

While the international women's movement has played a crucial role in forcing gender concerns on to the agenda of the UNDP, the World Bank, and the ILO, internal WID/gender advocates have tended to look either to supportive governing body representatives or to top management within the organization as key allies in promoting WID/gender. This section considers the impact of governance structures on response to WID/gender concerns within the UNDP, the World Bank, and the ILO and on the strategic alliances made by internal advocates. Particular emphasis is placed on the influence of political and financial accountability mechanisms.

It should be noted at the outset that there are mechanisms through which the UN system can to some degree exert 'external' pressure for attention to WID/gender on UN bodies. UNDP is a funding programme and ILO a specialized agency of the UN. Both are accountable to ECOSOC and the UN General Assembly. Each of the UN women's conferences has given rise to some form of action plan for the advancement of women which, in addition to guiding the measures to be taken by governments and NGOs, also stipulate action to be taken by the UN. In response, UN system-wide plans for WID/gender programming and monitoring have been adopted by ECOSOC. Such plans, monitored by the CSW, serve as the UN system's major WID/gender policy tools, and can be used by internal advocates to gain leverage within their individual organizations. While the World Bank is part of the UN system, it operates independently and is not formally obliged to implement UN system commitments to WID/gender concerns. The World Bank has none the less responded to such concerns, thus implying that external pressure has been exerted in some other form.

Many observers are of the opinion that the particular governance structure of the World Bank, with a weighted voting system rather than one country–one vote, allows G7 countries to exercise more 'voice' than developing country members on the Board of Executive Directors (Ayres, 1983; Mistry and Thyness, 1991). Although the Bank's management—like that of many other organizations—has a significant degree of control over policy directions, the Bank is more likely to respond to new issues if its major shareholders recommend that it pay attention to them (Kardam, 1993:1777). The United States, with its relatively large capital subscription, is in a particularly favourable position, reinforced by the fact that the Bank president has always been an American. Although the United States has lobbied the World Bank on environmental issues (Rich, 1994), it has been less willing to do so on WID/gender, for reasons that may relate to the strength of domestic lobbies in the United States. And in spite of increased NGO lobbying of the World Bank on environmental issues, NGOs have been less vocal about gender concerns (Siddharth, 1995), although as we saw earlier, this may be changing.

The ILO has the widest circle of accountability amongst all of the specialized agencies of the United Nations system. Its 'tripartite' structure enables employers' organizations and trade unions to be officially represented and to share power with governments in its main decision-making bodies, the International Labour Conference and the Governing Body. While the ILO's decision-making institutions are indeed more 'porous' than those of many other development agencies, the representation of women's interests has encountered some obstacles. For a start, despite a provision in the ILO constitution recommending the participation of women delegates, women are numerically under-represented in the two decision-making bodies, especially in the Governing Body (Riegelman Lubin and Winslow, 1990). Whether representatives of civil society, especially the trade unions, have been more adept than government delegates in prioritizing women's issues is also open to question. While many of the items on the agenda of trade unions have also been of interest to women workers, questions have periodically been raised by feminist advocates, both within the ILO context and beyond, as to the capacity of mainstream trade unions to represent the specific interests of women workers—such as childcare, or sexual harassment at work (Hosmer Martens and Mitter, 1994).

The UNDP is accountable to a 36-member executive board (formerly known as the Governing Council) that functions on a one member–one vote basis in which developing countries have a greater representation than developed countries. While this voting system is sometimes described as more 'democratic' than that of the World Bank, it has not necessarily provided greater openness to WID/gender concerns. This would require much greater support for WID/gender amongst developing country governments than has been evident thus far (Kardam, 1993:1776; Jahan, 1995:33). Certain developed country governments have, however, played a crucial role in conditioning response to WID/gender in the UNDP, as well as in the World Bank and the ILO. This is particularly evident

143

where donor countries have been able to use financial incentives to back up their demands for greater attention to WID/gender.

The UNDP is funded through voluntary contributions from member governments of the United Nations and its specialized agencies. Among the major contributors in the past decade were the Nordic countries.[5] Their status as key funders of the UNDP effectively gives the Nordic countries greater 'voice' in decisions over how the funds will be used (Childers and Urquhart, 1994:101). It is well known that the Nordic countries, with the support of Canada, the Netherlands and, more recently, Australia, have played a lead role in promoting the advancement of women in international fora. Their involvement in the UNDP is no exception. The Nordic countries have used UNDP executive board discussions to demand action and to censure the organization whenever actions have lagged behind policy commitments (Pietilä and Eide, 1990). In addition to pressure exercised through interventions of executive council representatives, Nordic countries, along with the Netherlands and Canada, have provided extra-budgetary funding for additional WID/gender staff, gender training and special activities.

Similiar influences are evident in the ILO. Questions relating to gender equality have been among the priorities of the Nordic Governing Body members (ibid.). As in the UNDP, ILO funding arrangements provide donor countries with some degree of leverage. The bulk of the ILO's operational activities are financed from extra-budgetary resources, the main contributors being the UNDP and the bilateral donors. In 1994, for example, the Nordic countries contributed almost half of the total bilateral extra-budgetary funding. Extra-budgetary funding is particularly critical at the ILO, where the regular budget has been on zero-growth since the early 1980s: in 1990/91, extra-budgetary resources constituted 47 per cent of total resources available to the ILO. In the period from 1987 to 1992 there was a significant increase in both the number and the financial size of projects financed by the bilaterals which were specifically targeted at women: in 1987 there were 21 projects representing a total of US$11.8 million, compared to 46 projects in 1992 at US$32.2 million (ILO, 1993a:16). During this period funding from the bilaterals accounted for between 46 and 58 per cent of total funding for WID/gender operational activities. The positive role played by bilateral donors supportive of women's issues was reiterated by several interviewees at ILO headquarters, some of whom had their WID/gender posts funded by these donors.[6]

At the World Bank, the Nordic governments, despite their weak voting power, have played an important role in trying to steer the Bank away from what they think are harmful trends for the institution and its borrowers, acting as the 'social conscience' by emphasizing poverty alleviation, social sector lending, and lobbying for reform in debt management. Nordic representatives have used debates of the Board of Executive Directors to push for more effective implementation of WID/gender concerns (Pietilä and Eide, 1990). As in the UNDP and the ILO, the Nordic governments have also used financial incentives to promote WID/gender through the provision of resources for additional staff as well as through grants and trust funds (World Bank, 1992c).

Political and financial pressure exerted by a handful of donor governments has thus been important in turning external demands for greater attention to WID/gender into concrete action by the organizations considered here. The fact that the WID/gender agenda has been excessively donor driven is not, however, unproblematic. Questions must be asked about how far these organizations have developed a sense of 'ownership' over the WID/gender agenda, and whether commitment has been sufficiently internalized so that progress would continue even in the absence of financial and political support from bilateral donors. Greater commitment from developing country governments is particularly crucial, an issue that is likely to be raised with greater urgency in the coming years as all three organizations further decentralize their activities to the country level.

Organizational culture

Although external pressure is a key factor in explaining organizational response, it is not in itself sufficient to explain the process by which WID/gender is taken up in specific institutions. As hinted at earlier, we must look more closely at 'organizational culture', including the mandate, ideology, and procedures of the organization in question. Some understanding of this nexus is important because it shapes the way in which WID/gender is assimilated and informs the strategies used by internal advocates to promote WID/gender concerns. According to organizational theory, an organization's mandate dictates its decision-making techniques. A concern for gender equity can be integrated more easily in decision-making procedures that use social analysis, although economic techniques, such as cost-benefit analysis, have also been used for promoting attention to gender concerns (Kardam, 1991). This section begins with a brief comparison of the organizational cultures of the UNDP, the World Bank, and the ILO[7] and then provides an account of how WID/gender concerns have been 'institutionalized' within these organizations.

The UNDP was established in 1966 to co-ordinate and administer United Nations resources for technical co-operation, the overall goal being to promote the self-determination and self-reliance of recipient countries. As a central co-ordinating agency of the United Nations, the UNDP has traditionally placed higher priority on good management than on substantive issues connected with programme/policy content. Although UNDP staff may be trained as social scientists, they are known as 'managers' and performance is based on good administrative skills. The co-ordination mandate and management culture has thus provided real challenges for the uptake of WID/gender concerns, as 'organizational fit' has been relatively difficult to demonstrate. One of the most important co-ordinating functions performed by UNDP is the country programming exercise. The country programme sets out the goals, strategies, and priorities for UN development assistance of a given country. It is prepared jointly by the recipient government, the UNDP Resident Representative, and participating multilateral and bilateral agencies. Getting WID/gender concerns included as an integral part of the programming exercise has been one of the main goals of internal advocates in recent years. Since the early 1990s, the UNDP has been engaged in a process of 're-inventing' itself. While still responsible for co-ordinating UN development assistance at the country level, under the leadership of the last two Administrators, it has also built a higher profile for itself around its 'sustainable human development' mandate. As we see below, this mandate has provided a more hospitable environment for promoting WID/gender concerns.

The World Bank has also seen some significant changes in its core mandate over the years which have had implications for response to WID/gender. Poverty alleviation and equity issues, which had been prioritized during the 1970s, were sidelined in the 1980s as the need for stability and structural adjustment gained ascendancy (Mosley *et al.*, 1991:23–4). By the late 1980s some further shifts were noticeable: certain priorities such as poverty alleviation and 'social costs of adjustment' were again being elevated, and human development and environmental concerns were on the agenda (ibid.). Despite the shifts and turns in the World Bank's mandate, most observers agree that the dominant language in the Bank remains economics (Lexow and McNeill, 1989:74). Although many staff members are interested in problems of social justice and equity, they are uncomfortable with these issues because they lack rigour, and are 'value-laden and subjective' (Kardam, 1991:72). In order to communicate effectively with their colleagues, policy advocates within the World Bank have needed to make hard economic arguments for attention to WID/gender. In recent years, however, more sociologists and anthropologists have been hired, and new procedures have been put in place that stipulate socially sensitive and culturally appropriate project design and implementation strategies.

Compared to the UNDP and the World Bank, the ILO's organizational mandate seems to provide a more fertile ground for addressing WID/gender concerns. Its original mandate was to promote social justice through the framing of international labour standards. Although social justice remains an overarching goal and standard-setting still retains an important place as one of the ILO's principal tasks, questions have been raised periodically about the relevance and usefulness of standard-setting, especially as far as developing countries are concerned (ILO, 1994b). The acceleration in international trade, the general deregulation of the economy, and corporate restructuring have all combined to prompt renewed debate on social regulation. Trade unions have urged the ILO to be 'rock solid' on its social justice mandate (Brett, 1994:22), but there have been increasingly strong pressures, especially from employers' organizations, to back down from promoting types of social and labour legislation which 'promote rigidities and hamper economic growth and employment' (IOE, 1993:3) and to embrace 'market realism' instead. As we see below, these tensions appear to have influenced the discursive strategies of WID/gender advocates.

While an organization's mandate clearly shapes the strategies of WID/gender advocates, their strategies are also influenced by the organizational structure. Two features are of particular relevance in this context. First, the organizational and spatial distance between policy development and operations may impact significantly on the integration of WID/gender policy into operational activities. Secondly, recent efforts in the UNDP, the World Bank, and the ILO to further decentralize their activities, with the aim of promoting greater 'national ownership' of the development process, may have contradictory implications for the WID/gender mandate.[8]

Compared to many other development agencies, the UNDP is remarkably decentralized. It has a small headquarters in New York and the majority of staff (over 85 per cent) are based in its 132 country offices, managed by Resident Representatives. Overall policy guidance for regional and country level work is provided by the Bureau for Programme and Policy Support (BPPS) located at headquarters. The operational side of UNDP's work is primarily the responsibility of the four regional bureaux at headquarters, and the country offices. While decentralization is often held up as a *sine qua non* of participatory development strategies, UNDP's decentralized structure has also been described as a factor-limiting response to WID/gender (Kardam, 1991). Even the most clearly formulated WID/gender policy directives by BPPS at headquarters may remain trapped on paper unless all the groups participating in UNDP country-level activities are committed to their full implementation.

At the World Bank, the main organizational division is that between Operations and the Central Vice-Presidencies.[9] The latter are responsible for setting policy and undertaking research—in theory, to strengthen Operations. Operations, as the name suggests, is the main body responsible for maintaining a steady stream of loans and all the work that it demands—identification, appraisal, negotiation, and supervision of projects. It is composed of six operational regions, with their respective country and technical departments. One of the aims of a Bank-wide reorganization in 1993 was to bridge the gap that existed at the headquarters level between research/policy work and Operations, in order to strengthen the direct operational relevance of the work performed by the research/policy departments— in particular to provide a clearer country focus in research/policy. While decentralization at the Bank has mainly taken place at the headquarters level, it reflects an overall concern with fostering 'partnerships' between the Bank and its borrowers aimed at enhancing their sense of 'ownership and commitment' to Bank projects. This constitutes a major challenge for the Bank, which has very often been criticized for its centralized structure and work methods. Compared to the UNDP, the Bank is a relatively centralized agency; it has 75 field offices and a smaller proportion of its staff members—18 per cent—are based in the field.[10]

In recent years the ILO has also made moves towards further decentralizing its management and programming from its Geneva headquarters to its regional, area, and branch offices in 40 countries. Since 1990, the percentage of staff based in field offices has increased from approximately 25 per cent to 36 per cent. Radical administrative and personnel changes are being made to establish in all regions multidisciplinary teams of experts (MDTs) which, in consultation with governments, employers' and workers' organizations and key donors, will determine the strategies and future programme activities of the ILO. Like the decentralization processes in other multilateral organizations, the weakness of women's constituencies at the local level is likely to emerge as a potential constraint for pursuing WID/gender activities in many national settings.

As in the UNDP and the World Bank, there are organizational divisions within the ILO that impact on response to WID/gender. In theory, all the work the ILO does—be it research, technical co-operation, or policy advice—is meant to reinforce its standard-setting mandate, and it has systematically tried to foster a synergy between its standard-setting and technical co-operation programmes. The division between standards and technical co-operation is reflected, however, in the bureaucratic structure, where one deputy director-general presides over Standards and another over Development and Technical Co-operation, giving rise to problems of lack of coherence and cross-fertilization. Reinforcing this division is a cleavage between different segments of ILO staff, with the technical and field segments having an 'essentially pragmatic' outlook, while those working in the standards segment, primarily headquarters-based, tend to possess an 'identity linked to the legal profession and are more likely to promote legal standards in their work' (Cox, 1973:123). Adding to this complexity, ILO's staff structure has since the 1960s also included a 'developmental' segment, which is composed mainly of economists. The range of approaches thus necessitates a degree of discursive flexibility on the part of WID/gender advocates.

This discussion highlights some of the features of the organizational contexts into which WID/gender concerns are being inserted. Two factors emerge as of particular importance for internal policy advocacy. First, a sound understanding of the organizational culture is needed to demonstrate the relevance of WID/gender concerns to the organization's mandate and to help forge alliances across the bureaucratic structure. Secondly, the structural location and functions of the central WID/gender advocacy unit and WID/gender staff may be crucial to the effective implementation of the WID/gender mandate. In the sections below we consider the strategies that have been pursued within the different organizational contexts of the UNDP, the World Bank and the ILO.[11]

Establishing an institutional presence

All three organizations responded to pressures and recommendations that emerged from the 1975 World Conference on Women held in Mexico City. Often, the first step was to appoint a WID adviser. The UNDP did this in 1976 and the World Bank in January of the following year. The role of the WID adviser in both organizations was mainly to 'sensitize' staff members about the costs of not taking women into account. At the World Bank, the WID adviser was also expected to provide operational support and to respond to outside requests for information (World Bank, 1994c:10). As in other institutions, the WID advisers were given broad mandates, with few resources to match. At the World Bank the post was situated in a project advisory unit in the research/policy part of the Bank, along with other advisers working on cross-sectoral issues. These project advisers were meant to provide intellectual and technical support to the Bank's operations. Given her location, the WID adviser could in theory play a monitoring and oversight role: she reviewed all projects at the preparation and appraisal stages, providing criticisms and suggestions that would have to be addressed before the projects could advance. Lacking any clear power to reject inappropriate projects, however, the WID adviser had to rely on persuasion and suggestion. With limited staff support, the WID adviser could only partially carry out the task of scrutinizing the 250 to 300 projects approved by the Bank each year, and monitoring the hundreds of ongoing ones.

Although women's issues had long been on the ILO agenda, and both research and operational activities had been carried out in this area, the declaration of the International Women's Year (1975) put pressure on the ILO to demonstrate further its commitment to women's concerns. In 1975 it adopted a Declaration on Equality of Opportunity and Treatment for Women Workers, and a Plan of Action for its implementation. One of the recommendations of the Plan was that a women's unit be set up. In 1976 the Office for Women Workers' Questions (FEMMES) was set up within the Promotion of Equality Department. The Equality of Rights Branch (EGALITE), of the same department, also worked to promote equality for women workers in addition to its activities to combat political and ethnic discrimination. In contrast to the WID posts in the UNDP and the World Bank, FEMMES was constituted as a separate unit. Its role was mainly an advocacy one, although it also consolidated and disseminated information. The Director, a D1-level post, was responsible for co-ordinating women workers' questions throughout the ILO. The means through which she could carry out the mandate were limited, however, especially in connection with technical co-operation activities, where specialized research and women's projects were expanding during this period.

Given the cross-cutting nature of gender concerns, it is important that commitment is fostered across the organizational context. Initial attempts to diffuse responsibility for WID/gender to other members of staff were made at the UNDP and the World Bank in the form of new programming guidelines. In 1977, UNDP's first guidelines on WID issues were produced as part of the UNDP *Programme Manual*. Staff were encouraged to examine all projects from the standpoint of women's role in development. At the World Bank, formal and fairly explicit guidelines on WID appeared for the first time in 1984, included under the 'Sociological Aspects of Project Appraisal' in the Bank's *Operational Manual*. The aim of the guidelines was to verify that project design took into account local factors impacting on women's participation, women's contribution to the project, and the likely impact of the project on women. As subsequent experience in the Bank and elsewhere was to confirm, without changes in incentives structures to enforce compliance, and without WID staff in operations to oversee compliance, the impact of such guidelines was limited.

The Nairobi Conference which marked the end of the Women's Decade in 1985 prompted some reflection on efforts to institutionalize attention to WID/gender concerns within multilateral agencies. A UNDP-sponsored evaluation in 1985 found limited progress in promoting women's participation in development projects and programmes of the United Nations system. It was estimated that fewer than one in six projects, reported to affect women, planned to involve women in project implementation, and that only four per cent of UNDP resources were allocated to projects related to women (Pietilä and Eide, 1990:42; Kardam, 1991:23). The report also indicated that women were primarily targeted for projects concerned with maternal and child health. At the World Bank, internal estimates suggest that projects with some type of gender-related action constituted seven per cent of the investment portfolio during the period of 1975 to 1985. The report notes a temporary increase in projects with some type of gender-related action between FY78 and FY83, when they constituted about 11 per cent of the entire investment portfolio (as opposed to three to four per cent before FY78), but the increase was not sustained after 1984—ironically the year the operational guidelines were issued (World Bank, 1994c).

Initial optimism that integrating WID/gender would be accomplished through the appointment of WID advisers to carry out mainly advocacy work gave way to the realization that unless these advisers could overcome their marginalization and impact on mainstream policy decisions, there would be little hope for the implementation of more gender-equitable policies. There was also a concern that a focus on women-specific projects helped to reinforce the marginalization of WID/gender issues. By the end of the Women's Decade there was greater emphasis on the need to 'mainstream' gender, a project that requires a radical overhaul of all organizational structures and procedures to ensure that women receive equal benefit from all the activities carried out by the organization.

Mainstreaming has involved primarily two main components: integrating gender issues into an organization's programmes and policies, and diffusing responsibility for attention to WID/gender concerns to staff members throughout the organization through the introduction of new institutions and procedures.[12] Goetz (Chapter 3) explored efforts to mainstream gender in state machineries of selected developing countries. Below we consider the manifestations of both dimensions of the mainstreaming strategy in the UNDP, the World Bank, and the ILO.

At the end of the Women's Decade there was also a growing concern within the women's movement, particularly among groups from developing countries, about the limitations of the 'integrationist' strategy that was being pursued by development agencies. According to such critiques, what was needed was not simply the 'adding on' of women to pre-existing mainstream programmes and policies, but a more transformative approach whereby adopting women's

150

concerns would promote a fundamental change in the mainstream (Jahan, 1995). UNIFEM responded with the argument that 'the incorporation of women into development—the mainstreaming of women—will change the mainstream' (Anderson, 1990:38). The extent to which gender mainstreaming within development institutions can have a transformatory impact on the development process remains a contentious issue among gender advocates.

Institutions and procedures for mainstreaming

Two main features characterize the mainstreaming strategy pursued by many organizations in the immediate post-Nairobi period: the creation or strengthening of WID/gender units, and the introduction of new procedures to diffuse responsibility for WID/gender concerns across the organizational context. In 1986, under the new UNDP Administrator, women in development became one of the four UNDP priority themes, along with the environment, NGOs, and the role of the private sector in development. This top-management support, itself a response to external pressures (Pietilä and Eide, 1990), provided the impetus for the creation of the Division of Women in Development. The Division was located in the Bureau for Programme and Policy Evaluation (now known as BPPS) where it was, in theory, strategically positioned to influence policy decisions. The head of the Division was assigned a Director-level post that made her part of the UNDP's top management. There were two professional staff, in addition to the Director. The overall responsibility of the Division was to 'assist in ensuring and monitoring through the UNDP's programmes and projects a substantially larger role for women, both as active participants at all levels and as beneficiaries of such projects' (ibid.:43). It was not involved in financing and implementing projects, which was the role of the UNDP-administered fund UNIFEM,[13] but worked instead to 'mainstream' WID into UNDP's work.

In order to promote cross-organizational responsibility, new policy guidelines prepared in 1986 and updated in 1987 referred to the importance of integrating WID issues into the country programming process, in particular during national consultations undertaken to identify the development priorities of recipient governments. The Director attempted to exercise an 'oversight' function on a top-management committee which discussed and approved projects over US$700 000, by using the opportunity to demonstrate the relevance of WID issues (ibid.:45). As was the case with the oversight function played by the Bank's WID adviser described above, the Division had neither the staff resources to adequately review the hundreds of new projects approved each year, nor the authority to ensure that its suggestions were followed by staff. The 'project review form' initiated by the Division to identify how far women's issues and the participation of women were included in UNDP projects was also seen by many staff as a *pro forma* activity rather than an *aide-mémoire* to be used in the course of project formulation, review, and evaluation (UNDP, 1990a:9–10). An organization-wide focal point system was also put in place in

151

the summer of 1987 to encourage attention to WID/gender across the organization, although for reasons we consider later, its impact was limited.

The first indication that WID/gender was to be taken more seriously at the World Bank came in September 1985 when a senior economist from inside the Bank was appointed the new WID adviser. Under the new adviser the previous functions of project monitoring, external relations, information dissemination and staff training were scaled back. Instead, her role was to demonstrate how attention to WID contributed to development objectives in a language that was acceptable to economists and to provide clear operational guidelines. In 1986 each region was instructed to appoint a WID co-ordinator (or focal point), often the assistant director of projects. The WID adviser was to 'provide leadership and seed money, but efforts on the ground would be led by the regions' (World Bank, 1994c:22). While this new division of labour provided a more focused strategy for the adviser, the adverse implication was that she lost the little oversight power that she had hitherto exercised. Focal points in the regions were not gender specialists and WID was added to their already full list of responsibilities. With weak WID representation in the regions, they could hardly be expected to play a lead role in 'efforts on the ground'. It is perhaps in these terms that the relative decline in WID action between FY84 and FY88 (ibid.) must be understood.

By 1987 the WID 'office' had grown into a Division with three professionals, and after a Bank-wide restructuring, was located in the Population and Human Resources Department (PHRWD), maintaining its association with what is seen as a 'soft' area in the Bank—human resources and social sector planning. Following UNDP's move a year earlier, in 1987 the new Bank president announced that WID would become one of the four formal 'areas of special emphasis' in Bank activities, along with poverty reduction, environment, and private sector development (World Bank, 1992d). This move helped to reinforce the work of the WID Division. In 1988 the WID Division put in place a new monitoring system whereby all projects were reviewed at approval to judge attention to WID. By 1990, it had eight professional staff members although there were still no full-time WID posts in Operations. There was also a boost in financial resources. WID's budget more than doubled in 1986, from US$80 000 to US$190 500. By 1988 it stood at US$620 000 (World Bank, 1994c:27). More than half the budget came from external sources—the UNDP and Norway, in particular (Lexow and McNeill, 1989).

The immediate post-Nairobi period also brought changes at the ILO. In 1985 the ILO adopted a resolution on equal opportunities and equal treatment for men and women in employment and in 1987 adopted a Plan of Action, which stands as its most comprehensive 'policy statement' on women's issues to date. The Plan committed the ILO to a 'mainstreaming strategy', and referred to the need for new institutional mechanisms and procedures to implement this strategy (ILO, 1994c). In 1989 FEMMES was closed down in response to demands for an institutional structure that could provide more co-ordinated and comprehensive policies for women workers throughout the ILO (ILO, 1989:89). A post of

152

Special Adviser for Women Workers' Questions, at Director level, was set up and funded through the regular ILO budget. The post was attached to the Office of the Deputy Director-General in charge of technical programmes, thereby giving the Special Adviser a stronger position from which to promote the co-ordination of women workers' questions within the technical co-operation side of the ILO's work, an area that FEMMES had found difficult to influence. At the same time that FEMMES was shut down, the Equality of Rights Branch (EGALITE) was moved to the International Labour Standards Department and became more involved in questions concerning the discrimination of women workers.[14] One staff member in EGALITE was assigned the responsibility for issues concerning gender equality, in addition to her other tasks.

Moves towards strengthening the technical co-operation activities had already been evident in 1986 when the post of Co-ordinator of the Women in Development Programme was created, with funding from Norway. The post was located in the Promotion of Technical Co-operation Branch and its function was to work with technical units and the field structure to integrate WID/gender into ILO's technical co-operation programmes. While this post was retained, the Special Adviser's more prominent location in the institutional structure meant that she was, in theory, better placed to provide overall policy advice and to promote interdepartmental collaboration on ILO priorities concerning women workers. As an indication of the cross-organizational responsibilities of the Special Adviser—both in technical co-operation and standard setting—she was responsible for servicing the Governing Body Committee on Discrimination for its standing agenda item 'ILO action for equality of opportunity and treatment for men and women in employment' (ILO, 1993b), and thus worked closely with EGALITE on this issue.

The cross-departmental nature of the Special Adviser's work in an organization reputed for its rigid bureaucratic structure raises obvious problems (Lotherington et al., 1991:67). One way to generate dialogue across bureaucratic divisions has been through inter-departmental committees or projects, such as the Inter-Departmental Project on Equality for Women in Employment.[15] As in the other organizations considered here, another 'bridge-building' strategy has been to appoint WID/gender focal points in other parts of the organization. In 1989, a focal point system was set up in all headquarters' departments and regional offices of the ILO. The position and terms of reference of the focal point differ from department to department. For example, some have the task of integrating gender into the department's mandate as part of their job description. Others have been asked to serve as focal points but do not have the role included in their job descriptions and therefore combine the task of raising gender issues with their own technical work; in other words, it becomes 'volunteer work', thus further reinforcing its marginalized status.

These problems are not unique to the ILO. In many organizations focal points are expected to assume the entire responsibility for integrating WID/gender into a department's work (Palmer and Jha, 1993:7). A difficult task under the best of circumstances, the problem is magnified where the focal point has no WID/gender expertise: although focal points may be committed to the promotion of gender issues, they are unlikely to have appropriate technical skills to draw out the gender dimensions of departmental work. And, unless they are well-positioned within the departmental decision-making structure, their recommendations will have little impact. In other words, the focal point system may be nothing more than 'window dressing' unless these staff members are given the appropriate tools to exercise influence.[16] A further problem in many agencies is the confusion among staff members over whether the focal point's role concerns substantive issues of programme content or the advancement of women employees within the organization. This confusion no doubt increases resistance amongst colleagues, especially where advocacy work of any sort is deemed 'unprofessional'.

Concerning the issue of women's representation, UN system agencies have responded to arguments concerning the importance of achieving a 'critical mass' of women in professional and senior-level posts by adopting targets for women's employment. According to feminist institutional analysts, the under-representation of women serves as an obstacle to the institutionalization WID/gender concerns (Staudt, 1990, 1995). While there is no evidence thus far to confirm that women in decision-making positions are likely to act in women's interests (Goetz, 1992: 13–14), it is undeniable that the majority of WID/gender advocates within development organizations have been women. Neither the UNDP nor the ILO have reached the 1995 UN target of 35 per cent women in professional posts and above, although the UNDP has come close with 31.8 per cent at the professional level in January 1995 (see Razavi and Miller, 1995b: Tables 1–3). The World Bank has not set targets but has committed itself to a greater gender balance in higher level staff: at present, the percentage of women staff increases the lower down the organizational ladder one goes. Given the relatively low level of women in senior posts, in all three organizations alliances with supportive male colleagues, particularly at the management level, have been crucial in efforts by internal advocates to institutionalize WID/gender concerns.

Decentralization

As noted above, since the beginning of the 1990s all three organizations considered here have become concerned with the issue of 'national ownership' of the development process. One of the consequences has been a greater decentralization of activities, in part to ensure that development assistance better reflects the national context. As part of this ongoing process of organizational change, moves have also been made to decentralize responsibility for the WID/gender mandate. In some ways this can be seen as a continuation of the mainstreaming strategy whereby efforts have been made to diffuse responsibility for WID/gender concerns across the organizational context. At the same time, the process of decentralization, especially to the field level, re-confirms the importance of strong system-wide procedures to ensure that WID/gender policy is implemented. It also raises important questions about national-level commitment to the WID/gender mandate, as explored by Goetz (Chapter 3).

Although the importance of making inroads in the country programming process was identified by UNDP as early as 1986, data collected in the late 1980s and early 1990s suggested that, in spite of the guidelines and focal point system, WID/gender concerns were still being subverted at the programming level. WID/gender concerns appeared to be included only in cases where the Resident Representative took an active interest in the issue (Pietilä and Eide, 1990:46). Interviews carried out in the late 1980s and early 1990s also reported that there was a widespread perception amongst UNDP staff members that unless financial or political incentives were involved, governments were likely to remain unin-terested in WID/gender issues (Kardam, 1991:33; Palmer and Jha, 1993:3). The fact that UNDP's main counterpart at the country level is usually the ministry of finance or planning, which tends to be less prepared to discuss WID/gender con-cerns than many other ministries and WID bureaux, has also been identified as a constraint on response to WID/gender at the country level (Pietilä and Eide, 1990:47).

In response to such concerns, in 1990 the UNDP Governing Council recom-mended the decentralization of WID activities to the field level (UNDP, 1990a) and pledged significant resources in support of this move.[17] As part of this trend, in 1992 the Gender in Development Programme (GIDP) replaced the WID Division. The name change indicated that GIDP would now focus on providing support to the country offices for 'strengthening national capacity in gender-responsive planning and programming' (GIDP, n.d., 1:3). GIDP's 'constituency' has been widened beyond the traditional interlocutors (field office staff, govern-ments, and international agencies) to include NGOs and individuals in national training institutions. GIDP's new mandate reflects the perceived importance of broad-based support for the WID/gender mandate.

Unlike the WID Division, the three-member GIDP does not exist as a separate division, but forms part of BPPS's new Social Development and Poverty Elimination Division (SDPED), established to consolidate all the dimensions of UNDP's 'sustainable human development' mandate—eliminating poverty, creat-ing employment and sustainable livelihoods, the advancement of women, and regenerating the environment. For the GIDP, a further organizational layer has been added between it and the director of BPPS, effectively decreasing GIDP's influence with top management. GIDP's location within SDPED, however, pro-vides new opportunities for promoting WID/gender concerns and alliance build-ing within the formulation of UNDP policy. Its operational role remains indirect, given the institutional (and spatial) distance separating the GIDP from operations at the country offices. It seeks to provide advice and support to the country offices in the form of policy papers, guidelines, and training.

By the late 1980s the World Bank President and the Board of Executive Directors, particularly members from the Nordic countries, also concerned that

WID issues were not well-enough integrated in Bank projects, were pushing for faster and more effective implementation (World Bank, 1994c; Pietilä and Eide, 1990). As with the UNDP, the Bank sought solutions in the decentralization of WID/gender. A first step in this direction was the appointment in 1990 of full-time WID co-ordinators in each of the Regions and the designation of resource persons in each country department whose duties would include the task of integrating WID concerns in departmental activities (World Bank, 1994c:28). With the overall Bank restructuring in 1993, aimed in part at providing a clearer country focus in operational work, the WID Division was closed down. According to some internal advocates this led to a 'temporary slowdown of momentum in building up and sustaining staff gender capacity' (World Bank, 1993b:2). A Gender Analysis and Policy (GAP) thematic group was set up in the Education and Social Policy Department (ESP) of the newly-created Vice-Presidency for Human Resources Development and Operations Policy.

The GAP team has six high-level positions, down from eight in the WID Division, but the monitoring function that was carried out by the WID Division between 1988 and 1993 has been allocated to a 'monitoring team' responsible for both poverty and gender. Like UNDP's GIDP, a signficant part of the GAP team's mandate is to support the mainstreaming of WID/gender in operations: through staff training, the preparation of 'best practice tool kits', and demon-stration of how gender concerns can be integrated into country assistance strat-egies (World Bank, 1994c:43). WID/gender capacity in the operational departments remains highly uneven. The strongest capacity is found in the Africa Region, which appears to make the greatest intellectual contribution to the Bank's WID/gender work (Razavi and Miller, 1995b:39–40). Although the new operational focus is a positive move, it also entails inevitable trade-offs. As the GAP team contributes more of its time to operationalizing WID/gender, capacity for its research and policy analysis is inevitably reduced, which may in fact deprive internal advocates of the opportunity to use new research findings to promote gender issues within the bureaucracy.

Organization-wide efforts to decentralize ILO's administrative and operational work have also had implications for the WID/gender mandate. A staff member in the Bureau for Active Partnership has been assigned the task of providing advice to regional and country offices on ways to integrate gender issues into their coun-try programming. Other measures have also been taken to make the field struc-ture more responsive to women's issues. In 1990–91 four high-ranking professional posts (P5) as Regional Advisers for Women Workers' Questions were set up in each of the regional headquarters. Although the Regional Advisers report to their regional directors, their mandate is to assist the Special Adviser in monitoring regional and national activities for their attention to women workers' questions. Their specific tasks include identifying areas and means for priority action, monitoring, and reporting on how gender issues are being promoted in the regions. Another manifestation of decentralization is the multi-disciplinary teams (MDTs). While most MDTs have WID focal points, only a few of them are gender specialists. There are, however, an increasing number of associate experts (donor government-sponsored posts) on MDTs who have a background in gender issues.

Strengthening procedures and accountability mechanisms

In all three organizations considered here, efforts to diffuse responsibility for WID/gender issues throughout the organizational structure, combined with the overall trend towards decentralization, necessitated effective procedures and accountability mechanisms to ensure that staff members, particularly at the field level, pay attention to WID/gender concerns. In recent years both the UNDP and the ILO have invested energy in updating and expanding their gender guidelines and training programmes, the aim of which is to foster responsibility amongst all staff members for promoting WID/gender concerns in their day-to-day work. Since 1993 a full-time post has existed in the ILO's Evaluation Unit of the Bureau of Programming and Management to promote attention to gender in the design, monitoring, and evaluation of ILO programmes and projects. In conjunction with other WID/gender staff, this staff member has been responsible for preparing a comprehensive set of guidelines intended for use in mainstreaming women's concerns across the organization (ILO/PROG/EVAL, 1995:1).

If we consider UNDP's long experience with guidelines, it is clear that guidelines alone are not a sufficient incentive for attention to WID/gender. ILO staff stress that their strategy has been to support a group of mutually reinforcing measures: guidelines, gender training, and sensitization. With funding from the Netherlands, the Office of the Special Adviser in late 1995 commenced a new gender training programme for staff across the organization (Groenen, 1995). Efforts are being made to tailor the training to the specific needs of the ILO, its 'social partners' and women's NGOs. The 'outreach approach' to gender training parallels that being pursued by GIDP at UNDP (GIDP, n.d., 7:16). Gender training has been of relatively low priority at the World Bank. Following its brief experience with gender training in the early 1980s, no training was offered for years. Since 1988 the training division has offered courses on gender, and included gender components in other courses, such as agriculture, nutrition, and environment. Many multilateral organizations have embraced gender training as a key procedure for mainstreaming, although recent assessments have raised questions about the overall benefits of such training (CIDA, 1993).

The strategy of 'persuading' staff of the importance of gender issues through guidelines and training was described by some ILO interviewees as more conducive to promoting change in behaviour than the alternative of building more formal staff incentives, such as staff performance appraisals, into the system. None the less, staff in other multilateral organizations have broached the issue of greater staff accountability mechanisms through which individual staff performance could be linked to 'gender responsiveness' (GIDP, n.d., 6:15–16; UN ECOSOC, 1995:29). According to the Operations Evaluation Department (OED) report, one of the flaws of past training efforts at the Bank has been the lack of attention to incentive structures; current thinking, it claims, 'is that more attention needs to be paid to the organizational context, and that incentives to use these new skills should be built into an organization's incentive structure' (World Bank, 1994c, Appendix C:75). Only in UNDP have tentative efforts been made to adopt staff incentives structures (Jahan, 1995:45; GIDP, n.d., 6:15–16).

In all of the organizations considered here, recent demands from member states, and especially from donors, for greater 'accountability' have set in motion efforts to improve monitoring and evaluation (see UNDP, 1994a; ILO, 1994b; World Bank, 1994c:55); this has been used by both internal and external advocates to raise issues about 'gender accountability' (UNGA, 1995; Jahan, 1995). The mainstreaming strategy has been problematic as far as gender accountability issues are concerned. Can 'mainstreamed' activities be monitored effectively for resources allocated to women and for attention to gender issues throughout the implementation process? In most organizations, only limited data exist on how far WID/gender concerns have been integrated into mainstream programmes and projects. The mere mention of the words 'women' or 'gender' may be sufficient to recommend a programme or project as 'WID/gender sensitive'. Information is even more sketchy on the extent to which WID/gender concerns included in project and programme design are prioritized in the implementation process. Most assessments to date are based on staff impressions and not on data collected at the field level (Jahan, 1995:53).

At the World Bank, WID's operational record in between FY86 and FY93 indicates that the proportion of projects with gender-related action increased to 24 per cent from the figure of 7 per cent for previous decade (World Bank, 1994c). These figures, however, refer to project documents at the appraisal stage and not to actual implementation. Internal assessments point to a 'significant' gap between objectives set out in appraisals and actual implementation of WID components (World Bank 1992d:10). One of the problems with 'mainstreamed' projects and programmes, at the World Bank and elsewhere, is that their WID/gender components tend to get marginalized during implementation. As one internal review of portfolio management for Latin American countries found, 'WID objectives are not matched by specific activities and actions to achieve them' (ibid.:16). As the same review noted, funds needed 'to undertake WID activities are not specified in a large number of project documents and, frequently, no Technical Assistance is available to support implementation capacity' (ibid.). Apparently in response to some of these problems, the Bank has for the first time in its history experimented with women-specific projects, two in Africa and one in Latin America (World Bank, 1994c).

The budgetary data provided by the ILO on its WID/gender activities covers women-specific projects only. Data for 1991 show that WID-specific projects account for six per cent of all projects, representing approximately four per cent of total budgetary allocations.[18] No figures are available on 'mainstreamed' projects at the ILO. In standard-setting work, however, there is evidence that a mainstreaming strategy is being pursued. While there have been no new conventions solely concerning women workers since 1985, there has been a focus on drawing attention to the way in which existing standards apply to women. Some recent conventions, while not women-specific, do in fact relate primarily to women, such as the Part-Time Work Convention, 1994 (No.175), and the proposed convention on home-work discussed at the 1995 International Labour Conference. According to one interviewee, standard-setting work now tries to take 'a holistic approach'; in other words, promoting equality for women workers involves a combination of legal standards that will create an enabling environment for women.[19]

Thus far UNDP has been unable to provide any data on how WID/gender concerns have been taken up in its activities or figures on resources allocated to WID/gender concerns. Aware of this problem, the Governing Council recommended in 1990 that a database be established. Although recent efforts have been made to put in place a system for the collection of thematic statistics on WID/gender (GIDP, n.d., 6:11–12), no data have yet been generated. The issue of accountability has also given rise to demands for measurable 'performance' indicators within development assistance. While emphasis on the clear definition of goals, targets, benchmarks and results, as promoted for instance in the UNDP's new Programme Support Document, is understandable, questions arise about the ability of indicators to capture WID/gender concerns. If emphasis is placed solely on easily measurable indicators, such as income, educational attainment, and life expectancy, for example, there is a danger that some of the less quantifiable dimensions of gender power relations will be overlooked in programming, a concern also addressed by Mayoux (Chapter 7). While measurable indicators and better reporting systems, especially on financial allocations, would provide both internal and external advocates with more leverage in their work, it is clearly important to guard against the possible adverse implications for WID/gender if multilateral agencies are forced by donor demands for 'performance' to focus solely on promoting outcomes that are easily quantified and, presumably, easily achieved. The challenge of changing gender relations requires thinking in the long term, well beyond the duration of the average project or programming cycle.

Policy dialogues and country programming

As noted above, until the mid-1980s, multilateral donors tended to tackle WID/gender issues with initiatives targeted mainly at the project level; this approach was linked to the perception that the macro-policy concerns of programme assistance had nothing to do with WID/gender. Thus a range of small, unconnected projects for women were often pursued while programme assistance carried on in a 'gender-blind' fashion, promoting macro and sectoral policies that often undid any of the positive gains for women that could be expected from project-level assistance. Since the early 1980s, aid negotiations have taken place in

159

the form of 'policy dialogues' between the donor agency and the government of the recipient country. Through these dialogues the macro-policy framework for the country programming process is designed. At both the UNDP and the World Bank, various policy documents are prepared as the basis for their aid allocation decisions. The analysis contained in these documents has far-reaching implications. The documents elaborate the organization's understanding of the recipient country's economic and social problems and the types of policy reform to be recommended. They also outline benchmarks for subsequent appraisal, monitoring and evaluation (Elson and McGee, 1995). In terms of WID/gender policy advocacy it is crucial that gender concerns are 'mainstreamed' in these policy documents. While the issue of mainstreaming gender at the policy level has been touched upon above, the subject warrants further discussion.

The GAP team at the World Bank has, among its main tasks, the role of strengthening the gender content of the Country Assistance Strategy Paper (CAS), a document which sets the tone for the 'policy dialogue' between the Bank and its borrowers. The data for FY94 shows that nearly 50 per cent of CAS statements contain gender analysis.[20] The GAP Team's efforts to demonstrate to selected country departments how gender concerns can be included in a meaningful way in CAS papers is considered an important step in making WID/gender policy statements operational (World Bank, 1994c; World Bank, 1994a). Analytical economic and sector work (ESW) carried out by the technical departments in the operational divisions is also intended to inform the Bank's policy dialogue and investment at the country level. A growing proportion of ESW addresses gender issues, especially sectoral reports on population, health and nutrition, education, and agriculture, as well as macro-economic reports and country economic memoranda covering these areas.

The WID Division calculated that nearly 50 per cent of ESW reports in FY92 contained discussion, analysis and/or recommendations on gender issues (World Bank, 1992d), nearly double the figures recorded for FY88 and FY89. The kind of mention that gender issues get in these reports, however, is highly varied. An internal review by the African WID Unit on work on population, health, and nutrition, areas where one would expect a full integration of gender concerns, indicated only limited consistency between the issues identified in the sector reports and their recommendations, and between the recommendations of the sector reports and the subsequent project designs (ibid.:7). A potentially critical subset of the Bank's ESW work, as far as gender issues are concerned, are the country-level WID assessments. While earlier reports were more descriptive, those produced in recent years have become more analytical and policy-oriented (World Bank, 1992d; World Bank, 1994c). Very often, however, WID assessments appear to stand alone, with weak links to the Bank's lending operations and policy recommendations at the country level—a criticism that also applies to other sectoral papers prepared by the Bank (IDS, 1994).

The UNDP's Country Strategy Note (CSN), intended to co-ordinate all the UN's operational activities (including ILO activities) in a given country, is a recent innovation and it is too early to assess how far WID/gender issues will be integrated into such documents. The other two main programming documents are the Resident Representative's 'advisory note', used as the basis for the country programming exercise, and the country programme itself. Again, very few data have been compiled on the content of these documents. In 1990 the UNDP Administrator reported that 37 per cent of the country programmes addressed WID/gender issues (cited in Jahan, 1995:69). A year later, in 1991, a desk review of 31 advisory notes, used as a basis for the country programming exercise for the programme cycle 1992–6, found that 'although there is some progress towards integration, WID issues are often regarded separately, or as a special concern rather than as an integral part of a plan' (Bernardes Davidson, 1991:i). While a few advisory notes systematically mainstreamed women's issues in all priority areas of the country programme to the extent that special provisions were made for gender-specific data and specific strategies to address women's concerns, in the majority gender issues were referred to only in passing as an important element of the sustainable human development mandate. On the whole, WID/gender concerns were unevenly integrated into country programmes of the 1992–6 programming cycle. Few targets were set and rarely were concrete projects and programmes outlined. Nor were figures set by UNDP for the allocation of resources to WID/gender concerns in country programming. Aware of these problems, GIDP has identified the Resident Representative's advisory note as a target for their support in coming years. It has also strongly recommended the preparation of a Gender Situation Analysis as a prerequisite for effective mainstreaming of gender concerns in the programming process in a given country (GIDP, 1995).

As for national-level policy dialogues, emphasis on promoting 'national ownership' of the development process has prompted some multilateral organizations to open up the process to a wider group of actors. In addition to donors and government representatives, civil society groups are in some contexts included as participants in policy dialogues, although it is still uncertain whether the highly secretive negotiations on adjustment programmes between Bretton Woods institutions and recipient governments will become more open. The aim of opening up the policy dialogue process is to facilitate constructive national debates involving all parties with a stake in the outcomes of macro-economic and policy reform. Many multilateral organizations are already talking about the importance of including women's groups in the policy dialogue process and this is seen by some gender advocates as an opportunity for inserting gender concerns into the policy formulation process (Elson and McGee, 1995). While the apparent moves, by development organizations, toward more participatory processes for determining the development agenda certainly provide 'political opportunity structures' for WID/gender advocacy, as Mayoux (Chapter 7) argues, participatory processes do not automatically guarantee that women's voices will be heard, a point we explore further in the next section.

This section provides an overview of some of the discursive strategies and alliances used by WID/gender policy advocates within the UNDP, the World Bank, and the ILO. Policy advocacy, and the institutional and procedural innovations discussed in the sections above, can be seen as interacting in a dynamic way. In other words, institutional and procedural innovations to some extent reflect the success of policy advocates in demonstrating the relevance of WID/gender concerns within the organizational context; even with such procedures in place, the issue of relevance remains a crucial one and internal advocates must constantly update their research and analytical skills in order to respond strategically to overall policy changes within the organization. In spite of a shared organizational culture, these institutions are not monolithic and allies have been more easy to find in some departments/sectors than in others. Alliance building has been crucial over the past decade in view of the focus on mainstreaming.

The importance of internal advocacy has been particularly striking in the case of the World Bank. In retrospect, the strategy adopted in 1985 by the new WID adviser was fairly effective: to provide solid intellectual justification for the Bank's WID/gender mandate. This approach contrasts significantly with that adopted by the first WID adviser who, as an institutional outsider (a senior UN official), was not sufficiently well-versed in the institutional language and value-system to facilitate internal bargaining (Kardam, 1991:77). The intellectual work that had to be done was demanding—arguing gender in efficiency terms was not easy, especially as data were scarce and not always supportive of the efficiency premiss. But in order to convince the Bank economists that WID was a legitimate concern for their organization, a sound conceptual and evidential base had to be built.

By the late 1980s internal advocates found an opening for raising the profile of gender concerns when the Bank, in response to criticisms of its adjustment programmes, began placing more focus on poverty and social sector considerations. In this context, the WID adviser and her colleagues decided to give top priority to investments in the social sectors where the evidence for 'high payoffs of investing in women's human capital' was strongest and the 'returns' were highest (World Bank, 1992b:5)—a focus reiterated in the Bank's first formal policy statement on WID/gender issued in 1994 (World Bank, 1994a). Based on research carried out in the Bank and outside, the positive synergies between investing in women and the Bank's main objectives—poverty reduction, increased productivity, more efficient use of resources, and social returns—were highlighted by internal advocates.

Internal advocacy has thus been based primarily on promoting efficiency gains by building 'human capital' through education and healthcare and 'equipping women' with credit and extension service (World Bank, 1989:iii). There has been some concern by external advocates of the dangers inherent in not recognizing gender equity as a valid objective in itself: it could, for example, limit interventions only to instances where the economic case was strong (Lexow and McNeill, 1989:89). For example, what if attention to gender issues did not enhance project success, as some advocates claimed? The Bank's OED report mentions, for example, that 'differences in overall performance between projects with and without gender-related actions were small' (1994c:47). Similarly, while some external advocates promoted women as the 'missing link' in economic development, policy advocates at the Bank have admitted that they have been unable to show in a sufficiently 'rigorous and convincing' manner that countries that have invested heavily in women have grown faster, in terms of GNP (World Bank, 1992b:9). There have been some attempts to revisit macro-economic programmes from a gender perspective, with economic arguments that go beyond the 'social cost' issues, as for example in the technical note *Paradigm Postponed* (World Bank, 1993c), prepared by the Gender Team in the Africa Region. The paper was intended to make a contribution to the World Bank's Women in Development policy paper (World Bank, 1994a), but failed to make an appearance there. In an institution where solid technical arguments command respect, documents that lack sufficient facts and figures will not find it easy to win the up-stream battle. In this regard, it is hardly surprising that internal advocates have moved only cautiously beyond areas where 'returns' to investment have already been proven.

Since the beginning of the 1990s, a number of issues have appeared on the World Bank agenda that would seem to provide openings for WID/gender advocacy; these include, for example, participatory development, governance and human rights and a heightened focus on poverty alleviation. The new Bank President has also challenged his staff to devote more attention to issues of social policy. With the close institutional links that exist between gender and poverty—they both fall under the Vice-Presidency for Human Resources Development and Operations Policy—the Bank's poverty work provides a potentially critical entry point for getting gender concerns into mainstream operations at the Bank. Through poverty assessments, for example, WID/gender advocates have been able to draw attention to such issues as women's education and health needs, and the alleviation of domestic labour constraints through investments in labour-saving technology and infrastructure, in addition to the importance of promoting women's legal rights. None the less, there have been serious criticisms of the Bank's understanding of the dimensions of women's poverty and the inappropriateness of its labour-intensive growth strategy as a means to alleviate women's poverty (Evans, 1994; Jackson, 1996). While such external criticisms and research findings can in theory be taken up by internal advocates and used to strengthen their work in this area, a further impediment remains. Like WID assessments, the Bank's Poverty Assessments do not have a sufficiently strong foothold inside the Bank to influence mainstream operations (IDS, 1994). Recommendations in Poverty Assessments for investments in social and physical infrastructure, for example, conflict with the overriding preoccupation with fiscal constraint in the Bank's public expenditure reviews, and calls for greater investment in social sectors may continue to be sidelined.

Efficiency concerns are also evident in the Bank's approach to participatory development. Although there is some evidence to suggest that women's organizations are being consulted in project formulation processes to allow them to identify their own priorities (World Bank, 1995a:45–7), the main concern has been to elicit the involvement of women's groups in relation to cost-effective service delivery—a trend that mirrors the Bank's engagement with NGOs in general (Siddharth, 1995). For example, national and local community-based NGOs are used to channel credit and microenterprise development services to increase poor women's income-earning capacities, and to implement projects concerning nutrition, primary healthcare, and vocational education and training. While such projects may increase women's participation in projects and their access to resources, they rarely provide opportunities for women's independent organizations to determine their own development goals and to undertake advocacy work in support of them.

Even as it affirms its commitment to poverty alleviation, participatory development, and governance, the Bank continues to assert staunchly that while its 'mandate is the promotion of sustainable economic and social development', its 'Articles of Agreement explicitly prohibit the institution from interfering in a country's internal political affairs and require it to take only economic considerations into account in its decisions' (World Bank, 1994b: vii). Whatever openings new agenda items may provide for policy advocacy, attention to WID/gender concerns must ultimately be justified on the grounds of cost-effective human capital development and productive efficiency, within the framework of the Bank's 'market optimism'. Perhaps the strongest evidence in support of this point is the way in which the issue of domestic violence has been taken up by the World Bank: the physical and mental abuse of women is described as having 'deleterious effects' on their productivity, causing 'women of reproductive age to lose a significant percentage of healthy days' (World Bank, 1995b:25–6).

Given the constraints within which policy advocates are working, the prospects that the mainstreaming strategy holds out for transforming the mainstream are somewhat limited. Internal advocates are in many ways confined to what has been described in other institutional contexts as avoiding 'worst case scenarios' and damage control (Sawer and Groves, 1994b). Nevertheless, as we have noted earlier, women's NGOs are stepping up their efforts to influence the policies and programmes of the World Bank and appear to have interpreted the new President's commitment to take social concerns more seriously as an opportunity for promoting change from within (DAWN, 1995). In the coming years it will be interesting to trace the work of the External Gender Consultative Group, which is described by the Bank as 'a step forward' in incorporating 'poor women's concerns' into the policy dialogue process.[21]

Compared to the World Bank, the ILO's social justice mandate has provided greater scope for WID/gender advocates to draw attention to women worker's concerns on the grounds of gender justice and equality. This is particularly evident in the context of standard-setting work. There is also evidence that policy advocacy, especially in connection with technical co-operation work, has involved demonstrating strategic linkages with other organizational goals. The ILO's 'basic needs' strategy of the 1970s provided an opportunity structure for greater attention to women's issues. The basic needs approach brought into focus the central role played by women in meeting their families' basic needs and in population growth. It has been argued that the emphasis on 'poor women' provided an opening for making the feminist agenda less threatening to male bureaucrats and programme implementers (Buvinic, 1983:26). In particular, the focus on female-headed households as the 'poorest of the poor' allowed intra-household redistributive questions to be circumvented.

None the less, by framing some of their concerns within the 'de-radicalized' context of basic needs and poverty alleviation, internal policy advocates were able to gain leverage to pursue new research on women. The shortcomings of the earlier focus on women's reproductive work became clearer as new studies by the ILO on the productive work of poor rural women began to appear. This new research involved efforts to assign a monetary equivalent to the bulk of women's labour that falls outside the scope of economic statistics and to capture the extent of women's participation in the 'informal' sector.[22] Because research and operations are largely carried out within the same departments within the ILO, it was possible to feed some of this new research into projects for women, mainly in the form of women's income-generating projects. Like policy advocates at the Bank, those at the ILO describe themselves as basing their case for attention to WID/gender on rigorous analysis and research findings. Internal research and analysis thus become tools in support of policy advocacy.

Against the backdrop of market liberalization in the 1980s and 1990s, internal advocates have also engaged economic efficiency arguments to promote attention to WID/gender. To some extent this can be interpreted as a response to the ILO's moves towards 'market realism' discussed earlier. In recent policy documents there is a mixture of discursive strategies. One pertinent example is a document on the changing role of women in the economy presented to the 1994 Governing Body, which goes quite far in highlighting the efficiency and growth implications of women's employment for households and enterprises, as well as for the national and global economies (ILO, 1994a:9). While the document celebrates the synergies between gender equality and economic growth/efficiency on lines that are somewhat similar to the arguments used by advocates in the World Bank, it does not go so far as to make its case for equality contingent upon such growth synergies. The document also devotes much attention to issues relating to the 'quality of work' and labour standards. In other words, 'market realism' at the ILO has not given way entirely to 'market optimism'.

Internal advocates have recently begun to re-emphasize interlinkages between gender and poverty, concerns that were first placed on the agenda in the context of the 'basic needs' strategy. Compared to the Bank, the ILO's mandate gives internal advocates wider scope in how they frame the linkages between gender and poverty. To some exent, the recommendations for reducing gender-based poverty are very similar to the interventions proposed by the World Bank: access and legal rights to land, credit, human capital investments (education and training), social funds, and extension of social protection (ILO, 1995; King Dejardin, 1996). The ILO's commitment to labour rights as an integral part of development, however, provides openings for raising feminist concerns such as maternity leave, childcare, and equal wages.

Similarly, while both organizations speak of promoting poor women's parti-cipation in development activities, there appear to be qualitative differences in their understanding of what this means in practice. According to one ILO docu-ment, the escape out of poverty requires more than productivity enhancement: instead, the organization of poor women is described as the essential ingredient for empowering them to break out of the circle of vulnerability and marginaliza-tion (ILO, 1995:i). The concern is to help build an enabling environment where-by women have the space to develop their organizational and negotiating capacity to articulate and promote their gender-related interests and concerns, including men's expropriation of women's land, labour, time, and income, and violence against women (ibid.:64). An interesting point that emerges from a reading of ILO policy documents is that in spite of considerable scope for poli-cy advocacy provided by the social justice mandate, there is none the less a reluc-tance to advocate interventions that radically change the configuration of gender relations and the gender division of labour in a given society (King Dejardin, 1996:21). At best, interventions seem aimed at 'initiating positive experiences', particularly through women's self-organization, that could ultimately lead to transformatory changes in existing gender relations (ibid.).

UNDP's co-ordination mandate has to some extent served as a constraint on policy advocacy. WID/gender staff tend to be strong in administrative and mana-gerial skills, but the absence of internally generated research and analysis upon which to base their claims for attention to WID/gender, has somewhat weakened their policy advocacy role (Kardam, 1991:38). Nevertheless, the organizational culture has encouraged internal advocates to promote WID/gender procedures as part of good project management. In fact, among the organizations considered here, the UNDP has gone the furthest towards putting in place gender-responsive bureaucratic procedures. This is not to suggest that other discursive strategies have not been pursued. In the context of structural adjustment programmes in the 1980s and early 1990s, for example, WID/gender staff adopted 'efficiency' argu-ments in their advocacy work. The 1993 WID/gender policy paper (GIDP, 1993) argued that failure to recognize women's economic contribution 'has often resulted in leaving a potential economic contribution untapped' (ibid.:1). Overall, internal advocates have tended to take a rather eclectic approach to

WID/gender. This is evident in GIDP's programming package *Programming through the Lens of Gender* (GIDP, n.d.), which encourages practitioners to choose freely from the range of different policy approaches to women and development (welfare, anti-poverty, efficiency, equality, empowerment). One reason for the all-embracing approach adopted by the GIDP is its wide constituency. Its guidelines on programming must accommodate the variety of needs and approaches of its different executing agencies, from the World Bank to local NGOs, as well as its diverse clients.

It is only since 1995 that internal advocates have begun to tap the opportunity structure provided by UNDP's human development mandate. The *Human Development Report*, UNDP's leading contribution to debates on human development, defines the basic objective of development as 'enlarging people's choices' by expanding their capabilities, such as improved health, knowledge, and skills, and opportunities to use these capabilities for productive purposes, for leisure, or for being active in cultural, social, and political affairs (UNDP, 1995:11). The designation of the advancement of women as one of the four focus themes of UNDP's sustainable development mandate implies a concern to enlarge women's choices. While there would appear to be an easy 'fit' between gender concerns and the human development mandate, this does not guarantee that gender concerns will receive attention. Although GIDP participates in the work of the co-ordination unit for sustainable human development, GIDP's capacity for strong policy guidance on WID/gender continues to be held back by resourcing problems. Nevertheless, tentative efforts are under way to develop the interlinkages between gender and sustainable human development (GIDP, 1995).

A useful tool in the hands of both internal and external advocates—and a symbol of UNDP's commitment to gender concerns—is the 1995 *Human Development Report* (HDR) which is devoted entirely to the issue of gender equality. A large proportion of the 1995 Report focuses on the theme of valuing women's reproductive work and the argument is made that if women's labour was properly valued, women's 'entitlements' to rights (legal, political, and social) and income would change radically (UNDP, 1995:98).[23] Overall, the analysis found in the HDR broadens the explanation of women's poverty, beyond their unequal access to the labour market, towards an understanding of how gender relations, especially those within the household, structure women's disadvantage. While the 1995 HDR implies that gender justice and economic growth are synergistic, there is recognition that 'the free workings of economic and political processes are unlikely to deliver equality of opportunity, because of the prevailing inequities in power structures' (ibid.:7). By introducing such issues into debates over 'human development', opportunities are opened up for policy advocates to adopt the language of gender equality and empowerment and to point to the need for a fundamental restructuring of gender relations.

As regards the issue of 'participatory development', UNDP has also encouraged the participation of women's organizations in the design and implementation of new projects and programmes as a means of improving sustainability. There appears, however, to be a recognition that effective implementation of WID/gender policies is critically dependent on two factors: the existence of active women's constituencies committed to these policies, and strong institutional capacity at the national level to ensure that the goods are delivered. In attempting to fulfil its mandate to build national capacity in WID/gender, the GIDP has thus adopted a two-pronged strategy to strengthen both national gender constituencies and national capacity in gender-analysis. GIDP has interpreted national capacity building to include 'building a gender constituency' capable of playing an effective advocacy role at the national level (UNDP, 1994b:10). For example, it promotes gender training for NGOs as 'an empowering tool for local women' through which they can 'learn to articulate their rights and concerns and to gain access to their share of resources and services' (GIDP, n.d., 4:4). This approach implies that special efforts are needed to strengthen women's negotiating skills if they are to take advantage of opportunities provided by participatory processes and to make their voices heard. In this sense, UNDP's approach to NGOs, like that of the ILO, appears to be moving beyond an understanding of a primarily 'collaborative' relationship with state agencies, in the form of service delivery, towards what Elson refers to as an 'adversarial' role. Elson's point seems to be that real policy reform and resource allocation in women's favour will only come when women have developed leadership and advocacy skills to defend their rights and to put pressure on state and private sector institutions for policy change (1992:18).

Recent 'constituency building' initiatives by UNDP are not unproblematic. It remains unclear whether the problems associated with the inherently political agenda have been fully grasped. Firstly, the assumption seems to be made that development interventions to build or strengthen social organizations will somehow overcome the power relations that marginalize certain social groups in the first place—a situation Cernea (cited in Vivian, 1994:21) describes as the fallacy of 'fiat lux' ('let there be light'). Secondly, according to Moore (1995), civil society organizations need political support in order to obtain the necessary resources and status to have an impact on policy and to do effective work. How far multilateral organizations are willing to go to support 'adversarial' NGOs challenging government behaviour is thus far unclear (Clark, 1995:596). For multilateral organizations, direct support to NGOs also raises a number of other concerns. In some cases, NGOs are being 'created' primarily in response to aid availability. This does little to overcome problems associated with donor-led development strategies that participatory approaches are meant to address, including the issue of sustainability once project funding ends. Nor does it counter allegations that the WID/gender mandate is a 'Western imposition' on developing countries. When involving women's NGOs in participatory processes, multilateral organizations may also make inaccurate assumptions about their representativeness. Women are not a homogeneous group and the diverse range of women's organizations may reflect different interests. The organizations that are invited to become 'partners' in poverty alleviation activities, for example, may not necessarily be those representing poor women, who often find it difficult to engage in advocacy work (Mayoux, Chapter 7; Jain, 1996).

To offset some of the more contentious aspects of 'constituency building', multilateral agencies could strengthen the gender analysis in their own policy documents, and invest more effort in improving country-level work in information generation, and gender policy analysis and formulation, in consultation with a wider network of national civil and research institutions. Such steps would help to initiate genuine policy debate on gender issues. This of course, would require approaches that are more process-oriented, time-consuming, and locally anchored. The decentralization process under way in all three organizations could facilitate such activities. As part of UNDP's 'capacity-building mandate' the GIDP seems to be moving in this direction. It has introduced a series of programmes aimed at both building national-level capacity in gender analysis and generating gender-disaggregated data and statistics. The idea behind these efforts is that improved skill levels at the national level will enable governments and civil society groups to identify their needs better and to develop programmes that are relevant and sustainable, to which they feel committed.

As we have seen above, policy advocates within the World Bank, the ILO, and the UNDP have tended to adopt two mutually reinforcing strategies: they have attempted to legitimize a concern with WID/gender by linking equity issues with other organizational goals, and they have made alliances with like-minded colleagues who appear to be pursuing goals that overlap with their own. Certain organizational mandates have provided greater discursive space for equity concerns, although even policy advocates at the ILO have found it necessary to demonstrate linkages with other organizational goals and to use efficiency-type arguments under some circumstances. Overall, linkages and alliances have been easier to develop in certain areas such as poverty alleviation, participatory development/good governance and, more recently, sustainable human development. Since UNDP adopted its human development mandate, there is evidence that some external advocates have begun to identify UNDP as an important ally in their lobby for more gender-equitable development (Beneria: 1995:1847; Wee and Heyzer, 1995). Opportunities for 'bridge-building' with the women's movement, which have been somewhat limited in the past, could ultimately strengthen the negotiating position of internal advocates. Alliances forged around the human development mandate also hint at ways in which the integration of WID/gender concerns can promote transformative change towards gender-equitable development.

Making connections

This chapter has attempted to illustrate connections between external and internal advocacy for policy reform. Both are indispensible for promoting change from within, although certain institutional mandates, as we have seen, hold out more promise for transformative change. Internal advocates are strategically positioned to channel external pressures and new research into organizations, and to build strategic alliances across the organizational context. Their role has been particularly crucial since the mid-1980s in connection with the adoption of the mainstreaming strategy. As Razavi (Chapter 2) has argued, internal advocates play an essentially conservative role. The examples of policy advocacy provided in this chapter confirm this observation. The institutional constraints within which advocates operate clearly limit the extent to which they openly engage in advocacy around a staunchly feminist agenda. Instead they often serve as mediators, translating feminist concerns and demands into issues and language that have legitimacy within the institutional context.

In doing so, they have been able to promote the establishment of new WID/gender institutions and procedures which serve as a constant reminder to bureaucratic 'resisters' (Staudt, 1990, 1995) of the need to take gender concerns into consideration. While WID/gender procedures, including guidelines and staff training, are important and could be further reinforced by stronger staff incentive structures, such procedures need to be constantly reinforced by solid policy advocacy on the part of skilled and well-located WID/gender staff. There is no 'blueprint' for the mainstreaming of gender concerns and the strategies pursued in each of the organizations have inevitably involved trade-offs. The UNDP's GIDP, for example, is well-placed to have an impact on policy and has introduced a number of procedural innovations; yet in the absence of internally-generated research and analysis upon which to base policy advocacy, its policy guidance role has thus far been limited. Policy advocacy work in both the World Bank and the ILO has been based on solid research and analysis, but the new operational emphasis in both organizations, while well-intentioned, may reduce staff incentives for research and policy work.

However crucial internal advocates may be in turning external demands into concrete institutional action, they can do little without constant pressure from strong national and international women's constituencies. Such external pressures were a considerable force in getting WID/gender issues on the development agenda in the 1970s. In the environment of structural adjustment programmes in the 1980s, the discursive strategies pursued by internal advocates often led to strained relations with the women's movement, and to some extent internal advocates appeared to have lost touch with the mainspring of their efforts. Instead, they looked primarily to top management and supportive donors to help promote gender concerns within their organizations.

As others have pointed out, this distancing from the women's movement is an inevitable part of the need to develop mainstream policy legitimacy (Sawer and Groves, 1994b). It also reflects the particular governance structures of the UNDP, the World Bank, and the ILO which have not encouraged direct contact between these national institutions and international women's organizations, although a more in-depth analysis of the influences which motivated those countries that we have referred to as supportive donors, would likely highlight the important role of national-level women's movements. As Sawer and Groves

(1994b) have suggested, contact with and accountability to the women's movement is important not only as a means to 'reaffirm the values' that inspired the project of fighting for women's concerns from within in the first place, but also to foster strategic alliances in support of shared goals. Since the beginning of the 1990s, the shift by some development organizations to more socially sensitive approaches to development have not only provided internal advocates with greater scope in their discursive strategies, but have opened up greater possibilities for dialogue with external advocates in support of transformative change towards more gender-sensitive development.

Whatever reservations feminists may have regarding engagement with multilateral development institutions, for those pursuing the goal of gender-equitable development these institutions are simply too important to ignore. Policy change is mediated through institutions. Free from the constraints imposed on internal advocates, external advocates are able to provide new research and knowledge that contributes to alternative ways of thinking about and doing development. Internal advocates help to feed new ideas into institutions—albeit often in a diluted form. According to some observers, gender lobbies have already contributed to perceivable shifts in development paradigms from economically inspired thinking towards a greater focus on sustainable development and gender concerns (Köhler, 1995:58). Opportunities for bridge-building activities between external and internal advocates noted above may help to push for further change in this direction in the activities of multilateral organizations.

7

Gender accountability and NGOs: avoiding the black hole[1]

LINDA MAYOUX

In the Platform for Action agreed at the Fourth World Conference on Women in Beijing in 1995, NGOs are seen as a 'driving force for change', mobilizing women's constituencies to challenge gender subordination at the local, national, and international levels (United Nations, 1995). This optimism is partly a result of the large and growing number of women involved in the NGO sector and the increasing influence of women's NGOs in national and international policy debates. Equally important, NGO organizational mandates generally focus on poverty alleviation and empowerment (rather than, for example, economic growth). This has enabled gender lobbies within a number of prominent Southern and Northern NGOs to formulate a common agenda for women's empowerment and for increasing gender accountability within their own organizations. These internal pressures have been paralleled by the introduction of gender policies within many donor agencies leading to increased support for gender initiatives of NGOs.

At the same time, over the past three decades, there has been a rapid increase in the number and size of NGOs, their political visibility, and the resources at their disposal. For some, NGOs are seen as key promoters of an alternative development agenda based on participation and empowerment. From this perspective, NGOs are regarded as representatives of the interests of the poor and disadvantaged, organizing them into a coherent movement for change and providing training grounds for activists (Rahman, 1993). They are also seen as an important source of opposition to the mainstream macro-level, neo-liberal agenda, with the independence, skills and motivation to challenge both the state and international donors (Clark, 1992; Edwards, 1993). There has been a growing involvement by NGOs in representation and (in some situations) formal party politics, as well as in mediation, advocacy, training, and 'civic education', particularly in relatively 'open societies' such as India and the Philippines (Fowler, 1991; Edwards, 1993).

Concurrently, within the neo-liberal agenda, NGOs (along with private-sector organizations) are seen as major providers of services to the poor in the process of 'rolling back the state' and as agents of democratization (Siddharth, 1995; Vivian, 1994; Moore, 1993). Since the early 1990s, the expansion of the NGO sector has been accelerated by increased funding for NGOs from multilateral and bilateral aid agencies, including the World Bank and UK Overseas Development Administration (ODA[2]). Particularly in countries undergoing structural adjustment policies and/or democratization, there has been a dramatic increase in the number of NGOs. There have been official statements of support for NGOs as service providers from a number of Southern governments including Bangladesh, India, Nepal, the Philippines, Ghana, and the Gambia (Edwards and Hulme, 1995). In the North, by 1988 there were over 2000 international NGOs based in Organization for Economic Co-operation and Development (OECD) countries engaged in development-related activities. About 500 were US-based while over 100 were based in Britain (ODI, 1988). In 1989 Northern NGOs transferred US$6.4 billion to the South, which accounted for twelve per cent of Western aid. This was greater than amounts disbursed to the South by the World Bank. An indication of the scale of NGO aid is given by the fact that the budget of the largest British development NGO was US$119 million, more than the aid programme of the government of New Zealand (Barton, 1992). Although some of the UK INGOs saw decreases in their budgets in the mid-1990s, the amount of resources at their disposal is still considerable.

Underlying this promotion of NGOs, there has been a general consensus that NGOs constitute a distinctive 'third sector' with a number of mutually reinforcing comparative advantages *vis-à-vis* other development agencies. These include firstly, their participatory nature, and/or ability to reach the poor and socially marginalized and represent their interests. Secondly, their independence, innovativeness, and efficiency to maximize (particularly for those on the left) impact on the wider development process and/or (particularly for those on the right) use of donor resources. These views are held by many NGOs themselves and underlie donor justifications for switching resources from the state to NGOs (Siddharth, 1995). Even if all NGOs do not possess all these characteristics, they are seen as having greater potential to achieve them than other development agencies (Fowler, 1988; Clark, 1991). As discussed in detail later, there are both internal and external pressures on NGOs to realize these assumed advantages in relation to participation, impact, and efficiency.

These advantages also have potentially positive gender implications, making NGOs potentially more responsive to women's needs, more likely to challenge underlying gender inequalities, and/or more flexible and efficient in achieving these aims than other development agencies. Current strategies by NGOs for increasing gender accountability are attempting to improve performance on all three counts. The triple combination of pressure from the gender lobby within NGOs themselves, the increasing prominence of NGOs as actors on the development scene, and their potential comparative advantages offers important opportunities for making the development agenda more accountable to women.

This chapter looks at both the challenges facing NGOs which are committed to women's empowerment, and the wider implications for donors. The paper does not claim to be a comprehensive overview. The NGO sector is large, diverse and changing rapidly. Typologies proliferate, and although, as discussed later, some general differences can be outlined between grassroots membership organizations (GROs), grassroots support organizations (GSOs) and international non-governmental organizations (INGOs), each organization is in many ways unique.[3] Within NGOs the quality of project and programme information is notoriously patchy (Edwards and Hulme, 1995; Riddell and Robinson, 1995). Much of this existing information is gender-blind. Where gender has been considered, information is mainly confined to numbers of women involved and numbers of organizations and activities.

This chapter is based on interview material, unpublished internal documents, and secondary literature, rather than commissioned focused research.[4] It concentrates on nine NGOs with an explicit commitment to women's empowerment: two Indian NGOs (SEWA and WWF), the Grameen Bank in Bangladesh, and six UK NGOs (Oxfam, ActionAid, Womankind, ACORD, Christian Aid and One World Action). Some of these organizations have developed strategies to address the tensions outlined in the paper. The problems described are, however, still very much current as highlighted in a recent pilot project by the author and a steering committee of UK NGOs and their Southern partners on women's empowerment and NGO micro-finance programmes (Mayoux, 1997).

What is gender accountability? Issues and strategies

Increasing accountability is inherently problematic for all development agencies in most areas of policy. Accountability is a complex and abstract concept. It is generally interpreted as the means by which individuals and organizations report to a recognized authority, or authorities, and are held responsible for their actions. But it also goes beyond narrow definitions of economic efficiency and accountancy or short-term functional accountability (accounting for resources, their use and immediate impacts) to include strategic accountability. For NGOs this means accounting for the impacts that their actions have on those of other organizations and the wider environment (Avina, 1993). In a recent formulation, effective accountability has been seen as requiring: firstly, a statement of goals; secondly, transparency of decision-making and relationships; and thirdly, honest reporting of what resources have been used (probity) and what has been achieved (performance). These conditions are underpinned by an appraisal process in which overseeing authority(ies) judge whether results are satisfactory, and by concrete mechanisms for holding to account (i.e. rewarding or penalizing) those responsible for performance (Edwards and Hulme, 1995).

Increasing gender accountability in NGOs is particularly contentious because the complexity of gender subordination exacerbates the problems inherent in any process touching on greater accountability. Although there is some degree of consensus on the elements of gender policy among gender lobbies within NGOs and donor agencies, these lobbies are generally in a weak position. At all levels there are considerable pressures to argue for gender policy in instrumentalist terms and, as discussed later, this has important consequences for the degree to which NGOs are able to realize their assumed 'comparative advantages'.

174

Gender subordination is characterized by its many interrelated dimensions, and the various ways in which gender interacts with other dimensions of inequality and disadvantage. It is all-pervasive, ranging from the level of the individual to households and communities, and local, national, and international development agencies. This exacerbates problems surrounding the establishment of goals and priorities, and raises questions about the linkages between the formulation, implementation, and evaluation of gender policy and the organization of development agencies themselves, particularly the employment of gender-aware staff.

Ensuring grassroots accountability for women cannot be assumed to be any less problematic than for men. Firstly, individual women, like individual men, have a range of needs and interests, some of which may either be conflicting or mutually reinforce each other in a vicious cycle of subordination. For women, particularly poor women, the wide range of needs includes increased access to income, reproductive health, childcare, and infrastructure provision which may be distinct from those of men. These needs are inextricably linked to underlying and mutually reinforcing gender inequalities in rights and responsibilities relating to resources, power, and people. The inequalities are often enshrined in ideological, religious, and cultural systems which make women's rights dependent on particular relationships with men, support male authority over women, and condone gender violence in support of men's rights. The establishment of goals and priorities is therefore extremely difficult.

Secondly, gender inequality means that women have generally had less exposure than men to alternative ways of acting and thinking. Women's own aspirations and strategies for change (like those of men) must be seen in the context of power relations which influence what is seen as desirable and/or possible. Most cultures have stereotypes of 'ideal' women and feminine behaviour, and many women have themselves internalized ideas of appropriate types of behaviour towards other men and women, including those which symbolize their own inferiority and enforce restrictions on their movements outside the home. Consequently, views expressed by women in initial consultative meetings with development agencies may not be as representative of their 'interests' as those expressed after women have had time to reflect or think, or once they have a greater awareness of possible options.

Moreover, for some women, the existing gender balance of rights and responsibilities, although unequal, offers a measure of security and emotional satisfaction. In situations where women have very few choices and little autonomy or direct access to resources for survival, their immediate interests may lie more in manipulating existing inequalities and stereotypes to their advantage than in openly challenging them (Moore, 1986; Thorbek, 1995). Where they are pursuing conscious strategies for change, these may rely on secrecy and subterfuge and may be jeopardized by public recognition (Mayoux and Anand, 1995). At the same time, the activities in which it is easiest for women to participate within existing structures of inequality (such as income-generation, mother and child healthcare) are unlikely to be sustainable without addressing more contentious underlying inequalities (such as rights over resources, mobility outside the home, or rights over reproduction). This is so whether or not overcoming these inequalities is seen as a priority or a possibility by the women involved.

Thirdly, it cannot be assumed that the views expressed by those women who have access to NGO decision-making processes are necessarily representative of other women, particularly the most disadvantaged. There are significant differences between women from different classes, of different ages and marital status, and from different cultures in all aspects of gender subordination. Certain categories of women, such as older women, mothers-in-law, first wives, and richer women, are often anxious to preserve their privileges within the system rather than challenge it, leading in some cultures to intense conflicts between women. Indeed, the continuance of structural gender inequality is often enforced by female networks of social control.

Development agencies are thus inevitably involved in making moral and political judgments. Even the apparently 'neutral' aim of 'increasing women's choices' inevitably begs the questions: *which choices?, whose choices?, how should these be prioritized? by whom?* Which views and whose views prevail is likely to be inextricably related to the organization of the decision-making process itself. Although it cannot be assumed that women NGO staff are necessarily gender-aware and/or represent the views of grassroots women, within many cultures the norms of gender propriety make it far more likely that women will be willing or able to express their views to female staff as opposed to male staff. There are also linkages between women's employment patterns within organizations and the degree of visibility of gender as an issue, the types of women's programmes adopted, and levels of resources allocated.[5] Increasing accountability to grassroots women is, therefore, likely to be highly dependent on levels of employment of women and their gender awareness and authority within decision-making structures.

Gender subordination affects not only women programme participants, however, but also staff within development agencies, as in other organizations. Although it is important to avoid stereotypes, many women are likely to have different career patterns and different employment needs because of their childbearing role, discrimination within their own households, and lack of state welfare provisions for education, health, and particularly childcare (Adler and Izraeli 1994). This is no less true of women within NGOs than other organizations. Gender accountability, therefore, has important implications for the staffing and organization of NGOs in ways which accountability in other areas of NGO activity may not.

NGOs and gender: Current strategies

Large and growing numbers of women are involved in the NGO sector. Many NGOs have been set up by women. Some NGOs have become increasingly organized around a common agenda concerned with women's empowerment (Sen and Grown, 1985) and/or increasing gender accountability within their own organizations. There are a growing number of large participatory women-only grassroots organizations and women's networks and movements (Vargas, 1992; Calman, 1992) nationally and internationally.[6] There are also an increasing number of influential women-only GSOs and INGOs, such as SEWA and the Working Women's Forum (WWF) in India, and Womankind, based in the UK, as well as mixed-sex GSOs such as the Grameen Bank in Bangladesh. In the North, a number of prominent INGOs have introduced their own organizational gender policy and guidelines for projects, and their own organizational structure. These include ACORD, Action Aid, Christian Aid, One World Action, and Oxfam. Further, in the early 1990s, preparation for the Beijing NGO Forum provided an important focus for mobilization both within and between these and other NGOs.

Common elements of such policies for women's empowerment and increased gender accountability are summarized in Box 1, in accordance with the practice and proposals for change in SEWA, WWF, the UK INGOs studied, and their Southern partners. In addition to formal statements of goals and aims in relation to gender, these proposals are designed to increase gender accountability through a combination of wider grassroots participation, greater impact on overcoming underlying inequalities and increased programme effectiveness. Although emphasis has varied, all the NGOs studied by the author were attempting in some way to combine the various strategies.

Some mixed-sex GSOs, such as the Grameen Bank, have argued that targeting and organizing poor women is a viable and efficient strategy for poverty alleviation. The Grameen Bank is a large GSO with over 14 000 staff, which focused on credit delivery to nearly two million beneficiaries in 1994. Over 90 per cent of its credit beneficiaries are women. Like SEWA and WWF, it has attempted to increase grassroots participation in decision-making, while growing rapidly and fulfilling donor demands for efficiency. All three GSOs have also made attempts to train and facilitate the employment of female staff (Holcombe, 1995).

SEWA and WWF provide good illustrations of efforts to increase the impact on the macro-level agenda. They are GSOs employing mainly women staff which have pioneered methods for mobilizing women informal sector workers and represent their interests at the national and international level. SEWA, set up in 1972, had about 40 000 members in 1992 (Rose, 1993). WWF, established in 1978, also focuses on credit provision and includes health and family welfare services and training and advocacy programmes; by 1995 it was said to have over 200 000 members (Ramesh, 1995). Its organizational leadership takes a strong stance against dowry, caste discrimination, and worker exploitation and has been influential in macro-level debates on women informal sector workers.

The INGOs in the UK all have a stated commitment to participatory development, influencing the macro-level agenda, and increasing their effectiveness as agents of development. They also all have an explicit commitment to gender equity enshrined in their organizational mandates. Womankind is a specifically

177

BOX 1: Gender accountability and NGOs: current strategies

Increasing grassroots participation

o support for women in participatory organizations, both women-only and
  mixed-sex organizations, particularly those addressing underlying gender inequalities
o participatory gender needs assessment and research
o participatory decision-making structures linking grassroots organizations
  with support organizations

Increasing impact on the macro-level agenda

o advocacy and lobbying to change macro-level policies, focusing particularly on women's human rights, on the basis of the 1979 United Nations
  Convention on the Elimination of all Forms of Discrimination against
  Women, to secure international agreement on the aims of gender policy
o acting as intermediaries to channel resources from governments and
  international agencies to the grassroots and influence policies in their
  favour
o federation and networking between women's organizations to increase
  the strength of the women's movement

Increasing programme effectiveness

o introduction of criteria for monitoring and evaluation
o introduction of gender guidelines for all programmes and projects covering project baseline data, design, and impact. Failure to comply with gender guidelines should lead to withdrawal of funding by donors

Organizational change within NGOs

o combining focal gender units/staff with gender mainstreaming, including
  sanctions and rewards for performance
o gender training at all levels for women and men and gender awareness as
  mandatory part of recruitment and promotion
o equal opportunities policies, including childcare facilities, changes in
  recruitment, and promotion practices and organizational culture

Sources: MacDonald, 1994; Hale *et al.*, 1993; Hadjipateras, 1995; Barrig
and Wehkamp, 1995; GOOD, 1992; Oxfam Gender Team, 1994.

woman-focused INGO channelling funds to projects for women's empowerment overseas. In Action Aid and One World Action promotion of gender issues relies on a combination of the activities of a small number of highly motivated women and the general levels of gender awareness of all staff. Other INGOs have more formal structures. Christian Aid, Oxfam, and ACORD all have special gender staff or gender units, institutional gender policies, formalized gender guidelines, and equal opportunities policies with influential networks to monitor gender issues within the organization.

To some extent NGO initiatives have been parallelled by an increasing focus on gender in many government and donor agencies. A certain degree of convergence in language and approach to gender issues can also be found in their official pronouncements. Parallelling debates elsewhere, a number of analytical distinctions are commonly made between 'women/gender'[7] and 'practical needs/strategic interests'.[8] These distinctions are particularly prominent in some recent INGO training manuals, handbooks, and workshop proceedings (Williams et al., 1994; Eade and Williams, 1995; MacDonald, 1994). It is stressed that gender programmes must address underlying inequalities and look not only at women but also at gender relations. This is echoed in the gender guidelines of some donor agencies (e.g. ODA, n.d.a). References to women's 'empowerment' are as prominent in recent publications of donors such as the World Bank and ODA (UK) as in those of NGOs.

At the same time there has been growing donor pressure on NGOs to capitalize on their assumed comparative advantages of participation, impact, and efficiency in relation to gender. Recent donor policy initiatives and proposals include attention to the development of participatory women's self-help organizations and the eliciting of women's local knowledge, especially in relation to service delivery (Narayan and Srinivasan, 1994; ODA, n.d.a; Robinson and Thin, 1993). Particular interest has also been shown in increasing the resources available to a number of large GSOs with a stated commitment to gender (including SEWA, WWF, and the Grameen Bank) and supporting NGOs as intermediaries to make governments more responsive to women's needs for services (Tendler 1989; Berger and Buvinic 1989). Further, many donors have introduced gender guidelines for all programmes and projects, at both the micro and macro-level (e.g. ODA, n.d.a), in an attempt to increase programme effectiveness.

Nevertheless, despite the apparent consensus between gender lobbies at the grassroots, in NGOs and donor agencies, gender policy continues to be a highly contentious issue. At the grassroots, women's 'interests' are as diverse and complex as those of men for the reasons outlined above. Within NGOs, despite the developments described above, gender lobbies are undeniably still in a very weak position.[9] This weakness means that implementation of any gender policy formulated by these gender lobbies within NGOs is often subject to the competition of demands from other interest groups at the grassroots and within NGOs and donor agencies. At all levels this has led to considerable pressures to promote gender in instrumentalist terms (i.e. stressing synergy with other development aims, such as poverty alleviation, environment, child welfare, and family planning) rather than in its own right (Jackson, 1996). Within projects and programmes, the focus on gender often has to be justified in terms of benefits to women's families and communities. Within NGOs themselves such arguments are common in policy statements and used to persuade the 'unconverted'. Instrumentalism is particularly prevalent in the context of donor emphasis on cost-effectiveness and NGO reliance on public 'charitable' donations. As convincingly argued (particularly by Jackson, 1993, 1996), the reliance on instrumentalism, although useful in positions of weakness, presents inherent problems where there are conflicts between gender policy and other issues.

NGO comparative advantages? gender dimensions

The so-called comparative advantages of participation, impact, and efficiency of NGOs all have the possibility of increasing gender accountability, thus making NGOs potentially more responsive to women's needs, more likely to challenge underlying gender inequalities, and/or more flexible and efficient in achieving these aims than other development agencies. The experience of the NGOs discussed here and in the extensive literature, however, indicates that each of these strategies also has possible negative implications for women. Participation, impact, and efficiency are all highly contested concepts, interpreted in different ways by different stakeholders and with organizational as well as policy implications. Although potentially mutually reinforcing, the 'advantages' are often experienced as 'competing imperatives'[10] between strategies to increase grassroots participation, impact on underlying inequalities, and achieve programme efficiency. The nature of gender subordination further exacerbates many of these ambiguities, tensions, and conflicts even for NGOs committed to women's empowerment. Where such commitment does not exist, these competing imperatives have even more ambiguous implications for gender accountability.

Gender, power and the politics of participation: Some questions about grassroots accountability

Increasing women's participation, particularly at the grassroots, is necessary for forming acceptable and achievable goals, increasing the transparency of the decision-making process, and ensuring the accurate and honest reporting of programme impacts on women. NGO gender lobbies have proposed and pioneered a range of strategies for increasing women's participation in the development process, including particularly: promoting women's participatory groups, increasing their participation in mixed-sex groups, using participatory research methods and planning, and increasing the representation of grassroots women in NGO decision-making. In NGO policy statements, increasing women's participation in programmes is generally seen as desirable in itself and an integral component of empowerment. Most current NGO literature on participatory development is very careful to make clear in their use of language that reference is to women as well as to men. In many cases women are named as a principal target group for participatory projects. A growing number of manuals exist on methods of promoting women's participatory groups and eliciting women's technological knowledge.[11] The contribution of NGO participatory initiatives for women to gender accountability cannot, however, be assumed. The experience of the NGOs studied and research by the author and others on GROs and GSOs indicate that much depends on what is meant by 'participation', who is participating, who is making the decisions, and in whose interests they are being made.

Women, gender inequality and participation: inherent dilemmas?

Even where there is an explicit prioritizing of gender issues, increasing women's participation may intensify rather than resolve tensions and conflicts surrounding the goals of gender policy. The complex nature of gender subordination means that increasing women's participation may exacerbate rather than reconcile contradictions in the position of individual women. Attempts to increase women's participation in decision-making may increase tensions between women themselves and between women and development agencies.

Further, increasing women's participation does not necessarily lead to an explicit and coherent strategy for change for all women involved. For many women, gender inequalities in access to productive resources, the burden of unpaid work, and lack of both mobility and autonomy continue to limit their possibilities for participatory involvement. Moreover, increasing women's participation cannot be assumed to be unambiguously beneficial or 'efficient' for the women concerned. Greater participation generally requires an increased commitment of time and resources and the development of participatory decision-making skills. Within women's groups, attempts to give all women control over all areas of decision-making may lead to inactivity and stagnation (Barrig and Wehkamp, 1995). Furthermore, the high costs of participation and low levels of immediate and tangible benefits mean that even poverty-targeted programmes often by-pass poor women, and particularly the poorest—many groups are by default set up by better-off women and/or dominated by them (Mayoux, 1995a; White, 1995).

In many NGOs there is a bias towards non-threatening mobilization of women's unpaid labour for family or community benefit (Barrig and Wehkamp, 1995; Hadjipateras, 1996; internal UK INGO project reports). In these cases women's participation is limited to special women's programmes in 'feminine' areas of activity, particularly income-generation programmes, mother and child health, and particular types of infrastructure development: housing, drinking water, and fuel production. These participatory programmes have often yielded negligible benefits to women and/or made some aspects of their lives more difficult, as they require women to contribute time, skills, and resources as unpaid or low-paid workers. Even women's income-generation groups frequently generate very little income and often significantly increase women's workload without increasing their access to resources (Piza-Lopez and March, 1990; Hadjipateras, 1996). But there has often been little attempt to involve women outside these activities.

Increasing women's participation may also threaten the sustainability of women's programmes. Some GSOs (including SEWA, WWF, and the Grameen Bank) have attempted to develop participatory forms of decision-making where grassroots groups are linked to support agencies, so that they control or at least have a say in policy design, implementation, and evaluation. Structures for involving grassroots women in decision-making have, however, proved problematic. For example, in production co-operatives, those elected to power may not be the ones with the greatest commercial expertise, and decisions made may threaten incomes (Mayoux, 1995a). In the case of SEWA, success in increasing the ability of women in production co-operatives to articulate and defend their interests led to tensions between women members and women trainers and managers, increased demands on SEWA, and unrealistic wage claims. These requests further undermined the sustainability of already commercially threatened co-operatives (Westwood, 1991; Rose, 1993).

Participatory development for women (as for men) must, therefore, be seen as an interactive process (Schrijvers, 1995) rather than a neutral response to 'grassroots spontaneity' or top-down imposition of particular participatory structures to address 'practical' or 'strategic' needs identified from outside. In this approach, no automatic benefits to women from participation *per se* are taken for granted but the potential costs and benefits of a range of types of collective activity are assessed, together with the women concerned. Given the inevitable position of power and authority of development agencies (even NGO gender lobbies) *vis-à-vis* women who are poor and disadvantaged, in many contexts this will require a delicate balancing of grassroots demands with considerations of feasibility and sustainability.

Beyond naivety: the politics of participatory development

Although participatory development is promoted by donors in terms of 'empowerment', their main implicit, if not explicit, interest is often ways in which resources, skills, and commitment of local people (both men and women) can be mobilized to increase the efficiency of development programmes and projects. It has been assumed that it is sufficient to change formal structures and entry requirements for women to be able to decide their own priorities and pressure for change. Findings suggest that increasing support for NGOs *per se*, however, will not necessarily increase the representation of women's interests within the development process. Evidence within INGOs, internal project reports, and the author's own research have shown that lack of intervention on gender is often justified in terms of 'cultural sensitivity', even where equally culturally alien

182

policies are being promoted in areas of, for example, class, ethnicity, and environment.[12]

The widespread assumption that NGOs are more participatory than other organizations is based partly on the frequent inclusion of large numbers of small local GROs within the definition of NGOs and the fact that support for and/or formation of participatory GROs has been one of the main aims of GSO and INGO programmes. The extensive literature on grassroots organizations and co-operative movements indicates, however, that membership organizations are frequently dominated by interested élites (Carroll, 1992). Within these organizations, men are not necessarily opposed to ideals of gender equality. Many mixed-sex participatory organizations and co-operatives, however, explicitly or implicitly exclude most women through membership requirements and/or because of the particular activities and work patterns around which they are organized (Mayoux, 1988, 1993; One World Action, 1993; Hajipateras, 1995). Moreover, male support for female participation has often been conditional on suppression of women's own demands, and the forms and aims of women's participation are frequently ultimately determined by male priorities, even where the women themselves are aware of gender inequalities and injustice (Fox, 1992; Mayoux, 1988, 1993). In some cases men have actively and violently opposed women's involvement in any type of activity which goes against their interests, either at household or community level (Andreas, 1985). Consequently, reinforcing men's participatory groups and/or their representation in organizational decision-making may also strengthen any existing opposition to gender empowerment.

In many contexts, challenging gender inequality depends on a focused strategy to question gender subordination by the NGO and/or specific space for such questioning as an integral part of training (Hadjipateras, 1995; GOOD, 1992; Blaker and Reichmann, 1994). More recently, some NGOs have been looking at broader approaches to women's participation, particularly ways of adapting participatory research methods to gender analysis. In the NGOs studied, this has included participatory training and project design, together with gender needs analysis. Internal INGO reports suggest that these initiatives have a much higher potential for success because of their greater acceptability to women themselves, and their greater realism in the context of the constraints they face. Nevertheless, gender needs assessments do not necessarily substantially challenge gender roles and the types of activities suggested by women continue to be traditionally 'female' ones (Bruggeman, 1993).

Some NGOs (including Oxfam, Action Aid, and ACORD) have been at the forefront of the development of participatory research techniques in many areas of policy (Chambers, 1994; Rahman, 1993), but despite the potential of participatory research to bring about change, it appears that this may not necessarily happen. In some cases, despite problems recruiting women researchers, the inclusion of skilled gender analysts has enabled full integration of gender issues within participatory research programmes

(Johnson and Mayoux, 1995). Particularly where gender needs assessment is only one of a more general participatory rural appraisal exercise, however, and for the reasons outlined above, women are often unable to publicly express their needs and interests (Mosse, 1994). And where gender is included as only one 'axis of difference', evidence suggests that gender is often addressed very superficially.[13]

Participatory research has little meaning unless there are participatory structures for decision-making within which the findings can be implemented. In GSOs and INGOs, despite their stated values and principles, evidence suggests that grassroots participation is generally limited to the formation of participatory groups at the local level in specific projects determined from outside. Grassroots constituencies and field staff have little influence over decision-making and debate at other levels of the organization (Lane, 1995; Griffith, 1987), and given the lack of participation by women in many GROs and the weakness of gender lobbies discussed above, women are even less likely to be represented than men. The geographical and social distance between the grassroots and the centres of decision-making is particularly great for INGOs, making grassroots participation particularly weak. Here the main moves towards increasing participation have been regional decentralization to partner NGOs or INGO offices overseas; in Oxfam, ACORD and Christian Aid the process of organizational decentralization has slowed the implementation of gender policy (GOOD, 1992; Hadjipateras, 1995; Oxfam Gender Team, 1994).

Increasing women's participation is thus inevitably a complex process involving potential conflicts of interest between women, between women and men, and between women and development agencies. The many interlinked and mutually reinforcing dimensions of gender subordination affect the forms which women's participation takes, the degree to which they are able to benefit, and the sustainability of many women's participatory programmes. Increasing women's participation in ways which benefit them will require considerable commitment of resources and a process of far-reaching organizational transformation. It will require the introduction of radically new procedures for decision-making at all levels, which will not only allow women to participate and to challenge gender inequality, but also to provide participatory structures of decision-making within which findings can be implemented.

Increasing impact: empowerment or exclusion?

Increasing gender accountability requires NGOs to work towards the provision of an enabling environment within which women have the space and power to articulate and negotiate their interests. This requires them to 'scale up' their impact on underlying gender inequalities, not only at the local level, but also at the national and international levels. The organizations studied have attempted to address some of the inherent limitations of local-level participatory projects through a range of strategies, including:

184

○ advocacy and lobbying of national and international development agencies on specific gender issues and/or the wider development agenda;

○ acting as intermediaries for government agencies, to channel resources from state programmes to grassroots women and/or to influence government programmes themselves; and

○ organizational growth through expansion of the organization itself and/or federating and networking with other like-minded NGOs.

Towards empowerment? Some questions about increasing impact

Some NGOs have been extremely successful in supporting or mobilizing large numbers of women with regard to specific demands on a range of issues, including changes in legislation on property rights, domestic violence, and pornography, particularly at the local level. At the international level, coalitions of women's organizations have been very influential in raising women's concerns in debates about the environment (Braidotti *et al.*, 1994), human rights, and population control (Corrêa and Reichmann, 1994), as well as at the 1995 Social Summit. Within the UK, the gender lobbies of the NGOs studied, particularly Oxfam and One World Action, have been very vocal internationally in urging special attention to the rights and interests of women.

Some organizations, particularly smaller ones, have concentrated on advocacy and lobbying or acting as intermediaries, allied to other organizations where possible for specific ends. Others, particularly large organizations such as the GSOs and INGOs discussed here, often employ all three strategies outlined above. These strategies for scaling up make considerable demands on organizational skills, time, resources and mobility, however. Promoting gender issues requires not only gender awareness but also skills in gender analysis and advocacy. Even more than at the local level, attempts to change inequalities at the macro-level requires contacts, knowledge of how institutional hierarchies work, and/or, in many contexts, considerable support from experienced gender advocates.

The increasing emphasis on gender advocacy and lobbying has also led to tensions within women's organizations and for gender lobbies within mixed-sex organizations. Within SEWA, for example, there is some disquiet amongst grassroots women members about the amount of time and organizational resources spent by the leadership on issues which are seen as being of no direct and immediate benefit to them (Rose, 1993). There are also tensions between urban middle class women and poor women within Southern NGOs over priorities and the appropriate balance between campaigning and practical assistance (Blaker and Reichmann, 1994; Vargas, 1992). Particularly among Northern INGOs, there are frequent questions about the relevance of the issues raised for poor women. Within ACORD, for example, attempts are being made to increase its advocacy role, but this was reportedly not supported by many women programme participants, who wanted practical interventions such as tube-wells.

185

Within INGOs, tensions are further heightened by perceived North/South divides on 'feminism'. Attempts have been made in Oxfam and Christian Aid to overcome this through networking and arranging visits from women in the South. Common agendas for action, focusing on women's human rights, have been agreed, and are now being promoted throughout the organization and in programmes in the South. The intervening dialogues highlighted, however, the dangers of assuming a common agenda or underestimating the barriers to be overcome (GOOD, 1992; de Wit, 1995).

Increasing impact: the dangers of exclusion

The gender dimensions of 'mainstream' strategies for scaling up have received little attention from NGOs, donors, or researchers.[14] Where gender is not explicitly prioritized, evidence suggests that strategies for scaling up are likely to bypass women, have negligible impact, or in some cases have adverse consequences for women. Within many NGOs, moves towards advocacy and lobbying have not included attention to gender. In many Indian GSOs lobbying has been conducted on specific issues, including local water supplies, housing, and land rights without any particular focus on women (ActionAid India, 1993; Griffith, 1987; Viswanath, 1991). A survey of advocacy by NGOs in Zimbabwe showed that gender issues were seldom raised (Moyo, 1991). In UK INGOs, notably Oxfam and One World Action, attempts are being made to integrate gender into lobbying and advocacy on macro-economic issues and human rights. This is taking place because skilled and experienced gender lobbyists are involved in their lobbying and advocacy units. In other organizations, however, even where women are prominent in advocacy units, they were not necessarily promoting gender issues. Advocacy staff (men and women) said they did not have the necessary skills and familiarity with gender issues to fully integrate them into advocacy campaigns. In some organizations there was also a continuing perception that gender was less important than poverty (internal UK INGO reports; Piza-Lopez and Wallace, 1994).

NGOs, which act as intermediaries for government agencies, are potentially able to increase women's ability to access state programmes and raise gender issues within them. SEWA and WWF have been relatively successful at this, having been a major force in making the Indian government credit programmes more responsive to women. In many societies, however, norms of social propriety and/or fear of discrimination against women often lead even women's organizations to relegate relations with government or distant donor agencies to men, as has been the case with a number of women's organizations and co-operatives in West Bengal (Mayoux, 1986). Where women are involved they are likely to be more professional and articulate women, and poor women are thus by-passed. Even for SEWA and WWF, most of the intermediary negotiations are of necessity conducted by skilled professional (and hence middle or upper class) women.

Within the neo-liberal agenda promoted by many international donors the main concern has been to enhance the role of NGOs as service contractors in the context of structural adjustment. Donors have increasingly urged NGO collaboration with state agencies to fill 'niches' in the gaps left by 'rolling back the state', or for NGOs to contribute their specific perceived expertise in participatory methods, training, etc. to state development programmes. This is seen as having the further advantage of increasing the resources available to NGOs at no cost to donors. In view of the well-documented gender bias of most government programmes, however, there are serious dangers of co-optation and dilution of women's demands in the attempt to gain government support for non-'women-specific' programmes. Moreover, where women's issues are being pursued, these are likely to be determined by the priorities of governments, and not necessarily by the women themselves.

The exclusion of women may be further reinforced by organizational growth. Despite its obvious potential for reaching more women and increasing solidarity, organizational growth is often accompanied by increasing bureaucratization, with potential adverse effects on both participation and efficiency (Korten, 1990). The potential benefits to women depend very much on the type of activities and the ways in which growth is managed.

In mixed-sex organizations, UK INGO project reports suggest that organizational growth often leads to the relegation of women to local affairs and organizations, leaving the major decision-making processes to men. In addition, the increasing size of organizations has often been coupled with the growing reliance on statistical measures of impact (Goetz and Sen Gupta, 1994). Particularly where large amounts of funding are being disbursed and the overriding concern of donors is cost efficiency, there are dangers that organizational growth will lead to a serious dilution of impact on women and on gender inequality. The expansion of some large and well-funded organizations in particular areas may lead to the dropping out of some smaller, more locally based organizations which have been less generously supported by donors. This has been evident in Bangladesh, where the expansion of Grameen Bank and BRAC, targeting small-scale credit to women's groups, has in some villages led to the demise of smaller groups, some of which had a much more specific empowerment and awareness-raising role (Ebdon, 1994; Arn and Lily, 1992).

Some questions about effectiveness

Alongside increasing grassroots participation and impact on underlying inequalities, there has also been growing emphasis on programme effectiveness. This again has potentially positive implications for gender accountability. Women frequently demand more tangible benefits from NGO programmes and, as noted above, their participation in NGO programmes is often dependent on obtaining these benefits. Within many NGOs there has been growing unease about the lack of critical evaluation of the aims and impacts of many women's programmes.

Pressure has also come from donors. Particularly since the beginning of the 1990s, the enhanced role and greater funding for NGOs has been accompanied by greater questioning of their effectiveness in the use of donor resources and in achieving the aims stated in their own policy documents and/or identified by their grassroots constituencies. The increasingly stringent efficiency stipulations imposed by donors have often included gender guidelines and checklists (for example ODA, n.d.a,b).

These measures could potentially provide the information necessary for an organizational learning process of how resources can be used to most benefit women and for an appraisal process which rewards good gender practice and discourages bad performance. As with participation, however, much depends on definitions, who is doing the defining, and in whose interests.

What is effectiveness? Some questions about definitions

Even where the predominant concern is women's empowerment, attempts to improve effectiveness face a number of dilemmas. Recent guidelines for monitoring and evaluation by both NGOs and some donors have stressed the importance of beneficiary participation and the need to move from simplistic rigid 'blueprints' to a 'process' approach where evaluation is an ongoing process integrated into organizational learning and change (Eade and Williams, 1995; ODA, n.d.b; Robinson and Thin, 1993). Nevertheless, even this more flexible and participative approach is still dependent on a number of assumptions. Firstly, that consensus about the criteria for assessment can be reached; as discussed above, increasing participation, although necessary, may make this a lengthy and contentious process. Secondly, that inputs and outcomes can be accurately assessed in such a way as to distinguish between different (and often competing) aims and strategies to judge whether the objectives have been achieved. Thirdly, that such assessments and judgements can be placed within a limited (albeit extendable) time frame. These assumptions are all problematic.

The collecting of any information about women's position presents well-documented problems. The amount and value of women's work both in production and reproduction are difficult to quantify. Women's paid work is likely to be under-evaluated because of women's low status and lack of power, and evaluating women's non-market contributions presents even more problems. Even greater difficulties are encountered with assessment of change in underlying gender inequalities in power, status, and cultural values. Although indicators can be devised, their interpretation may be difficult unless backed by long-term, in-depth, and costly research. These problems are not necessarily resolved by participatory methods (Johnson and Mayoux, 1995). Quantification and measurement are particularly troublesome when measuring the quality of participation and impact of advocacy and lobbying. The emphasis on quantification consequently leads to an inherent bias towards certain types of projects, particularly those giving fast, tangible benefits to large numbers of people.

The price of efficiency? Some questions about donor interests

Even for NGOs with a stated commitment to women's empowerment, there are questions about how success is being measured and in whose interests. For example, the credit programmes of SEWA, WWF, and Grameen Bank have been hailed as particular successes both in terms of poverty targeting and loan repayment for donors. The emphasis on efficiency benefits of women's programmes is particularly prominent in statements by large donors such as the World Bank (Jackson, 1996) and underlies much of their recent enthusiasm for women's participatory projects. Women's very 'efficiency' in loan recovery may, however, be more in the interest of donors than of the women themselves. The presumed efficiency contributions of women are often reliant on undervaluing their non-market contribution. This means that many programmes attempt to increase efficiency for donors by increasing women's unpaid contribution (in terms of skills and labour time).

Even in women-only credit programmes, group loan systems may create problems and tensions. Noponen's study of WWF (1990) found that the loan groups often in fact disguised higher levels of default and shifted the burden of repayment on to group leaders, who were themselves not necessarily in a good position to bear the loan. Moreover, the overriding emphasis on repayment rates disadvantaged very poor women. In mixed-sex programmes, such as those of the Grameen Bank, a significant proportion of women's loans was invested directly by their male relatives, with women borrowers bearing the liability of repayment although lacking meaningful control over their investment activities. The costs of loan repayment had thus been merely shifted from the development agencies on to women (Goetz and Sen Gupta, 1994).

The multidimensional nature of gender subordination means that many programmes may have conflicting impacts on women. Different women (participants and NGO staff) may have differing priorities. Questions, therefore, arise about how different programme aims and achievements are to be compared, and who should decide priorities. As discussed earlier, within women's income-generation programmes, attempts to address easily quantifiable 'practical' needs are likely to be seriously constrained by underlying and less tractable 'strategic' inequalities. There is overwhelming evidence that women's access to healthcare and education is similarly constrained by underlying aspects of gender subordination, such as lack of autonomy, the unequal division of reproductive/non-market labour, restrictions on female mobility, and gender violence. Prioritizing easily quantifiable 'practical' strategies may therefore risk undermining the sustainability of women's programmes. It may also miss opportunities to increase the benefits to women.

Attempts to introduce gender guidelines as part of wider moves to increase efficiency and effectiveness within mainstream programmes are likely to be particularly problematic. The effect of the shift from 'blueprint' to 'process' is to considerably increase the complexity and sophistication of the parameters used and to introduce multiple time frames and multiple actors into what was already a difficult process for grassroots NGOs. Gender guidelines are therefore likely to be seen as yet one further imposition and irritant to be dealt with as quickly as possible and with minimal effort. Collecting information on gender issues is likely to be more costly than collecting data from or about men because many aspects of women's position and work are very difficult to measure or quantify. In many contexts it is also difficult for male staff to collect reliable information on gender. Evidence suggests that many NGOs simply fail to comply. Internal UK INGO reports on their overseas partners as well as academic research (Griffith, 1987) indicates that within many NGOs, internal systems of regulation are very lax and there are continual allegations of mismanagement, incompetence, and corruption against members of staff. Misinformation to donors is frequent.[15] Even where the involvement of women is stressed as an important element in project reports, reference is mainly to the number of women involved and the number of organizations, rather than any account of what the organizations are doing or the benefits to women. Such reports are far less detailed in their analysis than equivalent information for men.

Thus, questions arise about appropriately comprehensive guidelines (which involve greater costs) versus more manageable guidelines (which risk imposing a straitjacket on policy). An appropriate balance must also be found between administrative costs to develop necessary skills and implementation. In both cases, increasing effectiveness cannot be seen in purely 'rationalist' terms, but as a complex balancing of competing interests and priorities.

These issues become particularly important in the context of competition for donor resources. The problems of assessment lead to an inherent bias towards easily demonstrable impacts rather than less tangible long-term change. There is also a serious danger of concentrating on 'easy' situations, where such impacts are most immediate. Those most likely to obtain the greatest benefit with regard to income and position are women who, although poor and disadvantaged, are nevertheless not the poorest or most oppressed (Mayoux, 1997). It is the view of some analysts that concentration on these women should be the main priority (Tendler, 1989; Kraus-Harper and Harper, 1992). It must be asked whether donor resources should be used in situations where little success is likely. It is equally important, however, to consider how to ensure that the poorest and most oppressed women are not excluded. Questions also arise as to how far emphasizing effectiveness for donors (as in the case of credit) compromises commitment to other aims.

Avoiding the black hole: the wider implications

For all development agencies, increasing gender accountability is a contentious balancing of competing demands where different stakeholders may have different interpretations and priorities. NGOs' intermediary status between grass-roots constituencies and donors, however, along with the pressures to simultane-ously increase participation, impact, and efficiency, in many ways exacerbates these ambiguities and conflicts. The evidence suggests that the concept of gen-der accountability, and hence the formulation and implementation of gender pol-icy, are in many ways more complex for NGOs than for other development agencies.

Where explicit commitment to women's empowerment does not exist there is a serious danger that gender policy will fall into a 'black hole' between compet-ing accountabilities and imperatives. Multiple accountability to donors as well as trustees, staff, and programme participants/members means that in some con-texts NGOs are required to 'over account' (because of multiple demands) and in others they are able to 'under account', as each overseeing authority assumes that another authority is taking a close look at actions and results (Edwards and Hulme, 1995). In relation to gender the evidence suggests that on the one hand women and gender lobbies are often required to over account, simultaneously responding to the demands of divergent grassroots and NGO stakeholders and the efficiency demands of donors. On the other hand, where explicit commitment and institutional support for women's empowerment do not exist, NGO staff and/or donors are able to under account, excusing inaction by reference to the need to satisfy all these different interest groups and/or leaving responsibility to grassroots or donor pressure.

Where attention to women's empowerment is dependent on synergy with other development aims it is likely that the exclusion or marginalization of women will continue. Such synergy may exist for certain activities, particularly those where women are already substantially involved. The usefulness of women in fulfilling other development aims is often dependent on the continuance of these inequal-ities, particularly their performance of unpaid work. This is no less true of NGOs than other development agencies. Increasing women's participation has mainly taken the form of increasing the numbers of women in local-level participatory projects, especially those involving mobilization of their unpaid labour or intens-ification of low-paid economic activity. At the same time, as this chapter has attempted to demonstrate, the requirements for scaling-up and efficiency may lead to further marginalization of gender issues. These trends are particularly apparent in many micro-finance programmes targeting women (Mayoux, 1997).

The organizational implications of increasing gender accountability within NGOs go beyond formal mechanisms like adoption of a gender policy, gender officers/gender units, increasing numbers of women staff, and gender training programmes. Although all are necessary, they are not sufficient. All the INGOs discussed here had gender policies or firm statements of intent in their organiza-tional mandates. The degree to which these statements were integrated into all areas of policy, however, was extremely variable within organizations, between departments, geographical areas, and individual programmes (Hale *et al.*, 1993; Oxfam Gender Team, 1994; Hadjipateras, 1995).

The appointment of gender staff and/or the setting up of gender units or networks are unlikely to be effective without adequate resources and authority. Gender training for men as for women must go beyond analytical frameworks; it needs to include awareness and strategies for implementation, with appropriate follow-up, and thus become an integral compulsory part of all aspects of NGO training, staff assessment, and recruitment.

Avoiding the 'black hole' will require a change not only in NGOs but in donor policies. There are a number of extremely disturbing features of the current enthusiasm for NGOs from international donors. First, the overwhelming emphasis in the agendas of the largest donors like the World Bank is on service provision and/or programmes in sectors where women already predominate, rather than support for organizations addressing gender inequalities at the macro-level or women's integration into 'male preserves' (Siddharth, 1995). In some cases the formal separation of service provision from advocacy and lobbying has been proposed as an explicit policy, as in UK Home Office recommendations of the mid-1990s and current financial self-sustainability approaches to micro-finance (Mayoux, 1997). Indeed, in some countries this separation is already taking place. The emphasis on cost-efficiency further militates against broader definitions of participation and addressing contentious gender inequalities as discussed above. Some donors (including ODA UK) have also reportedly questioned the degree to which women-only projects are discriminatory in the context of recent emphases on 'gender'. Although some NGOs (particularly large well-known NGOs such as Oxfam, SEWA, and WWF) are in a position to choose between donors and can raise independent sources of funding to pursue their own agendas, others are very dependent on a few sources. This is particularly true of small NGOs in the South whose agendas are likely to be heavily influenced by donor priorities.

Secondly, this expansion of NGO activity is taking place in the context of withdrawal of support for state welfare provisions on which women depend. Mainstream literature on NGOs gives grounds to question NGO capacity to substitute for state welfare and service provision. Precisely because of NGO independence and flexibility there are dangers of creating a 'patchwork quilt' of services of varying quality without any overview of overall needs (Edwards, 1993). In some areas large, influential, and well-funded NGOs are able to concentrate resources on particular villages and social groups which are not the poorest or the most important for national development (Robinson, 1995). In other areas, large numbers of small NGOs lead to uncoordinated provision and duplication (Hanlon, 1991). The increased funding to NGOs has coincided with decreased state funding for social welfare, and NGOs have often attracted significant numbers of skilled staff from the state sector through higher salaries (Edwards and Hulme, 1995; Farrington and Lewis, 1993). The effectiveness of NGO programmes is not a justification for withdrawal of state provision, but is dependent upon the ability of NGOs to influence and supplement a well-resourced and responsive state system (Carroll, 1992). This is no less true for women than for men. The effects of increased NGO funding may be merely to substitute one inadequate and unresponsive system of service and welfare provision for women for a system which is even less well-resourced, less co-ordinated and dependent on women's own unpaid 'participatory' input.

There are serious dangers in the over-reliance on NGOs as the main representatives of women's interests without changes in other development agencies and the wider development agenda. The degree to which increasing support to NGOs will increase women's representation in the development agenda will depend crucially on the types of NGO promoted, the reasons for this promotion, and the levels of explicit commitment to women's empowerment by both NGOs and donors. In many contexts it may not be possible to demonstrate the cost savings or efficiency gains of addressing gender issues, particularly for very disadvantaged women.

The conclusions of this chapter point to a three-fold strategy for improving gender accountability. Firstly, there needs to be far greater support for organizations and programmes specifically addressing gender inequities through grassroots mobilization, advocacy, and lobbying. Secondly, there needs to be a much firmer commitment to the inclusion of gender criteria for the funding of all programmes, with impact assessments beyond mere numerical statements of women's participation. Thirdly, it is unlikely that these changes will take place without parallel changes in the structure of donor agencies and the dominant development agenda. Support for NGOs cannot be seen as a 'soft alternative' to macro-level change.

Notes

Chapter 1

1. A useful definition of the 'politics of meaning-making' (also referred to as 'discursive politics') is provided by Katzenstein (1995): 'it is discursive in that it seeks to reinterpret, reformulate, rethink, and rewrite the norms and practices of society and the state' (p.35). At a more general level the work of feminist social theorists like Nancy Fraser (1989) highlights 'struggle over meaning' as one of the most important arenas of contemporary politics.
2. The concept of 'entryism' gained currency among Marxist political activists in the post-war period as some militant groups, frustrated by what they saw as the conservatism of their societies, felt that the best way to speed up the prospects of socialist transformation was to enter established social democratic parties and work towards taking them over (Bangura, 1997). Activist groups, Bangura maintains, often adopt this strategy because of their general weakness, and the realization that independent forms of organization, advocacy, and mobilization would not secure the desired objectives.
3. The inspiration for the title of this book comes from Ann Summers who talked of two possible models for feminist policy advocacy within the state—the missionary and the mandarin approaches (Summers, 1986 cited in Sawer and Groves, 1994a).
4. Institutional innovations include the setting up of new structures (WID bureaux, units, focal points, etc.), issuing new procedures (gender guidelines and checklists), and providing gender training programmes.
5. Bangura (1997) also draws attention to the way in which different political systems/cultures shape possibilities for policy dialogue on gender issues.
6. Femocrats, or feminist bureaucrats, refers to feminists who went into the women's policy positions created in Australia in the 1970s. The word is now in common usage.
7. While the discussion in this section focuses on relations between women inside state institutions and women's movements on the outside, the tensions described regarding the dual loyalties of femocrats (*vis-à-vis* their professional colleagues *and* the women's movement) also apply to women working inside other institutions explored in this volume (e.g. multilateral institutions and non-governmental organizations).
8. It is significant to note that this is not only at the level of official rhetoric; it is also reflected in the growing proportion of development funding handled by the NGO sector (see UNRISD, 1994).

Chapter 2

1. The term 'internal advocate', rather than 'practitioner', is used here to refer to WID/gender staff because their work entails a significant amount of advocacy for gender issues inside the bureaucracy.
2. Needless to say a wide gulf separates this anti-interventionist discourse and the highly interventionist policies of its proponents. As Elson (1994) observes, workers' rights are very often removed in the name of removing 'distortions'.
3. The most comprehensive being the Convention on the Elimination of All Forms of Discrimination against Women of 1979.

4. The equality discourse is clearly dominant in the Beijing Platform for Action, for example.
5. For a comprehensive account and critique of Boserup's thesis see Beneria and Sen (1981) and Huntington (1975).
6. It is important to note that in the WID literature 'welfare' often takes on a pejorative meaning, incorporating the concept of residualism (as opposed to institutionalism).
7. In response to the failures of the growth orthodoxy, by the late 1960s the 'basic needs strategy' had emerged on the development agenda. According to its proponents, the primary aim of development was to meet basic human needs—food, clothing, shelter, and fuel, as well as education, human rights, and 'participation' through employment and political involvement. In this approach, the focus was placed squarely on these ends rather than on household income. A set of selective policies, it was argued, makes it possible to satisfy the basic human needs of the whole population at levels of income per capita substantially below those required by a less discriminating strategy of overall income growth.
8. Synergism is 'the assertion of a positive, mutually beneficial, relationship between gender equity and other development objectives' (Jackson, 1996:491).
9. We refer to this literature as '*gender* efficiency' because gender *relations* are taken on board.
10. Many of the points raised here apply to the writings of both Palmer (1991) and Collier (1989), but in this section we are mainly concerned with the former. For a thorough discussion of Collier's model see Lockwood (1992) and Elson (1995).
11. Needless to say, social expenditure cuts which have often worked against women are justified in terms of 'economic efficiency'.
12. Palmer, like Boserup, makes an *ad hoc* use of 'culture' (prejudice, values, ideology) to fill in the gaps that cannot be explained by the neo-classical framework. A similar weakness can be seen in Collier's (1989) model, where 'social convention' becomes the exogenous explanation for the creation and perpetuation of gender hierarchies (Lockwood, 1992). In all three cases the explanation for gender hierarchies is placed outside the model.
13. The useful distinction between *gender ascriptive relations* and relations that are *bearers of gender* which was first made by Whitehead (1979) is applicable here. The former are constructed intrinsically in terms of gender (e.g. husband–wife), while the latter can become gendered even though they are not intrinsically so (e.g. employer–employee).
14. The term 'public action' should not be confused with government action only; it also includes the activities of non-government organizations (Drèze and Sen, 1989:18–19)
15. This seems to be the case in Vietnam and Singapore, for example (see comments of feminist researchers/advocates from these two countries in DAWN, n.d.).
16. A similar argument was made by Marjan Kroon (DGIS) at the UNRISD/CPD workshop, Working Towards a More Gender Equitable Macro-economic Agenda, held in Dhaka, Bangladesh, 26–28 November 1996.
17. Personal communication, Alison Evans.
18. Personal communication, Cynthia Hewitt de Alcantara.
19. This observation also applies to other 'new' issues, such as the environment. For an illuminating discussion of the role of external pressure in facilitating the up-take of environmental issues by the World Bank see Rich (1994). It needs to be added that external pressure can also be exerted by other actors, such as states. In the take-up of gender issues by multilateral agencies, for example, Scandinavian governments have often given critical moral and financial support (see Razavi and Miller, 1995b).

20. As Köhler (1995) points out, UNICEF's *Structural Adjustment with a Human Face* was extremely important in terms of institutional politics—being the first frank inter-agency critique within the UN system.
21. Although the World Bank's *World Development Report* of 1990 (on poverty) confirmed this shift in discourse, the Bank's Operational Guidelines had already been amended in 1987 to require analysis of the impact of adjustment on the poor (Ribe and Carvalho, 1990, cited in Vivian, 1995).
22. But it is by no means confined to the World Bank; a similar line of reasoning was evident in the basic needs strategies of the 1970s. Female education, for example, was seen as a cost-effective means of solving the population problem. For a feminist critique of basic needs strategies see Beneria and Sen (1982) and Palmer (1977).
23. One of the most ambitious attempts at providing estimates for the incidence of poverty amongst rural women is the IFAD study, *The State of World Rural Poverty* (Jazairy *et al.*, 1992).
24. Direct measures of poverty which rely on well-being indicators (e.g. life expectancy, health status, education, etc.) are more conducive to measuring gender differences in poverty given that they are based on the individual rather than the household (Kabeer, 1996a). Some of the recent attempts at constructing gender-specific indices of well-being, such as UNDP's gender-related development index (GDI) and IFAD's women's status index (WSI) take this alternative route.
25. To emphasize the importance of such technical and political skills, organizational theorists have used the term 'policy *entrepreneur*' to refer to internal advocates (see Kardam, 1991).
26. Although some research had been carried out in-house, a substantial body of evidence was available outside the Bank from which the WID advocates drew.
27. A point that was strongly confirmed by one internal advocate in the ILO (personal communication, Azita Berar-Awad). Similarly, in a meeting of the Indian Women Studies Association in Jaipur, poverty was identified as a concern that could unify the different strands of the Indian women's movement (personal communication, Naila Kabeer).
28. See Monica Das Gupta's (1987) village-level study in Punjab for evidence of pronounced sex differentials in early age mortality despite an economic environment that has been conducive to improved survivorship. The evidence on the relations between class status and anti-female bias (in nutrition and early age mortality) is very mixed (Harriss, 1990; Jeffery *et al.*, 1987; Sen and Sengupta, 1983; Wadley and Derr, 1987).
29. Comparisons of GDI relative to HDI reveal that in most countries in Sub-Saharan Africa gender inequality in basic capabilities is less severe than in Latin America, despite the former's lower achievements in basic capabilities (UNDP, 1995:79).
30. It also makes the parallel drawn by Jackson (1995) between 'efficiency' and 'poverty' problematic, i.e. poverty is a serious concern for a significant number of women in a way that efficiency may not be.
31. As Beneria (1995) puts it, there is considerable convergence between feminist demands for a more humane economics centred around the provisioning of human needs, and other forces pursuing similar objectives. Are these arguments synergistic, instrumental, or both?
32. The distinction has been made in relation to markets; for the distinction between 'real' vs 'abstract' in the context of politics, I am grateful to Naila Kabeer (personal communication).
33. The research/advocacy linkage seems to work best where gender units in development institutions have their own in-house capacity for research and policy analysis, as in the ILO and the World Bank (Miller, Chapter 6).

Chapter 3

1. This chapter draws on interviews commissioned by UNRISD and conducted by researchers in each of the seven countries: Nadira Barkillil (Morocco); Lalla Ben Barka (Mali); Joy Kwesiga (Uganda); Mohsena Islam (Bangladesh); Christine Mariott (Jamaica); Molly Pollack (Chile); Van Anh Tran Thi (Vietnam). The interviews were held in 1994 with members of state bureaucracies, NGO representatives, members of women's organizations, and academics, almost all of whom in one way or another were involved in promoting improved state attention to women's needs and interests in development. The interview data are rich in subjective assessments of official policy efforts, but perhaps because of this, there is considerable unevenness in the detail provided on formal policy measures, and their impact. Also largely missing are detailed 'insider' accounts of efforts to pursue gender policy agendas at particular instances, accounts which would illuminate aspects of the gendered politics of policymaking, although I have made some inferences. The absence of this kind of data is unsurprising, as bureaucratic decision-making is notoriously impervious to outside scrutiny; it dwells in the minutiae of everyday slights and omissions, of memos unsent or 'not received', of forgotten meetings, of secret alliances. This report also draws on national and sectoral policy statements, on a wide range of documents from multilateral and bilateral agencies working in these countries, and on secondary literature on gender and development issues in each country.
2. Important contributions include Franzway *et al.* (1989), Connell (1990), and MacKinnon (1989). Texts developing feminist perspectives on non-Western states include Kandiyoti (1991), Agarwal (1988), Charlton *et al.* (1989), and the essays in Parts 2 and 3 of Mohanty *et al.* (1991).
3. This is not to deny, of course, that fruitful collaboration has occurred on an *ad hoc* basis between women's organizations, NGOs, and various government departments in Morocco.

Chapter 4

1. The term 'strategy' used here and in other sections does not necessarily refer to a structured and voluntary process, but to choices which are not considered as such or are not voluntary.
2. These are the parties which participated in the national independence movement, i.e. the Istiqlal Party (pro-traditional party of the centre); the Socialist Union of Popular Forces (left nationalist and socialist party); the Party of Progress and Socialism (Marxist socialist party); the Organization of Democratic and Popular Action (formed recently by secession of the leftist movement, this is a strong pan-Arabic supporter, resembling Arab nationalism with socialist leanings).
3. This word is commonly used to describe authority. Historically Morocco has often been separated into two areas: the *Makhzen* areas were under the authority of the central power and of the Sultan, and the Siba areas were the regions of the tribes which refused the authority of the central power. By semantic extension these two concepts have been used to describe the authority of the central power (order) and of rebellion (disorder).
4. The number of these associations varies enormously, depending on the source (from 17 698 to 30 000).
5. According to the Department of Statistics (1994), the number of unemployed has reached 1 347 552, 39 per cent of which are women and 13.6 per cent graduates of higher institutions of education.

6. A new development is taking place in Morocco: the apparent 'depoliticization' of the university. In her survey of students from the University of Rabat, Rahma Bourqia shows that only a small minority of students identify the term 'protest' as the characteristic which best defines youth. Unlike preceding generations, 'Third World' and Marxist ideologies apparently have little resonance with contemporary youth. In no way does this signify indifference to national and international concerns. In the survey, a majority of students spoke of non-political associations as being the ideal framework for expression and mobilization (See Bourqia et al., 1995).

7. Ibid. Bourqia shows that most of the students opt for associations for purposes of mobilization.

8. An intense debate, as yet unresolved, is taking place on the definition of the concept of civil society in the Arab and Maghrebin context. See the Annuaire de l'Afrique du Nord, Vol.28, 1989, and particularly the contributions of Camau, Goudron and Zghal.

9. Freedom of worship is acknowledged only for other religions, since Muslims cannot change their religion.

10. Tozy (1989) extends his analysis to all the political and religious trends. In our opinion this analysis seems better adapted to the situation of the religious forces.

11. Network composed of independent women's associations and individuals from the Maghreb (Algeria, Morocco, and Tunisia).

12. The French Protectorate did not favour the propagation of education in general, nor that of women in particular.

13. There is an extensive literature on the subject. It is impossible to refer to all the publications on women's condition, status and roles in Morocco. For further information see Rachid, No. 33, 1985. For more recent works see Hadraoui and Monkachi, Mernissi, 1991.

14. According to the latest population census (GOM, 1994), half of the Moroccan population is urban.

15. In the urban areas, the average number of children per woman, 4.28 in 1982, had decreased to 2.56 by 1994 (GOM, 1994).

16. See the study by a group of researchers from three countries of the Maghreb (Algeria, Morocco, and Tunisia), FNUAP/IREP, 1991. The study is based on an investigation which aims to measure the degree of the break with tradition and the strategies used by graduate women in order to assert themselves as individuals in the family, at work, and in society.

17. Fatima Mernissi (1992) shows how the leaders of the Muslim Arab countries have throughout history singled out women and persecuted them whenever their countries underwent serious economic and social crises.

18. The ongoing debate within the women's movement in Morocco on the attitude to be adopted with regard to women wearing the *hijab* and desiring membership in the women's associations is very significant and deserves further analysis.

19. In Morocco, Fatima Mernissi, Farida Bennani (University of Marrakech) and Zineb Miadi (University of Casablanca) were among the first to adopt this approach.

20. The *Ijtihad* is the attempt to interpret the Koran and the words of the Prophet.

21. Reservations were also made with regard to Article 9 (nationality), Article 16 (equality in marriage and divorce), and Article 29 (national sovereignty in settling disputes).

22. The Malékite rite is a school of Muslim law. Malékism, founded in 795, is based on a particular interpretation of the Koran and the tradition of the Prophet (*la Sunna*). Applied in all of the Maghreb region, because of certain dispositions related to the status of women and the family, it is considered to be one of the most conservative.

23. Some months ago the obligation of women to obtain marital authorization in order to go into business was abolished, as was the obligation for married women to obtain marital authorization before receiving a passport. This has been replaced by the possibility for the husband to oppose his wife's demand for a passport by written request.
24. For example, according to the results of the latest General Census (1994), two out of ten heads of household are women.
25. The World Bank no longer hesitates to reduce or cut aid to a number of developing countries because of non-respect of human rights or freedoms. Thus, in 1990 the Bank reduced its activities in Zaire and it refused new loans to Malawi in 1992, as well as to China following the events of Tiananmen Square.
26. These articles concern in particular equal status in regard to inheritance; the right of Muslim women to marry non-Muslims; and abolition of the duty of obedience to the husband as well as abolition of responsibility of the husband for the wife.

Chapter 5

1. The author would like to thank Carol Miller and Shahra Razavi for their helpful comments on an earlier draft; Jill Vickers and Wendy Robbins in Canada; and Prue Hyman and Patti O'Neill in New Zealand.
2. The idea of bureaux which would provide information on women's labour market participation was much older, dating back to the creation of the Women's Bureau in the United States Department of Labour in 1920 and replicated in other countries over time—e.g. Canada (1954) and Australia (1963), thanks to the lobbying of women's international non-governmental organizations. In New Zealand the body was not a bureau as such but a National Advisory Committee on the Employment of Women (1967).
3. In all three countries the 'first wave' of the women's movement welled up in the 1890s and was largely pro-state in orientation, particularly with regard to issues of moral and social reform. By contrast, the 'second wave' which arrived in the 1970s (women's liberation) tended to have a more anti-state or anarchical tendency. None the less, by 1973 many of the founders of women's liberation in Australia were candidates for the position of Women's Adviser to the Prime Minister and soon after became femocrats themselves.
4. The spelling of Labour differs in Australia and New Zealand—Australia having dropped the 'u' early this century. Where the Labour parties of both countries are being referred to the 'u' will be used. The equivalent in Canada is the New Democratic Party which has been in government at provincial but not at the federal level. Women's policy machinery was initially fostered in Canada at the federal level by the Liberal government of Pierre Trudeau. The conservative parties in Australia are called the Liberal and National Parties (usually in Coalition and referred to thus), in Canada the Progressive Conservative Party and in New Zealand the National Party.
5. For example, Australian femocrat arguments for increased childcare expenditure increasingly had to be couched in terms of macro-economic benefit. The major new childcare commitment for the 1993 federal election was announced in the Prime Minister's Economic Statement 'Investing in the Nation' (9 February 1993). The downside of the construction of childcare as an economic issue was the subsequent restriction of hours available to the children of non-working parents. For a more positive view of the construction of childcare as a macro-economic issue see MacDonald (1995).
6. The appointee was Elizabeth Reid, a philosophy tutor active in women's liberation. She resigned in late 1975 over a government decision to move her into the bureaucracy. The public controversy which surrounded her position meant that almost all

subsequent Australian governments appointed their women's advisers to head policy units within prime minister's/premier's departments rather than within the more overtly political prime minister's or premier's offices within parliament (one exception was within the Northern Territory). Subsequently Reid became a senior United Nations official.

7. One of the reasons that the story of Australian feminist interventions in the state is relatively well known is that a number of those who headed the Office were themselves important writers—such as novelist Sara Dowse, who was to write both fictional and non-fictional accounts of her experience, and Anne Summers, a high-profile journalist and editor.

8. The idea was to go beyond a common denominator platform of action by getting in addition three or four new practical commitments from each country.

9. NAC was described as 'the model most compatible with Australia' in the 1995 government-sponsored feasibility study into the establishment of a peak women's body. As pointed out by Jill Vickers, however, NAC's increased radicalism under its minority policy may disrupt its government lobbying (personal communication, January 1996).

10. When Helen Clark was elected Party Leader in late 1993 there was an attempt to depict her as lesbian as well.

11. In the early days of OSW in Australia and of the Women's Program in Canada there were similar attempts to subvert hierarchy.

12. In New Zealand, as in Australia and Canada, the universal benefit had decreased significantly in value, due to a failure to index it, and it was argued that an increase in support for low-income families would be more equitable. As noted in relation to Australia, this discounted the fact that even in relatively wealthy families the universal benefit paid to mothers was often the only income over which they exercised control. Canada was the last of these three countries to abolish the universal benefit—in 1992.

13. As noted earlier, the Employment Equity Act of 1990 both required companies to prepare EEO programs and made provision for pay equity assessments at the request of employees.

Chapter 6

1. Although the term 'international women's movement' fails to capture the diversity of women's international organizing and the variety of interests that are represented, it is none the less commonly used in the literature and by activists and thus has been retained throughout this chapter.

2. A record number of NGOs were accredited to the Fourth World Conference on Women, Beijing, 1995. Whereas 154 NGOs were accredited to the Mexico City Conference (Stephenson, 1995:140), some 3000 NGOs were eligible to attend the UN Conference in Beijing (WEDO, n.d.: 2).

3. This information is taken from the World Bank Web site: http://ftp.worldbank.org/html/hcovp/gender/gnets.htmo

4. For a discussion of the international efforts to advance the status of women see Tomasevski, 1993 and Pietilä and Vickers, 1994.

5. In 1992 the Nordic countries provided a combined total of US$344.2 million, followed by the United States with US$107.4 million, and Japan with US$92.1 million (UNDP, 1993).

6. In 1992 a document was prepared by the Promotion of Technical Co-operation Branch to inform staff of the women in development policies of the major bilateral donors (ILO/PROMOTEC, 1992). The document provides a formidable tool for

internal advocates to use financial incentives in order to promote attention to WID/gender concerns within the ILO.

7. For a fuller account see Kardam (1991; 1993) and Razavi and Miller (1995b).

8. The description of organizational structures presented here represents our assessment of the picture in late 1995. We have been unable to incorporate changes that have undoubtedly taken place since then, as all three organizations continue their restructuring processes.

9. The thematic vice-presidencies are: Environmentally Sustainable Development; Finance and Private Sector Development; and Capital Development and Operations Policy.

10. World Bank figures were obtained from a Spokesman for the World Bank, 15 June 1995.

11. Among the organizations considered here, only the World Bank has made an effort to record the emergence and evolution of gender issues within the organization (World Bank, 1994c). For the UNDP and the ILO, external efforts to document this history are at best sketchy (Kardam, 1991; Lotherington et al., 1991; Pietilä and Eide, 1990; Whitworth, 1995), and interviews with agency staff suggested that, on the whole, 'institutional memory' within these organizations is poor.

12. It is worth noting that as early as 1975 the World Bank emphasized the need to mainstream women's issues in regular projects, and was critical of special WID projects being pursued by other agencies (World Bank, 1994c). The Bank's position may have been aimed at averting the 'marginalization' of women's projects, although it seems more likely that there was some resistance to women-only projects on the grounds that they are 'political' rather than 'technical' projects.

13. Initially called the Voluntary Fund for the United Nations Decade for Women, in 1985 UNIFEM joined the United Nations system as a 'separate and identifiable entity in autonomous association with the United Nations Development Programme' (NGLS, 1994: 73).

14. The Branch took over the application and implementation of the main equality conventions (No.100, No.111, and No.156), which had previously been the responsibility of the Application of Standards Branch.

15. The ILO's Interdepartmental Project on Equality for Women in Employment adopted a multidisciplinary approach to analysing some of the critical concerns regarding equality for women in employment with a view to generating comprehensive data that could form a solid basis for further work programmes.

16. This point was made by the Deputy Focal Point for Women of the United Nations Geneva office, who was in January 1996 frustrated by her lack of effective power to execute her role.

17. The Governing Council also pledged US$8 million for initiatives in building national capacity in WID/gender.

18. These data were provided by the Promotion of Technical Co-operation Branch based on their computerized list of projects, May 1995. The figures may underestimate total spending on women because they are calculated on the basis of projects with WID in their titles.

19. One example used in this context is that the Discrimination (Employment and Occupation) Convention, 1959 (No.111) may not be complete without attention to issues raised in the Workers with Family Responsibilities Convention, 1981 (No.156) which, thus far, has had only 20 ratifications.

20. GAP Manager, personal communication, 17 July 1995.

21. This information is taken from the World Bank Web site: http://ftp.worldbank.org/html/hcovp/gender/gnets.htmo.

22. See for example, Beneria (1982).

23. Elson criticized the 1992 *Human Development Report* for its lack of analysis concerning 'the way in which women are socially assigned the indispensible *nurturing* role in human development, and yet are not assigned control over the resources necessary to discharge this role' (1992:14).

Chapter 7

1. I would like to thank UNRISD and the Open University, Milton Keynes for making this paper possible through financial support. I would particularly like to thank Carol Miller and Shahra Razavi of UNRISD for editing the paper and Alan Thomas of the Open University, Milton Keynes for his continual encouragement and assistance in getting an OU grant for part of the research on which this paper is based. I would also like to thank Kate Young, Fiona Thomas, Laura Kelly, Helen O'Connell, Angela Hajipateras, Eugenia Piza-Lopez, Deborah Eade, and Kirsti Floor for their critical comments on an earlier draft. On a practical level I would not have been able to produce the paper without the generous help of Tim Read, Howard Andrews, Henri Mayoux, and Jacqui André in overcoming the limitations imposed by RSI. Responsibility for the views expressed in the paper, however, lies entirely with the author.
2. ODA UK became the Department for International Development (DFID) following the election of the Labour Government. References to ODA in this paper refer to policies before this date.
3. In this paper the term NGO is used generically to refer to both grassroots membership organizations (GROs) and grassroots support organizations (GSOs), following the usage in the Beijing Platform for Action and many recent discussions of NGOs and gender (Karl, 1995). The most important difference between GROs and GSOs is in their accountability structures: GROs are formally accountable to their members while GSOs are not. Where it is necessary to distinguish between different types of NGO, as in our discussion of participation, this is explicitly stated.
4. In addition the paper draws on the author's own research on women's grassroots organizations in India, Nicaragua, and Africa. On UK-based NGOs, the secondary literature was supplemented by exploratory interviews with key gender staff and others on organizational tensions within NGOs in 1995 and updated through correspondence to the time of writing. Some of the INGOs discussed (particularly Oxfam and ACORD) are in the process of collating their organizational experience on gender, but existing material does not follow a standardized format to allow cross-cultural comparisons of context or detailed comparisons of organizational structure. The author has respected the confidentiality of some of the more critical observations by interviewees at the expense of specificity of some of the assertions made in this text. Despite the inevitably incomplete and to some extent arbitrary nature of the material discussed, it is hoped that the paper will be useful in adding to pressures for more detailed, systematic, and open research by NGOs and donors on the issues raised.
5. For a preliminary discussion of some of the literature see Goetz, 1992. The experience of other development agencies is discussed in some detail in other chapters in this volume.
6. Some of the most active include DAWN, Red Entre Mujeres in South America, and AAWORD and Abantu in Africa (Abantu for Development, 1994; Carbajal, 1994) and CHANGE and Women Working Worldwide based in the UK.
7. This marks a shift from Women in Development (WID) discourse concerned with increasing women's access to existing development programmes to Gender and Development (GAD) where the concern is to transform the development agenda to

eliminate inequities and power asymmetries between women and men. This approach stresses that men as well as women must be included in gender policies (see Razavi and Miller, 1995a). This shift has been particularly marked in some recent INGO publications (Eade and Williams, 1995) but the concepts of gender, gender roles, and gender relations also feature in donor agency guidelines (ODA, n.d.a).

8. The original formulation of analytical distinctions between 'women's interests', 'practical gender interests', and 'strategic gender interests' was by Molyneux (1985) in her discussion of Sandinista policies for women. The distinction aimed to explain women's responses to particular political ideologies and to highlight the shortcomings of looking at 'women' rather than 'gender'. The practical/strategic distinction was then applied by Moser (1994) to women's needs in gender planning. It has been widely adopted by development agencies for gender training and analysis of development programmes, see for example GOOD, 1992, Williams *et al.*, 1994, ODA, n.d.a.

9. The levels required for women to present a 'strategic presence' within organizations is obviously difficult to determine and within the UK INGOs women were undoubtedly influential. Nevertheless, apart from One World Action, women within the mixed-sex UK INGOs were in a minority on the management committees. Within Christian Aid, following the reorganization in 1995, two of the six-member Senior Management Team were women but most team leaders were men and gender awareness was not a criterion for selection. In Oxfam in 1994 the Director and all five members of the corporate management team were men and overseas most senior positions were occupied by men (Oxfam Gender Team, 1994). In Grameen Bank considerable difficulty was experienced in recruiting female staff, and despite constituting the majority of clients, women were very poorly represented within the NGO hierarchy (Holcombe, 1995)

10. I owe the suggestion of the idea of 'competing imperatives' to discussions with Alan Thomas at the Open University, Milton Keynes.

11. For manuals looking explicitly at methods of mobilization of women see May, n.d.; Williams *et al.*, 1994. For a discussion of participatory technology development and women in farming systems and environmental improvement see Guijit, 1992; Reijntjes *et al.*, 1992; Thomas-Slayter *et al.*, 1993. For women and methods of participatory health research see Welbourn, 1992.

12. For example, in a recent book which shows no such qualms about class and race, Burkey (1993:67) writes: 'Is it the role of international development agencies to fight for women's liberation in the Third World? Wouldn't that be cultural imperialism at its worst? It isn't necessary to campaign for women's liberation; it is necessary that agencies make sure that their programmes and projects do not make the situation of women worse. The second crucial step is to ensure that women genuinely do have at least equal opportunity to participate in development projects with men. If rural women have genuine opportunities for participating in their own development, then they will take care of the when and how of women's liberation'. He fails to say what he means by 'women's liberation' in this context or how women can have equal opportunities to participate without it. Similar hostile attitudes are also reported for Oxfam and Christian Aid in Piza-Lopez and Wallace, 1994; GOOD, 1992 and reported to the author by female staff in other organizations.

13. The inclusion of gender as one of the 'axes of difference' (others being age, class, ethnic group, etc.) was originally proposed by Welbourn as a less politically sensitive approach in the context of her work in Somalia (Welbourn, 1991a,b). It was then embraced by NGOs working in much less sensitive environments where grassroots women's organizations had already been directly and successfully raising feminist issues.

14. Discussion of gender is notably absent from one of the most important reference works on scaling-up (Edwards and Hulme, 1992).
15. A particularly glaring example of this is in a cattle breeding development project in the Andes where donors had demanded that a significant percentage of the community authorities be women. This had led male leaders to ask a number of women to come forward, but also to stamp their fingerprint on a separate document naming the men the community authorities. It was only by chance that the donor authorities found out that the women had not been elected, or allowed to participate in decision-making or even the project itself (Barrig, 1994).

Bibliography

Abantu for Development (1994) 'Southern Women's Networks: Their own priorities' *Focus on Gender* Vol.2 No.3, October:34–6.

ABS (Australian Bureau of Statistics) (1994) *Australian Women's Year Book 1994.* (Cat. no.4124.0), Australian Government Publishing Service, Canberra.

Acker, Joan (1990) 'Hierarchies, Jobs, Bodies: A theory of gendered organisation' *Gender and Society* Vol.2 No.4:139–58.

ActionAid India (1993) 'Understanding Advocacy'. Report of the First ActionAid India Advocacy Workshop, Whitefield, 6–8 December, ActionAid, Bangalore.

Adler, Nancy J. and Dafna N. Izraeli (ed.) (1994) *Competitive Frontiers: Women managers in a global economy.* Basil Blackwell, Oxford.

ADB (African Development Bank) (1993) *Governance and Development in Africa: Issues and the role of the African Development Bank and other multilateral institutions.* ADB, Abidjan.

Agarwal, Bina (1986) 'Women, poverty, and agricultural growth in India' *Journal of Peasant Studies* Vol.13 No.4:165–220.

Agarwal, Bina (ed.) (1988) *Structures of Patriarchy: State, community and household in modernising patriarchy.* Kali for Women, Delhi.

Alam, Bilquis Ara (1987) 'Women in Local Government: Profiles of six chairmen (sic) of Union Parishads' *The Journal of Local Government* Vol.16 No.1, Dhaka.

Alam, Bilquis Ara (1992) *Statistical Pocketbook of Bangladesh*, Bangladesh Bureau of Statistics, Dhaka.

Alter Chen, Martha (1996) 'Engendering World Conferences: The international women's movement and the UN' in Thomas G. Weiss and Leon Gordenker *NGOs, the UN and Global Governance.* Lynne Rienner, London.

Anderson, M. (1990) *Women on the Agenda: UNIFEM's experience in mainstreaming with women 1985–1990.* UNIFEM, New York, May.

Andreas, C. (1985) *When Women Rebel: The rise of popular feminism in Peru.* Lawrence Hill, Connecticut.

Arn, A. L. and F.B. Lily (1992) 'Evaluation Report of Saptagram Nari Swanirvar Parishad'. Oxfam, Dhaka.

Ardener, E. (1975) 'Belief and the Problem of Women' in S. Ardener (ed.), *Perceiving Women.* Malaby Press, London.

Avina, J. (1993) 'The Evolutionary Life Cycle of Non-governmental Development Organisations' *Public Administration and Development* Vol.13 No.5 December:453–74.

Ayres, R. (1983) *Banking on the Poor: The World Bank and world poverty.* MIT Press, Cambridge.

Backhouse, Constance and David Flaherty (ed.) (1992) *Challenging Times: The women's movement in Canada and the United States.* McGill-Queen's University Press, Montreal.

BBS (Bangladesh Bureau of Statistics) (1992) *Statistical Pocketbook of Bangladesh.* Dhaka.

Bangura, Y. (1994) 'Economic Restructuring, Coping Strategies and Social Change: Implications for institutional development in Africa'. Discussion paper No. 52, UNRISD, Geneva.

Bangura, Y. (1997) 'Policy Dialogue and Gendered Development, Institutional and Ideological Constraints'. Discussion Paper, No 87. UNRISD, Geneva.

Banks, Olive (1981) *Faces of Feminism.* Basil Blackwell, Oxford.

Barkallil, Nadira (1994) 'Technical Cooperation and Women's Lives: Integrating gender into development policy: Morocco'. Mimeo, UNRISD, Geneva.

Barrig, Maruja (1994) 'Gender in institutions: An inward look' in M. Barrig and A. Wehkamp (ed.) op. cit. pp.73–98.

Barrig, Maruja and Andy Wehkamp (ed.) (1995) *Engendering Development: Experiences in gender and development planning.* NOVIB, The Hague.

Barton, T. (1992) 'British-based NGOs: Gender issues in policy and practice'. Unpublished MA dissertation, University of East Anglia.

Bashevkin, Sylvia (1989) 'Free trade and Canadian feminism: The case of the National Action Committee on the Status of Women' *Canadian Public Policy* Vol.15 No.4.

Bashevkin, Sylvia (1993) *Toeing the Lines: Women and party politics in English Canada.* Oxford University Press, Toronto.

BAW (Branch for the Advancement of Women) (1987) *The Development of National Machinery for the Advancement of Women and their Characteristics in 1985.* United Nations, Vienna.

Bégin, Monique (1992) 'The Royal Commission on the Status of Women in Canada: Twenty years later' in Backhouse and Flaherty (ed.), op. cit.

Belhassen, Souhayr (1989) 'Les femmes Tunisiennes islamistes' *Annuaire de l'Afrique du Nord* Vol.28.

Bell, Susan G. and Karen M. Offen (1983) 'General Introduction' in S.G. Bell and K.M. Offen (ed.) *Women, the Family, and Freedom.* Stanford University Press, Stanford.

Ben Barka, Lalla (1994) 'Mali: La problematique du genre dans les politiques de développement'. Mimeo, UNRISD, Geneva.

Beneria, Lourdes (1982) *Women and Development: The sexual division of labour in rural societies.* ILO/Praeger, New York.

Beneria, Lourdes (1995) 'Towards a Greater Integration of Gender in Economics' *World Development* Vol.23 No.11:1839–50.

Beneria, Lourdes and Gita Sen (1981) 'Accumulation, Reproduction, and Women's Role in Economic Development: Boserup revisted' *Signs: Journal of Women in Culture and Society* Vol.7 No.21:279–98.

Beneria, Lourdes and Gita Sen (1982) 'Class and Gender Inequalities and Women's Role in Economic Development: Theoretical and practical implications' *Feminist Studies* Vol.8 No.1:157–76.

Bennani-Chraibi, Mounia (1994) *Soumis et rebelles, les jeunes au Maroc.* Edition La Fennec, Casablanca.

Bennis, A. (1994) 'Elements de Strategie Pour La Promotion de la Femme Rurale'. Draft Statement, Ministry of Agriculture, Rabat, Morocco.

Berger, Marguerite and Mayra Buvinic (1989) *Women's Ventures: Assistance to the informal sector in Latin America.* Kumarian Press, Boulder, Colorado.

Bernardes Davidson, W. (1991) 'Desk Review of Advisory Notes for the Fifth Country Programme Cycle'. Unpublished report, Women in Development Division, UNDP, New York.

Bessis, Sophie and Souhayr Belhassen (1992) *Femmes du Maghreb: l'enjeu.* JC Lattés, Paris.

Blaker, C. and R. Reichmann (1994) 'Gender Evaluation, Oxfam (UK/I) Brazil 1990–1993'. Oxfam, Brazil.

Boserup, Ester (1970) *Women's Role in Economic Development.* St. Martin's Press, London.

Bourquia, Rahma, Mokhtar El Harras and Driss Bensaid (1995) *Jeunesse estudiantine Marocaine: Valeurs et stratégies.* Series: Essays and Studies No.14, Faculté des Lettres et Sciences Humaines, Rabat.

206

Braidotti, R., E. Charkiewicz, S. Hausler and S. Wieringa (1994) *Women, the Environment and Sustainable Development: Towards a theoretical synthesis.* Zed Books in association with INSTRAW, London.

Brett, Bill (1994) *International Labour in the 21st Century: The ILO Monument to the past or beacon for the future.* Epic Books, London.

Bruggeman, H. (1993) 'Pastoral Associations in Chad: Experiences from an Oxfam project'. Oxfam Research Papers No.7, Oxford.

Burkey, Stan (1993) *People First: A guide to self-reliant, participatory rural development.* Zed Books, London.

Burt, Sandra (1990) 'Organized Women's Groups and the State' in W.D. Coleman and G. Skogstad (ed.), *Policy Communities and Public Policy in Canada: A structural approach.* Copp Clark Pitman, Mississauga, Ontario.

Buvinic, Mayra (1983) 'Women's Issues in Third World Poverty: A policy analysis' in M. Buvinic, M.A. Lycette and W.P.McGreevy, *Women and Poverty in the Third World.* Johns Hopkins University Press, Baltimore. pp.14–31.

Buvinic, Mayra (1986) 'Projects for women in the Third World: Explaining their misbehaviour' *World Development* Vol.14 No.5.

Cagatay, Nilüfer, Diane Elson and Caren Grown (1995) 'Introduction' *World Development* Vol.23 No.11:1827–36.

Calman, Leslie J. (1992) *Toward Empowerment: Women and movement politics in India.* Westview Press, Boulder, San Francisco and Oxford.

Camau, Michael (1989) 'Changements Politiques et Problématique du Changement' *Annuaire de l'Afrique du Nord* Vol.28. CNRS, Paris.

Carbajal, C. (1994) 'A Women's Approach to North South Co-operation' *Focus on Gender* Vol.2 No.3, October:82–6.

Carroll, Thomas F. (1992) *Intermediary NGOs: the supporting link in grassroots development.* Kumarian Press, West Hartford.

Cernea, Michael M. (1993) *Sociological Work Within a Development Agency: Experiences in the World Bank.* World Bank, Washington D.C.

Chambers, Robert (1994) 'Participatory Rural Appraisal (PRA): Analysis of experience' *World Development* Vol.22 No.9:1253–68.

Charlton, Sue Ellen, Jana Everett and Kathleen Staudt (ed.) (1989) *Women, The State, and Development.* State University of New York Press, New York.

Childers, Erskine and Brian Urquhart (1994) *Renewing the United Nations System.* Dag Hammarskjöld Foundation, Uppsala.

Chowdhury, Najma (1985) 'Women in Politics in Bangladesh' in Ahmed *et al.* (ed.) *Situation of Women in Bangladesh.* Ministry of Social Welfare and Women's Affairs, Dhaka.

CIDA (Canadian International Development Agency) (1993) 'Gender as a Cross-Cutting Theme in Development Assistance: An evaluation of CIDA's WID policy and activities, 1984–1992'. Final report, prepared by F. Mailhot, July.

Clark, John (1991) *Democratising Development: The role of voluntary organisations.* Earthscan, London.

Clark, John (1992) 'Democratising Development: NGOs and the State' *Development in Practice* Vol.2 No.3:150–62.

Clark, John (1995) 'The State, Popular Participation, and the Voluntary Sector' *World Development* Vol.23 No.4.

Cockburn, Cynthia (1991) *In The Way of Women: Mwn'a resistance to sex equality in organisations.* Macmillan, London.

Cohen, Marjorie (1992) 'The Canadian Women's Movement and its Efforts to Influence the Canadian economy' in Backhouse and Flaherty (ed.), op. cit.

Collier, Paul (1989) 'Women and Structural Adjustment'. Unit for the study of African economics, Oxford University, Oxford.

Connell, R.W. (1990) 'The State, Gender and Sexual Politics' *Theory and Society* Vol.19:507–44.

Cornia, Giovanni, Richard Jolly and Frances Stewart (ed.) (1987) 'Adjustment with a Human Face: Protecting the vulnerable and promoting growth' cited in J. Vivian (ed.) *Adjustment and Social Sector Restructuring.* Frank Cass, London, 1995.

Corrêa, Sonia and Rebecca Lynn Reichmann (1994) *Population and Reproductive Rights: Feminist perspectives from the South.* Zed Books in association with DAWN, London.

Cox, Roger (1973) *The Anatomy of Influence: Decision making in international organizations.* Yale University Press, New Haven.

Curtin, Jennifer (1992) 'The Ministry of Women's Affairs: Where feminism and public policy meet'. Unpublished thesis, University of Waikato, New Zealand.

Curtin, Jennifer and Marian Sawer (1996) 'Gender Equity and the Shrinking State: Women and the great experiment' in Francis G. Castles *et al.* (eds.) *The Great Experiment: Labour Parties and Public Policy Transformations in Australia and New Zealand.* Allen and Unwin, Sydney.

Dahlerup, Drude (1988) 'From a Small to a Large Minority: Women in Scandinavian politics' *Scandinavian Political Studies* Vol.11 No.4:275–98.

Das Gupta, Monica (1987) 'Selective Discrimination Against Female Children in Rural Punjab India' *Population and Development Review* Vol.13 No.1:77–100.

Davis, S. (1996) 'Evolution of the Women's Caucus from Miami to Beijing' in *Women, Gender and the United Nations: Views from NGOs and activists.* NGLS, Geneva.

DAWN (n.d.) Alternative Economic Framework.

DAWN (1994) 'Challenging the Given: DAWN's perspectives on social development'. Prepared for World Summit on Social Development, Copenhagen.

DAWN (1995) *Dawn Informs* (4) Barbados.

Devere, Heather (1990) 'Women and the Fourth Labour Government of New Zealand'. Paper presented at the Canadian Political Science Association Conference, Victoria, British Columbia.

Dey, Jennie (1981) 'Gambian Women: Equal patterns in rice development projects?' *Journal of Development Studies* Vol.17 No.3.

Dowse, Sara (1975) 'Power in Institutions: The public service'. Paper presented at the Women and Politics Conference, Canberra.

Dowse, Sara (1983) *West Block.* Penguin, Ringwood, Australia.

Drèze, Jean and Amartya Sen. (1989) *Hunger and Public Action.* Clarendon Press, Oxford.

Eade, Deborah and Suzanne Williams (eds.) (1995) *The Oxfam Handbook of Development and Relief.* Oxfam, Oxford.

Ebdon, Rose (1994) 'Gender Implications of NGO Expansion in Bangladesh'. Paper presented to IDS workshop: Getting Institutions Right for Women in Development, November 3–5, IDS, Sussex.

Edwards, Michael (1993) 'Does the Doormat Influence the Boot?: Critical thoughts on UK NGOs and international advocacy'. Save the Children Fund, London.

Edwards, Michael and David Hulme (eds.) (1992) *Making a Difference: NGOs and development in a changing world.* Earthscan, London.

Edwards, Michael and David Hulme (1995) 'NGO Performance and Accountability: Introduction and overview' in M. Edwards and D. Hulme (eds) *Non-Governmental Organisations: Performance and accountability.* Earthscan, London.

Eisenstein, Hester (1995) *Inside Agitators: Australian femocrats and the state.* Temple University Press, Philadelphia.

Elson, Diane (1991) 'Male Bias in Macro-economics: The case of structural adjustment' in D. Elson (ed.) *Male Bias in the Development Process.* Manchester University Press, Manchester.

208

Elson, Diane (1992) 'Public Action, Poverty and Development: A gender aware analysis'. Prepared for Seminar on Women in Extreme Poverty (SWEP/1992/ WP.11), Vienna.

Elson, Diane (1993) 'Structural Adjustment with Gender Awareness: Vulnerable groups, gender based distortions, and male bias'. Gender Analysis and Development Economics Paper No.2. University of Manchester, Manchester.

Elson, Diane (1994) 'People, Development and International Financial Institutions: An interpretation of the Bretton Woods system' *Review of African Political Economy* Vol.62:511–24.

Elson, Diane (1995) 'Gender Awareness in Modeling Structural Adjustment' *World Development* Vol.23 No.11:1851–68.

Elson, Diane and Rosemary McGee (1995) 'Gender Equality, Bilateral Program Assistance and Structural Adjustment: Policy and procedures' *World Development* Vol.23 No.11:1987–94.

Elson, Diane and Ruth Pearson (1981) 'The Subordination of Women and the Internationalization of Factory Production' in K. Young *et al.* (eds.), op. cit.

Evans, Alison (1994) 'Growth and Poverty Reduction in Uganda'. Paper presented at Poverty Reduction and Development Cooperation, Copenhagen, 23–4 February.

Farrington, John and David Lewis (ed.) (1993) *Reluctant Partners? NGOs, the State and the Rural Poor: NGOs and agricultural development.* Routledge, London.

Ferchiou, Sophie (1995) 'Femmes Tunisiennes entre Feminisme d'Etate et Résistance' in Andrée Dore-Audibert and Sophie Bessis (ed.) *Femmes de Méditerranée: Politique, Religion, Travail.* Khartala, Paris.

Ferguson, Kathy (1984) *The Feminist Case Against Bureaucracy.* Temple University Press, Philadelphia.

Findlay, Sue (1987) 'Facing the State: The politics of the women's movement reconsidered' in Heather Jon Maroney and Meg Luxton (ed.) *Feminism and Political Economy: Women's work, women's struggle.* Methuen, Toronto.

Findlay, Sue and Melanie Randall (1988) 'Feminist Perspectives on the Canadian State' *RFR/DRF* Vol.17 No.3.

FNUAP/IREP (1991) *Femmes Diplômées du Magreb: Practiques novatrices.* A study by a group of researchers from three countries of the Maghreb (Algeria, Morocco, Tunisia), Tunis.

Fowler, Alan (1988) 'Non-governmental Organizations in Africa: Achieving comparative advantage in micro-development'. IDS Discussion Paper No.249, IDS, Sussex, August.

Fowler, Alan (1991) 'Building partnerships between Northern and Southern development NGOs: Issues for the 1990s' *Development in Practice* (Vol. 1, No. 1):5–18.

Fox, J. (1992) 'Democratic Rural Development: Leadership accountability in regional peasant organizations' *Development and Change* Vol.23 No.2:1–36.

Fraser, Nancy (1989) *Unruly Practices: Power, discourse, and gender in contemporary social theory.* University of Minnesota Press, Minneapolis.

Franzway, Suzanne, Diane Court and R.W. Connell (1989) *Staking a Claim: Feminism, Bureaucracy, and the State.* Polity Press, Cambridge.

Gascoigne, L. (1991) 'Finding Ways of Working with Women in Patriarchal Societies' in Tina Wallace and Candida March (ed.) *Changing Perceptions: Writings on Gender and Development.* Oxfam, Oxford.

Gelb, Joyce (1995) 'Feminist Organization Success and the Politics of Engagement' in M.M. Ferree and P.Y. Martin (ed.) *Feminist Organizations: Harvest of the New Women's Movement.* Temple University Press, Philadelphia.

Geller-Schwartz, Linda (1995) 'An Array of Agencies: Feminism and state institutions in Canada' in Stetson and Mazur (ed.), op. cit.

GIDP (Gender in Development Programme) (n.d.) 'Programming through the Lens of Gender, Parts 1–8'. UNDP, New York.

GIDP (Gender in Development Programme) (1993) 'Integrating Gender Concerns in Programming' Policy paper, UNDP, New York, June.

GIDP (Gender in Development Programme) (1995) 'Gender and Sustainable Human Development: Policy perspectives'. Draft paper. UNDP, New York.

Goetz, Anne Marie (1995) 'Institutionalizing Women's Interests and Gender-sensitive Accountability in Development' *IDS Bulletin* Vol.26 No.3.

Goetz, Anne Marie (1992) 'Gender and Administration' *IDS Bulletin* Vol.23 No.4:6–17.

Goetz, Anne Marie (1994) 'From Feminist Knowledge to data for development: The bureaucratic management of information on women and development' *IDS Bulletin* Vol.25 No.2: 27–36.

Goetz, Anne Marie and R. Sen Gupta (1996) 'Who Takes the Credit? Gender, power and control over loan use in rural credit programmes in Bangladesh'. Mimeo, IDS, Sussex.

GOB (n.d.) 'Five-Year Plans from 1973 to 1990'. Ministry of Planning, Government of Bangladesh.

GOJ (1987) 'National Policy Statement on Women'. Bureau of Women's Affairs, Government of Jamaica, Kingston.

GOJ (1990) 'Summary of the Five Year Plan on Women'. Bureau of Women's Affairs, Government of Jamaica, Kingston.

GOM (1989) *Strategie Nationale de Promotion de la Femme Marocaine a l'Horizon 2000.* Ministry of Employment and Social Affairs, Government of Morocco, Rabat.

GOM (1993) *Stratégie de Développement Social Pour la Décennie 90'* Ministère du Plan, Government of Morocco, Rabat, June.

GOM (1994) *Recensement Général de la Population et de l'Habitat.* Government of Morocco, Rabat.

GOOD (Gender Orientation on Development Working Group) (1992) 'Report on - Conference on Gender Training Frameworks'. GOOD, 14–18 September, Rhondorf, Germany.

GOU (1990) 'Women and the New Constitution: Field training manual'. Department of WID, Government of Uganda, Kampala.

GOU (1991) 'Recommendations by the Women of Uganda to the Constitutional Commission'. Government of Uganda, Kampala.

GOU (1993) *Rehabilitation and Development Plan 1993/4 1995/6, Vol.1.* Ministry of Finance and Economic Planning, Government of Uganda, Kampala.

GOU (1994) 'National Policy Statement on Gender Issues'. Draft, mimeo, Ministry of Employment and Social Affairs, Government of Uganda, Kampala.

Goudron, Henri (1989) 'Trois Comptines à propos de la Société Civile'. *Annuaire de l'Afrique du Nord*, Vol. 28.

Griffith, G. (1987) 'Village Women Cooperators: An Indian women's village producer cooperative as educator and agent of social change'. Unpublished thesis, University of Sussex, Sussex.

Groenen, Riet (1995) 'Training of Trainers Workshop on Gender Issues in the World of Work'. Report on the workshop, Turin, 5–16 December 1994.

Guijit, Irene (1992) 'Gender Differences and PRA'. Mimeo, IIED, London.

Hadjipateras, A. (1995) 'Gender in ACORD: Report of a survey of ACORD programmes'. September-December 1994, ACORD, London.

Hadjipateras, A. (1996) 'Gender Review-Interim Report'. ACORD, London.

Hadraoui, Touria and Myriam Monkachi (1991) *Women's Studies, Index and bibliography,* Fatima Mernissi (ed.). Collections Femmes Maghreb, UNU/WIDER. Le Fennec, Casablanca.

Hale, A., M. Makris and J. Goldsmith (1993) 'Equality and Development: Report of a survey and research on gender policies of aid and development agencies in the UK'. National Alliance of Women's Organisations, London.

Hale, Mary M., and Rita Mae Kelly (ed.) (1989) *Gender, Bureaucracy, and Democracy: Careers and equal opportunity in the public sector.* Greenwood Press, New York.

Hanlon, Joseph (1991) *Mozambique: Who calls the shots?* James Curry, London.

Harriss, Barbara (1990) 'The Intrafamily Distribution of Hunger in South Asia' in Jean Drèze and Amartya Sen (ed.) *The Political Economy of Hunger, Volume 1: Entitlement and well-being.* Clarendon Press, Oxford.

Heitlinger, Alena (1993) *Women's Equality, Demography and Public Policy: A comparative perspective.* St. Martin's Press, London.

Hewitt de Alcantara, Cynthia (1993) 'Introduction: Markets in principle and practice' in C. Hewitt de Alcantara (ed.) *Real Markets.* Frank Cass, London.

Hirschman, David (1991) 'Women and political participation in Africa: Broadening the scope of research' *World Development* Vol.19 No.12:1679–94.

Hodgson, Geoffrey (1988) *Economics and Institutions: A manifesto for a modern institutional economics.* Polity Press, Cambridge.

Holcombe, Susan (1995) *Managing to Empower: The Grameen Bank's experience of poverty alleviation.* Zed Books, London.

Hopkins, Jane, Carol Levin and Lawrence Haddad (1994) 'Women's Income and Household Expenditure Patterns: Gender or flow? Evidence from Niger' *American Journal of Agricultural Economics* Vol.76:1219–25, December.

Hosmer Martens, Margaret and Swasti Mitter (ed.) (1994) *Women in Trade Unions: Organizing the unorganized.* ILO, Geneva.

Humphrey, John (1987) *Gender and Work in the Third World: Sexual divisions in Brazilian industry.* Tavistock Publications, London.

Huntington, S. (1975) 'Issues in Women's Role in Economic Development: Critique and alternatives' *Journal of Marriage and the Family* Vol.37 No.4:1001–12.

Hyman, Prue (1994) 'New Zealand since 1984: Economic restructuring feminist responses, activity and theory' *Hecate* Vol.20 No.2:9–35.

IDS (1994) 'Poverty Assessment and Public Expenditure: A study for the SPA Working Group on Poverty and Social Policy'. Summary report, IDS, Sussex, September.

IDS (1995) 'Getting Institutions Right for Women in Development' *IDS Bulletin* Vol.26 No.3.

IDS (1997) *IDS Bulletin* Vol.28 No.3, July.

ILO (1989) 'Special Adviser on Women Workers' Questions'. Circular, ILO, Geneva, 20 July.

ILO (1993a) 'The Role of the ILO in Technical Cooperation'. Report IV, International Labour Conference, 80th Session, ILO, Geneva.

ILO (1993b) 'Special Adviser on Women Workers' Questions'. Internal memo, DGA/TEC, ILO, Geneva, 19 February.

ILO (1993c) *Workers with Family Responsibilities.* ILO, Geneva.

ILO (1994a) 'The Changing Role of Women in the Economy: Employment and social issues'. ILO Governing Body, (GB.261/ESP/2/2), Geneva, November.   .

ILO (1994b) 'ILO Strategy for Technical Cooperation'. ILO Governing Body, (GB.261/TC/2.5), Geneva, November.

ILO (1994c) 'Women and Work: Selected ILO policy documents'. ILO, Geneva.

ILO (1995) *Gender, Poverty and Employment: Turning capabilities into entitlements.* ILO, Geneva.

ILO/PROG/EVAL (1995) 'Guidelines for the Integration of Gender Issues into the Design, Monitoring and Evaluation of ILO Programmes and Projects'. ILO, Geneva, January.

ILO/PROMOTEC (1992) 'The Women-in-Development Policies of Multi-Bilateral Donors'. ILO, Geneva, October.

IOE (1993) 'Proposals for a Thorough Reform of the ILO'. International Organisation of Employers, Geneva, February.

Islam, Mohsena (1994) 'Technical Cooperation and Women's Lives: Integrating gender into development policy: Bangladesh'. Mimeo, UNRISD, Geneva.

Jackson, Cecile (1993a) 'Questioning Synergism: Win-win with women in population and environment policies?' *Journal of International Development* Vol.5 No.6:651–68.

Jackson, Cecile (1996) 'Rescuing Gender From the Poverty Trap' *World Development* Vol.24 No.3:489–504.

Jacquette, Jane (1990) 'Gender and Justice in Economic Development' in I. Tinker (ed.) *Persistent Inequalities.* Oxford University Press, Oxford. pp.54–69.

Jacquette, Jane (1994) 'Women's Movements and the Challenge of Democratic Politics in Latin America' *Social Politics* Vol.1 No.3, Fall.

Jahan, Rounaq (1982) 'Purdah and Participation: Women in the politics of Bangladesh' in Hannah Papanek and Gail Minault (eds.) *Separate Worlds: Studies of purdah in South Asia.* South Asia Books, Missouri.

Jahan, Rounaq (1995) *The Elusive Agenda: Mainstreaming women in development.* Zed Books, London.

Jain, Devaki (1996) 'The United Nations Needs Structural Adjustment: Some experiences in working together' in *Women, Gender and the United Nations: Views from NGOs and activists.* NGLS, Geneva.

Jazairy, Idriss, Mohiuddin Alamgir and Therese Panuccio (eds.) (1992) *The State of World Rural Poverty: An inquiry into its causes and consequences.* IT Publications, London.

Jeffrey, Patricia, Robin Jeffrey and Andrew Lyon (1987) 'Domestic Politics and Sex Differences in Mortality: A view from rural Binjor District, U.P.'. BAMANEH/ American SSRC Workshop on EFM, Dhaka.

Joekes, Susan (1995) 'Women's Employment and Moroccan Competitive Advantage'. Report on the National Workshop for Morocco Mimeo, UNRISD, Geneva.

Johnson, Hazel and Linda Mayoux (1995) 'The Problem of Power: Issues in participative research' in A. Thomas, J. Chataway and M. Wuyts (eds.) (1995) *Finding Out Fast: Investigative skills for development policy and public action.* The Open University, Milton Keynes.

Jonasdottir, Anna (1988) 'On the Concept of Interest, Women's Interests, and the Limitations of Interest Theory' in Kathleen Jones and Anna Jonasdottir *The Political Interests of Gender: Developing theory and research with a feminist face.* Sage, London.

Kabeer, Naila (1989) 'Monitoring Poverty as if Gender Mattered: A methodology for rural Bangladesh'. Discussion Paper No.313, IDS, Sussex, UK.

Kabeer, Naila (1991) 'Gender Dimensions of Rural Poverty: Analysis from Bangladesh' *Journal of Peasant Studies* Vol.18 No.2, January.

Kabeer, Naila (1994) *Reversed Realities: Gender hierarchies in development thought.* Verso, London.

Kabeer, Naila (1996a) 'Agency, Well-being and Inequality: Reflections on the gender dimensions of poverty' *IDS Bulletin* Vol.27 No.1:11–21.

Kabeer, Naila (1996b) *Gender, Economics and Demographic Transitions : Making connections for a human-centered development.* Occasional Paper No. 7, Fourth World Conference on Women, UNRISD, Geneva.

Kandiyoti, Deniz (1988) 'Women and Rural Development Policies: The changing agenda'. Discussion Paper No. 244, IDS, Sussex.

Kandiyoti, Deniz (1990) 'Women and Rural Development Policies: The changing agenda' *Development and Change* Vol.21 No.1:5–22.

Kandiyoti, Deniz (1991) 'Introduction' in Deniz Kandiyoti (ed.) *Women, Islam and the State.* Temple University Press, Philadelphia. pp.1–21.

Kardam, Nüket (1991) *Bringing Women In: Women's issues in international development programs.* Lynne Rienner, Boulder, Colorado.

Kardam, Nüket (1993) 'Development Approaches and the Role of Policy Advocacy: The case of the World Bank' *World Development* Vol.21 No.11:1773–86.

Kardam, Nüket (1995) 'Conditions of Accountability for Gender Policy: The organizational, political and cognitive contexts' *IDS Bulletin* Vol.26 No.3:11–22.

Kardam, Nüket (1997) 'The Emerging International Women's Regime'. Mimeo, UNRISD, Geneva.

Karl, Marilee (1995) *Women and Empowerment: Participation and decision making.* Zed Books, London.

Katzenstein, Mary Fainsod (1995) 'Discursive Politics and Feminist Activism in the Catholic Church', in Myra Max Ferree and Patricia Yancey Martin (ed.) *Feminist Organizations: Harvest of the New Women's Movement.* Temple University Press, Philadelphia.

King Dejardin, Amelita (1996) 'Public Works Programmes, A Strategy for Poverty Alleviation :The gender dimension' *Issues in Development.* Discussion Paper 10, ILO, Geneva.

Köhler, Gabrielle (1995) 'The UN and Development Thinking: From optimism to agnosticism and back again' *IDS Bulletin* Vol.26 No.4:54–63.

Korten, David (1990) *Getting to the 21st Century: Voluntary action and the global agenda.* Kumarian Press, West Hartford, CT.

Kraus-Harper, Uschi and Malcolm Harper (1992) *Getting Down to Business: A training manual for businesswomen.* IT Publications, London.

Krut, Riva (1997) 'Globalization and Civil Society: NGO influence in international decision-making'. Draft paper prepared for Globalization and Citizenship: An International Conference, UNRISD, Geneva.

Kwesiga, Joy C. (1994) 'Technical Cooperation and Women's Lives: Integrating gender into development policy: The Uganda case study report'. Mimeo, UNRISD, Geneva.

Lane, Jan-Erik (1995) 'Non-governmental organizations and participatory development: The concept in theory versus the concept in practice' in Nici Nelson and Susan Wright (ed.) *Power and Participatory Development: Theory and practice.* IT Publications, London. pp.181–91.

Leaveau, Remy (1989) 'Eléments de Reflexion sur l'Etat au Magheb' *Annuaire de l'Afrique du Nord* Vol.28.

Leaveau, Remy and Mounia Bennani-Chraibi (1996) *Maroc 1996: Institutions, economie, société.* Marc Bloch Centre, Berlin.

Lemrini, Amina (1993) 'L'image de la Femme dans les Manuels Scolaires: Il lit, elle cuisine' in *Femmes et Système Educatif au Maroc: Blocages et impacts.* Le Fennec, Casablanca.

Levi, Margaret and Meredith Edwards (1990) 'Dilemmas of Femocratic Reform' in Mary F. Katzenstein and Hege Skjeie (ed.) *Going Public: National histories of women's enfranchisement and women's political participation within state institutions.* Institute for Social Research, Oslo.

Lexow, J. and D. McNeill (1989) 'The Women's Grant'. Desk Study Review, NORAD Oslo, February.

Lockwood, Matthew (1992) 'Engendering Adjustment or Adjusting Gender? Some new approaches to women and development in Africa'. Discussion Paper No.315, IDS, Sussex/ London-Edinburgh Weekend-Return Group.

London-Edinburgh Weekend Return Group (1979) *In and Against the State.* Pluto Press, London.

Lotherington, A.T., M.Haug and A.B. Flemmen (1991) *Implementation of Women-in-Development (WID) Policy.* Forut, Oslo.

MacDonald, Martha (ed.) (1994) *Gender Planning in Development Agencies: Meeting the challenge.* Oxfam, Oxford.

MacDonald, Martha (1995) 'Economic Restructuring and Gender in Canada: Feminist policy initiatives' *World Development* Vol.23 No.1.

MacKinnon, Catharine (1989) *Towards a Feminist Theory of the State.* Harvard University Press, Cambridge, Massachusetts.

Mackintosh, Maureen (1989) *Gender, Class and Rural Transition: Agribusiness and the Food Crisis in Senegal.* Zed Books, London.

Mackintosh, Maureen (1990) 'Abstract Markets and Real Needs' in Henry Bernstein, Ben Crow, Maureen Mackintosh and C. Martin (eds.) *The Food Question: Profit versus People.* Earthscan, London.

Marand-Fouquet, Catherine (1995) 'French Women and Politics' in Andrée Dore-Audibert and Sophie Bessis (ed.) *Femmes de Méditerranée, Politique, Religion, Travail.* Khartala, Paris.

Mariott, Christine (1994) 'Technical Cooperation and Women's Lives: Integrating gender into development policy: The Jamaican report'. Mimeo, UNRISD, Geneva.

May, N. (n.d.) *No Short Cuts: A starter resource book for women's group field workers.* CHANGE, London.

Mayoux, Linda (1986) 'Employment Generation for Women in West Bengal'. Unpublished report presented to ODA, London.

Mayoux, Linda (ed.) (1988) *All Are Not Equal: African women in cooperatives.* Institute for African Alternatives, London.

Mayoux, Linda (1993) 'Integration is not Enough: Gender inequality and empowerment in Nicaraguan agricultural co-operatives' *Development Policy Review* Vol.11:67–89.

Mayoux, Linda (1995a) 'Alternative Development or Utopian Fantasy? Cooperation, empowerment and women's cooperative development in India' *Journal of International Development* Vol.7 No.2:211–28.

Mayoux, Linda (1995b) 'From Vicious to Virtuous Circles: Gender and micro-enterprise development'. UNRISD Occasional Paper Series: Fourth World Conference on Women, UNRISD, Geneva.

Mayoux, Linda (1997) 'Micro-Finance Programmes and Women's Empowerment: Approaches, issues and ways forward'. Discussion Paper, Open University, Milton Keynes, UK.

Mayoux, Linda and Anand, Shri (1995) 'Gender Inequality, Revolving Credit Societies and Sectoral Employment Strategies: Some questions from the South Indian silk industry' in S. Ardener and S. Burman (ed.) op.cit.

McKinlay, Robin (1990) 'Feminists in the Bureaucracy' *Women's Studies Journal* Vol.6 No.1/2:72–95.

Meer, Shamin (1997) 'Gender and Land Rights: The struggle over resources in post-apartheid South Africa' *IDS Bulletin* Vol.28 No.3, July.

Mernissi, Fatima (1991) *Women and Islam: An historical and theological enquiry.* Basil Blackwell, Oxford.

Mernissi, Fatima (1992) *La Peur-Modernité: Conflict islam démocratie.* Albin Michel, Paris.

Mistry, Percy S. and Paul Thyness (1991) 'Options for Funding the UN System and the Development Banks' in *The United Nations: Issues and Options: Five studies on the role of the UN in the economic and social fields.* Commissioned by the Nordic UN Project, Almqvist & Wiksell International, Stockholm.

Moghadam, Valentine (1994) 'Market Reforms and Women Workers in Vietnam'. WIDER Working Paper No.116, United Nations University, Helsinki.

Mohanty, Chandra T., Ann Russo and Lourdes Torres (1991) *Third World Women and the Politics of Feminism.* Indiana University Pess, Bloomington.

Molyneux, Maxine (1985) 'Mobilisation Without Emancipation? Women's interests, the state, and revolution in Nicaragua' *Feminist Studies* Vol.11 No.2:227–54.

Moore, Henrietta (1986) *Space, Test and Gender: An anthropological study of the Marakwet of Kenya.* Cambridge University Press, Cambridge.

Moore, Henrietta (1994) 'Is There a Crisis In The Family?' Occasional Paper 3, Prepared for World Summit on Social Development, UNRISD, Geneva.

Moore, Mick (1993) 'Good government? Introduction' *IDS Bulletin* Vol.24 No.1:1–6.

Moore, Mick (1995) 'Promoting Good Government by Supporting Institutional development?' *IDS Bulletin* Vol.26 No.2.

Morris, Cerise (1980) 'Determination and Thoroughness: The movement for a Royal Commission on the Status of Women in Canada' *Atlantis* Vol.5 No.2.

Moser, Caroline O.N. (1989) 'Gender Planning in the Third World: Meeting practical and strategic needs' *World Development* Vol.17 No.11:1799–825.

Moser, Caroline (1994) *Gender Planning and Development: Theory, practice and training.* Routledge, London.

Mosley, Paul, Jane Harriagan and John Toye (1991) *Aid and Power: The World Bank and policy-based lending, Vol.1.* Routledge, London.

Mosse, David (1994) 'Authority, Gender and Knowledge: Theoretical reflections on the practice of participatory rural appraisal' *Development and Change* Vol.25 No.3:497–526.

Moyo, Sam (1991) 'NGO Advocacy in Zimbabwe: Systemising an old function or inventing a new role?' Paper presented to the workshop NGO and Development Advocacy, 29 January-1 February.

Mugyenyi, Mary (1994) 'Gender, Empowerment, and Development in Uganda'. Mimeo, Makerere University, Uganda.

Narayan, Deepa and L. Srinivasan (1994) *Participatory Development Tool Kit: Materials to facilitate community empowerment.* World Bank, Washington.

Nathan, Judith (1989) 'Establishment of the Ministry of Women's Affairs: A case study of the creation of a new organisation'. Unpublished thesis, Victoria University of Wellington, New Zealand..

National Council of Women of New Zealand, (1992) 'Submission to the Ministry of Women's Affairs on New Zealand's Report to the Monitoring Committee of the Convention on the Elimination of All Forms of Discrimination against Women'. NCWNZ, Wellington, New Zealand.

Nelson, Penny (1989) 'The Ministry of Women's Affairs: Role, process and change, 1985–1989'. Unpublished thesis, University of Otago, Dunedin, New Zealand.

NGLS (United Nations Non-Governmental Liaison Service) (1994) *The NGLS Handbook of UN Agencies, Programmes and Funds Working for Economic and Social Development.* NGLS, Geneva.

Noponen, H. (1990) 'Loans to the Working Poor: A longitudinal study of credit, gender and the household economy', PRIE Working Paper No. 6, Rutgers University, New Brunswick, New Jersey.

North, Douglas (1990) *Institutions, Institutional Change and Economic Performance, Political economy of institutions and decisions.* Cambridge University Press, Cambridge

ODA (n.d.a.) 'Checklist for the Participation of Women in Developmental Projects'. ODA, Glasgow.

ODA (n.d.b) 'The Joint Funding Scheme: Guide-lines and procedures'. ODA, Glasgow.

ODI (1988) 'Development Efforts of NGOs' *Development* No.4:41–6. Society for International Development, Rome.

Office of the Ministry of Women's Affairs (1985) 'The 1984 Women's Forums: What women want of the Ministry'. Ministry of Women's Affairs, Wellington, New Zealand.

Olin, Ulla (1988) 'Needs Assessment of Women in Development in Vietnam'. Unpublished report for UNIFEM.

One World Action (1993) 'Cape Verde: The challenge of change'. One World Action, London.

O'Regan, Mary (1991) 'Radicalised by the System' in Maud Cahill and Christine Dann (ed.) *Changing our Lives.* Bridget Williams Books, Wellington, New Zealand, 1991.

O'Regan, Mary (1992) 'Daring or Deluded?' in Rosemary du Plessis and Phillida Bunkle *Feminist Voices.* Oxford University Press, Auckland, 1992.

215

Oxfam Gender Team (1994) 'Oxfam's Gender Revolution: Past and future struggles'. Oxfam, Oxford.

Pal, Leslie A. (1993) *Interests of State: The politics of language, multiculturalism, and feminism in Canada.* McGill Queen's University Press, Montreal.

Palmer, Ingrid (1977) 'Rural Women and the Basic-Needs Approach to Development' *International Labour Review* Vol.11 No.5:97–107.

Palmer, Ingrid (1991) *Gender and Population in the Adjustment of African Economies: Planning for change.* ILO, Geneva.

Palmer, Ingrid (1992) 'Gender Equity and Economic Efficiency in Adjustment Programmes' in H. Afshar and C. Dennis (ed.) *Women and Adjustment Policies in the Third World.* Macmillan, London.

Palmer, Ingrid (1993) 'Report on World Bank Phase 1 Interviews: Changes in the approach to WID or gender over the years'. Mimeo, UNRISD, Geneva.

Palmer, Ingrid (1995) 'Public Finance from a Gender Perspective' *World Development* Vol.23 No.11:1981–6.

Palmer, Ingrid and Jha, R. (1993) 'Changes in the Approach to WID or Gender Incorporation over the Years'. Mimeo, UNRISD, Geneva.

Pateman, Carol (1992) 'Equality, Difference, Subordination: The politics of motherhood and women's citizenship' in G. Bock and S. James (ed.) *Beyond Equality and Difference: Citizenship, feminist politics and female subjectivity.* Routledge, London.

Pearson, Ruth (1995) 'Bringing It All Back Home: Integrating training for gender specialists and economic planners' *World Development* Vol.23 No.11.

Phillips, Susan D. (1991) 'Meaning and Structure in Social Movements: Mapping the network of national Canadian women's organizations' *Canadian Journal of Political Science* Vol.21 No.4:755–81.

Pietilä, Hilkka. and Ingrid Eide (1990) 'The Role of the Nordic Countries in the Advancement of Women within the United Nations System'. Report No.16, Commissioned by the Nordic UN Project, Stockholm.

Pietilä, Hilkka and J. Vickers (1994) *Making Women Matter: The role of the United Nations.* Zed Books, London.

Piza-Lopez, E. and Candida March (ed.) (1990) *Gender Considerations in Economic Enterprises.* Oxfam, Oxford.

Piza-Lopez, E. and Tina Wallace (1994) 'Oxfam's Gender Revolution: Past and future struggles'. Mimeo, Oxfam, Oxford.

Pollack, Molly (1994a) 'Technical Cooperation and Women's Lives: Integrating gender into development policy: Chile, civil servants report'. Mimeo, UNRISD, Geneva.

Pollack, Molly (1994b) 'Technical Co-operation and Women's Lives: Integrating gender into development policy: Chile NGOs'. Mimeo, UNRISD, Geneva.

Polsby, Nelson W. (1985) *Policy Innovation in the US.* Yale University Press, New Haven.

Preddy, Elspeth (compiler) (1985) 'Women's Electoral Lobby: Australia/New Zealand, 1972–1985'. WEL Australia and WEL New Zealand, Wellington.

Rachid, Abderazak Moulay (1985) *Women's Condition in Morocco.* Collection of the Faculty of Law of Rabat, No.33.

Rachid, Abderazak Moulay (1991) *Femmes et Lois au Maroc.* Le Fennec, Casablanca.

Rahman, A. (1993) *People's Self-Development: Perspectives on participatory action research.* Zed Books, London.

Ramesh, J. (1995) 'Strategies for Monitoring and Accountability: The Working Women's Forum model' in M. Edwards and D. Hulme (ed.) op. cit.

Razavi, Shahra (1997) 'Fitting Gender into Development Institutions' *World Development* Vol.25 No.7.

Razavi, Shahra and Carol Miller (1995a) 'From WID to GAD: Conceptual shifts in the women and development discourse'. UNRISD Occasional Paper Series, Fourth World Conference on Women, UNRISD, Geneva.

216

Razavi, Shahra and Carol Miller (1995b) 'Gender Mainstreaming: A study of efforts by the UNDP, the World Bank and the ILO to institutionalize gender issues'. Occasional Paper No.4, Fourth World Conference on Women, UNRISD, Geneva.

Reijntjes, Coen, Bertus Haverkort and Ann Waters-Bayer (1992) *Farming for the Future: An introduction to low-external-input and sustainable agriculture.* ILEIA, Leusden.

Reinelt, Claire (1995) 'Moving onto the Terrain of the State: The battered women's movement and the politics of engagement' in M.M. Ferree and P.Y. Martin (ed.) *Feminist Organizations, Harvest of the New Women's Movement.* Temple University Press, Philadelphia.

Rich, Bruce (1994) *Mortgaging the Earth.* Earthscan, London.

Riddell, Roger and Mark Robinson (ed.) (1995) *Non-Governmental Organizations and Rural Poverty Alleviation.* Clarendon Press, London.

Riegelman Lubin, Carol and Anne Winslow (1990) *Social Justice for Women: The International Labor Organization and women.* Duke University Press, Durham, North Carolina.

Robinson, Mark (1995) 'India' in Ridell and Robinson (ed.) *Non-Governmental Organizations and Rural Poverty Alleviation.* Clarendon Press, London.

Robinson, M and N. Thin (1993) 'Project Evaluation: A guide for NGOs'. ODA, Glasgow.

Rogers, Barbara (1980) *The Domestication of Women: Discrimination in developing societies.* Tavistock, London.

Ronquillo-Nemenzo, Ana Maria (1996) 'International Activism and National Activities' in Women, Gender and the United Nations: Views from NGOs and Activists, - UNNGLS, Geneva.

Rose, Kalima (1993) *Where Women are Leaders: The SEWA Movement in India.* Zed Books, London.

Saith, Ashwani (1996) 'Poverty: How does measurement measure up?' Mimeo, UNRISD, Geneva.

Sawer, Marian (1990) *Sisters in Suits: Women and public policy in Australia.* Allen and Unwin, Sydney.

Sawer, Marian (1993) 'Reclaiming Social Liberalism: The women's movement and the state' *Journal of Australian Studies* No.37:1–21.

Sawer, Marian (1994) 'Feminism and the state: Theory and practice in Australia and Canada' *Australian Canadian Studies* Vol.12 No.1:49–68.

Sawer, Marian (1996) 'Femocrats and Ecorats: Women's policy machinery in Australia, Canada and New Zealand'. Occasional Paper No.6, Fourth World Conference on Women, UNRISD, Geneva.

Sawer, Marian and Abigail Groves (1994a) 'The Women's Lobby: Networks, coalition building and the women of middle Australia' *Australian Journal of Political Science* Vol.29 No.3.

Sawer, Marian and Abigail Groves (1994b) 'Working From Inside: Twenty years of the Office of the Status of Women'. Australian Government Publishing Service, Canberra.

Sawer, Marian and Marian Simms (1993) *A Woman's Place: Women and Politics in Australia.* Allen and Unwin, Sydney.

Schreader, Alice (1990) 'The State-funded Women's Movement: A case of two political agendas' in Roxana Ng, Gillian Walker and Jacob Muller *Community Organization and the Canadian State.* Garamond Press, Toronto.

Schrijvers, John (1995) 'Participation and Power: A transformative feminist research perspective' in N. Nelson and S. Wright (ed) *Power and Participatory Development: Theory and practice.* IT Publications, London. pp.19–29.

Sen, Amartya (1981) *Poverty and Famines: An essay on entitlement and deprivation.* Oxford University Press, Oxford.

Sen, Amartya (1989) 'The Nature of Inequality, Presidential Address to the Ninth World Congress of the International Economic Association'. Mimeo, Harvard University, Cambridge, Mass.

Sen, Amartya and S. Sengupta (1983) 'Malnutrition of Rural Children and the Sex Ratio' *Economic and Political Weekly* Vol.18:855–65.

Sen, Gita (1995) 'Women Taking Hold of the Opportunities' in *Dawn Informs* No.4.

Sen, Gita (1996) 'Globalization and Citizenship: Health and reproductive rights'. Draft paper prepared for Globalization and Citizenship: An International Conference, UNRISD, Geneva.

Sen, Gita and Caren Grown (1985) *DAWN, Development Crisis and Alternative Visions: Third World women's perspective.* Stavenger Verbum.

Sen, Gita and Caren Grown (1987) 'Development, Crises, and Alternative Visions: Third World women's perspectives' *Monthly Review Press.* New York.

Sen, Gita and Caren Grown (1988) *Development, Crises and Alternative Visions.* Earthscan Publications, London.

Siddharth, V. (1995) Gender participation: NGOs and the World Bank' *IDS Bulletin* Vol.26 No.3:31–4.

Siddiqui, Theniath (1995) 'The Women's Movement and Democratization in Pakistan (1977–1988): Opportunities and limitations for political participation.' Unpublished MSC thesis, London School of Economics, University of London.

Spalter-Roth, Roberta M. and Ronnie Schreiber (1995) 'Outsider Issues and Insider Tactics: Strategic tensions in the women's policy network during the 1980s' in M.M. Ferree and P.Y. Martin (ed.) *Feminist Organizations, Harvest of the New Women's Movement.* Temple University Press, Philadelphia.

Staudt, Kathleen (1978) 'Agricultural Productivity Gaps: A case study of male preference in government policy and implementation' *Development and Change* Vol.9 No.3.

Staudt, Kathleen (1985) *Women, Foreign Assistance, and Advocacy Administration.* Praeger Special Studies, New York.

Staudt, Kathleen (1990) 'Gender politics in bureaucracy: Theoretical issues in comparative perspective' in Kathleen Staudt (ed.) *Women, International Development and Politics: The bureaucratic mire.* Temple University Press, Philadelphia.

Staudt, Kathleen (1995) 'Bringing Politics Back In: Bilateral assistance efforts to mainstream women'. Mimeo, UNRISD, Geneva.

Stephenson, Carolyn M. (1995) 'Women's International Nongovernmental Organizations at the United Nations' in A. Winslow (ed.) *Women, Politics, and the United Nations.* Greenwood Press, Westport.

Stetson, Dorothy M. and Amy Mazur (ed.) (1995) *Comparative State Feminism.* Sage, Newbury Park, California.

Stienstra, Deborah (1994) *Women's Movements and International Organizations.* St. Martin's Press, New York.

Summers, Anne (1986) 'Mandarins or Missionaries: Women in the federal bureaucracy' in Norma Grieve and Ailsa Burns (ed.) *Australian Women: New feminist perspectives.* Oxford University Press, Melbourne.

Tendler, Judith (1989) 'Whatever Happened to Poverty Alleviation?' *World Development* Vol.17 No.7.

Thomas, N. (1991) 'Land, Fertility and the Population Establishment'. Population Studies, Vol. 45.

Thomas-Slayter, Barbara, A. Lee Esser and M.D. Shields (1993) *Tools of Gender Analysis: A guide to field methods for bringing gender into sustainable resource management.* Clark University, Virginia.

Thorbek, Suzanne (1995) *Gender and Slum Culture in Urban Asia.* Zed Books, London.

Tomasevski, Katarina (1993) *Women and Human Rights.* Zed Books, London.

Tomlinson, Marlene H. (1992) 'Jamaica: Context report, WID Evaluation Study'. Mimeo, Canadian Cooperation Office, Kingston, Jamaica.

Townsend, Kathy (1995) 'Sex, Lies and Videotape'. Address to the Sydney Institute, 8 November.

Tozy, Mohamed (1979) 'Monopolisation de la Production Symbolique et Hièrarchisation du champ Politico-Religieux au Maroc' *Annuaire de l'Afrique du Nord* Vol.XVIII.

Tozy, Mohamed (1989) 'Représentation/Intercession: Les Enjeux de Pouvoir dans les "Champs Politiques Désamorcés" au Maroc'. *Annuaire de l'Afrique du Nord*, Vol. 28.

Tran Thi, Van Anh (in collaboration with Nguyen Nhat Tuyen) (1994) 'The Vietnam Case Study Report for UNRISD'. Mimeo, UNRISD, Geneva.

UNDP (1990a) 'Fifth Programming Cycle'. Governing Council Decision 90/34, in ECOSOC Official Records, Supplement No. 5, (E/1990/29), UNDP, New York.

UNDP (1990b) *Human Development Report 1990*. UNDP New York.

UNDP (1993) 'Human Development at Work: 1992 UNDP Annual Report'. UNDP, New York.

UNDP (1994a) 'Dear Colleague Letter: Programme of change, from the Administrator James Gustav Speth'. Internal memo, e-mail, 20 May.

UNDP (1994b) 'Making Beijing Successful: UNDP's strategy for the Fourth World Conference on Women, Action for Equality, Development and Peace'. Mimeo. UNDP, New York.

UNDP (1995) *Human Development Report 1995*. Oxford University Press, Oxford.

United Nations (1995) 'Report of the Fourth World Conference on Women, Beijing, 4–15 September'. Preliminary Version.

UN ECOSOC (1995) 'Technical Assistance and Women: From mainstreaming towards institutional accountability'. Note by the Secretary General, (E/CN.6/1995/6), New York.

UN GA (1995) 'The Advancement of Women Through and In the Programmes of the United Nations System: What happens after the Fourth World Conference on Women?' Note by the Secretary General, Joint Inspection Unit, UN General Assembly (A/50/509), Geneva.

UNICEF/UNDP (1995) 'Pay, Productivity and Public Service: Priorities for recovery in Sub-Saharan Africa'. Study for UNICEF and UNDP.

UNRISD(1994) 'State and Institutions of Civil Society in a Changing World: Problems of regulating social development'. Mimeo, UNRISD, Geneva.

USAID (1996) 'Renforcement des ONG pour la Démocratisation et le Développement Durable au Maroc'. DIS, Rabat.

Vargas, V. (1992) 'The Feminist Movement in Latin America: Between hope and disenchantment' *Development and Change* Vol.23 No.3:195–214.

Vickers, Jill McCalla (1988) 'Politics as if Women Mattered: The institutionalisation of the Canadian Women's Movement and its impact on federal politics, 1965–1988'. Paper presented to the ACSANZ Conference, Canberra, 23 June.

Vickers, Jill McCalla (1992) 'The Intellectual Origins of the Women's Movement in Canada' in Backhouse and Flaherty (ed.) op. cit.

Vickers, Jill McCalla, Pauline Rankin amd Christine Appelle (1993) *Politics As If Women Mattered: A political analysis of the National Action Committee on the Status of Women*. University of Toronto Press, Toronto.

Viswanath, Vanita (1991) *NGOs and Women's Development in Rural South India: A comparative analysis*. Westview Press, Oxford.

Vivian, Jessica (1994) 'Social Safety Nets and Adjustment in Developing Countries'. Occasional Paper No.1 for the World Summit for Social Development, UNRISD, Geneva.

Vivian, Jessica (ed.) (1995) 'How Safe are 'Social Safety Nets'? Adjustment and social sector restructuring in developing countries' in *Adjustment and Social Sector Restructuring*. Frank Cass, London.

Wadley, Susan and Bruce Derr (1987) 'On Differential Childhood Mortality in a U.P. Village : A preliminary report'. BAMANEH/ American SSRC Workshop on EFM, Dhaka.

Washington, Sally (1988) 'Great Expectations: The Ministry of Women's Affairs and public policy' *Race Gender Class* No.7:7–16.

Waylen, Georgina (1992) 'Rethinking Women's Political Participation and Protest: Chile 1970–1990' *Political Studies* Vol.40.

Waylen, Georgina (1995) 'Women's Movements: The state and democratization in Chile *IDS Bulletin* Vol.26 No.3.

Wee, Vivienne and Noeleen Heyzer (1995) *Gender, Poverty and Sustainable Development.* Engender, UNDP, Singapore.

WEDO (Women's Environment and Development Organization) (n.d.) 'A Brief Analysis of the UN Fourth World Conference on Women Beijing. Declaration and Platform for Action'. WEDO, New York.

Welbourn, Alile (1991a) 'A Non-Threatening Approach to Gender-Awareness training? Some possibilities'. Mimeo, IIED, London.

Welbourn, Alile (1991b) 'RRA and the Analysis on Difference'. Mimeo, IIED, London.

Welbourn, Alile (1992) 'Rapid Rural Appraisal, Gender and Health: Alternative ways of listening to needs' *IDS Bulletin* Vol.23 No.1.

Westwood, Sallie (1991) 'Gender and the Politics of Production in India' in H. Afshar (ed.) *Women, Development and Survival in the Third World.* Longman, London. pp.288–308.

White, Sarah (1995) 'Bangladesh' in Riddell and Robinson (ed.) op. cit. pp.101–37.

Whitehead, Ann (1979) 'Some Preliminary Notes on the Subordination of Women' *IDS Bulletin* Vol.10 No.3:10–13.

Whitworth, Sandra (1995) *Feminism and International Relations: Towards a political economy of gender in interstate and non-governmental institutions.* St. Martins Press, New York.

Williams, Suzanne with J. Seed and A. Mwau (1994) *The Oxfam Gender Training Manual.* Oxfam, Oxford.

Wilson, Elizabeth (1977) *Women and the Welfare State.* Tavistock, London.

Wilson, Margaret (1992) 'Employment Equity Act 1990: A case study in women's political influence, 1984–1990' in John Deeks and Nick Perry (ed.), *Controlling Interests: Business, the state and society in New Zealand.* Auckland University Press, Auckland.

de Wit, D. (1995) 'An Evaluation of the Oxfam Women's Linking Project (WLP): An important step in the process'. De Beuk, the Netherlands.

Wolfe, Marshall (1994) 'Social Integration: Institutions and actors' Occasional Paper for the World Summit for Social Development, UNRISD, Geneva.

World Bank (1989) 'Women in Development: Issues for economic and sector analysis'. Working Paper, WPS 269, PHRWD (Women in Development Division), World Bank, Washington, D.C., August.

World Bank (1992a) *Governance and Development.* World Bank, Washington D.C.

World Bank (1992b) 'Initiating Memorandum: Women and development, a best practice paper'. Mimeo, World Bank, Washington D.C., 27 September.

World Bank (1992c) 'Norwegian Support to WID Activities in Africa'. AFTSP/WID (Women in Development Unit in the Poverty and Social Policy Division of the Technical Department), World Bank, Washington, June 30.

World Bank (1992d) 'Programs of Special Emphasis: Implementation of women in development (PSE)'. Mimeo, World Bank, Washington D.C.

World Bank (1993a) *Governance: The World Bank experience.* Operations Policy Department, World Bank, Washington D.C., November 29.

World Bank (1993b) 'Making the GRADE: Transforming the development agenda in the Africa Region'. Technical note, GT/AFR (Gender Team, Africa Region), World Bank, Washington, D.C., September.

World Bank (1993c) 'Paradigm Postponed: Gender and economic adjustment in Sub-Saharan Africa'. Technical note, HRPD/AFR (Human Resources and Poverty Division, Africa Region), World Bank, Washington, D.C.,August.

World Bank (1993d) *World Development Report 1993.* Oxford University Press, Oxford.

World Bank (1994a) 'Enhancing Women's Participation in Economic Development'. Policy paper, World Bank, Washington, D.C.

World Bank (1994b) *Governance: The World Bank's experience*, Development in Practice. World Bank, Washington D.C., May.

World Bank (1994c) OED (Operations Evaluation Department) 'Gender Issues in Bank Lending: An overview'. Report No. 13246, World Bank, Washington, D.C., 30 June.

World Bank (1995a) *Advancing Gender Equality: From concept to action.* World Bank, Washington D.C., August.

World Bank (1995b) *Toward Gender Equality: The role of public policy,* Development in Practice. World Bank, Washington D.C., July.

Yeatman, Anna (1990) *Bureaucrats, Technocrats, Femocrats: Essays on the contemporary Australian state.* Allen and Unwin, Sydney.

Young, O.R. (1989) 'The Politics of International Regime Formation: Managing natural resources and the environment' *International Organization* Vol.43 No.3:349–75.

Zghal, Abdelkader (1989) 'Le Concept de Société Civile et la Transition vos Multipartisme', *Annuaire de l'Afrique du Nord*, Vol. 28.

Index

operation] [Netherlands] 29
discourses 22–37, 39, 40, 49, 106, 107, 114
discrimination 27, 28, 36, 102, 121, 134
discursive strategies 2–3, 20–2, 96, 106–7, 139, 162, 169
disengagement 3, 4, 6, 90, 139
distortions 10, 11, 27, 40
Division of Women in Development [UNDP] 151–2
donors 60–1, 82–3, 144–5, 159, 179, 188–90, 192
  see also budgets; funding

economic & social change 47–54
economics 7, 10, 21
  see also market; macro-economics; neo-classical economics
economists 26, 27, 152
'ecorats' & economic rationalism 10, 114, 120
ECOSOC [Economic and Social Council] 140
education 11, 32, 33, 38, 48, 49, 53, 92, 97–8
effectiveness 187–8
efficiency 10, 11, 23, 25–31, 40, 162–6, 180, 182, 189–90
EGALITE [Equality of Rights Branch] 149, 153
elections and voting 107, 109, 110, 114, 115, 122, 129, 135, 136–7
employment 28, 47–8, 50–1 65, 67–8, 83, 104, 132, 152–3
  see also work
empowerment 184–7, 191
engagement 3, 4, 5, 6, 37, 87, 139
  see also engagement
entryism 2, 6
equal opportunities 50, 65, 72, 132, 133, 153
equal rights 25, 28, 44, 134, 149, 153
equality/inequalities 23, 39, 165, 167, 175–6, 181, 183
equity 24, 42–3, 68–9, 83, 114, 132
exclusion 16, 99–102, 103, 107, 186
  see also constraints; resistance
external pressure 13, 22, 30, 36, 54, 62, 135–6, 138–45, 170–1

family 27, 38, 44, 49, 51, 52, 98, 100
  see also households; parental leave
federal systems 113, 124, 127
female-male relations 27, 52, 101, 167
  see also gender relations
'feminism' 45
Feminist Majority 11–12
feminist movement see women's movements
feminists 43–7, 96, 100, 136, 186
femininity & feminine behaviour 28, 51, 106, 175
feminization of poverty 32, 33, 35, 39
FEMMES [Office for Women Workers' Questions] 149, 153

femocrats 6, 7, 8, 9, 115, 117, 136
  see also gender advocates
FHH [female-headed households] 32, 33–4, 165
'fit' organisational 14, 29, 30, 37, 138, 145, 167
focal points 42, 63, 64, 75, 152, 153–4
funding 13, 58, 62, 68, 125–6, 143, 152, 172–3, 192–3
  see also budgets; donors

GAD [Gender and Development] 13–14, 34, 42–3, 47–54, 56–62, 71–80
'gender' 13, 53, 82
gender 35, 44, 54, 176–84, 186, 192
  accountability 174–6, 191
  advocates/advocacy 7, 31–2, 36, 37
  analysis 82, 125, 131, 169, 183
  gap 117, 122, 129, 136
  hierarchies 1–2, 28, 29
  justice 23–4, 35, 36, 39, 139, 167
  relations 1, 4, 14, 37, 95, 101, 159, 167
  relevance of 25, 27
  see also female-male relations; femocrats; men; women
GIDP [Gender in Development Programme] 155, 167, 168
globalization 12–15, 85
Grameen Bank 174, 177, 189
grassroots 16, 17, 18, 58, 179, 180–4
  see also GROs; GSOs
GROs [Grassroots Organizations] 16, 173, 182
GSOs [Grassroots Support Organisations] 173, 177, 184

health/healthcare 32, 49
hijab [veil] 6, 100, 101
household 1, 27, 32, 165
  female-headed households 32, 33–4, 165
  see also family
human capital/development 30, 32, 33, 34–5, 48, 162, 164, 167, 169
Human Development Report 9, 36, 85, 167
human rights 10, 14, 38, 90–1, 97, 134, 185

identity 4, 44, 53, 98
ILO [International Labour Organisation] 22, 138, 141–9, 152, 153, 156, 162, 165, 169
impact 112–15, 117, 118, 119, 131, 149, 184–7, 189
implementation units 56
incentives 157–8
incomes and wages 2, 32, 33, 51, 114
India 174, 177, 186
INGOs [International Non-Government Organisations] 14, 17, 173, 177, 179, 184, 185–6, 191
insider-outsider relations/dynamics 6–9, 12–19, 30, 71–80, 134, 141
institutions 1, 2, 6, 42–3, 45, 54–5, 151–4, 162
  see also organisations

institutionalizing 2, 42–3, 46–7, 54–71
instrumentalism 9–12, 37–41, 54, 138, 179
integration 31, 42, 46, 47, 65–71, 123–4, 150, 158, 161
'interest' 46
internal advocates 20–2, 30, 34, 116, 138–9, 148, 162–7, 169
international community/scrutiny 12, 13, 43, 121
investing in women 9, 10, 30, 32, 35, 162
Islam 5–6, 38, 52–3, 79, 87, 91–3, 97, 99–102

Jamaica 14, 43, 48–51, 53, 55, 61, 63, 66–7, 72, 78

Koran 11, 97, 101
Koutla 90, 91, 93, 103

labour/labour markets 27–9, 48–9, 59, 114, 132, 146, 165, 167
  see also work
language 9, 13, 29, 30, 35, 53, 128
  see also definitions
law/legislation 44, 58, 77, 79, 102, 103, 121, 132, 134
legitimacy 7–10, 13, 21, 42, 68, 83, 91
location, structural 56–62, 81, 116, 118, 126, 148, 149, 152, 153
  see also ministries

machineries 42, 55, 112–15, 122, 131, 136
  see also women's machineries
macro-economics 7, 29, 120
mainstreaming 10, 26–37, 47, 62–5, 139, 150–4, 158–60, 164
male domination 45, 98, 103, 106
  see also patriarchy; subordination
male-female relations 27, 52, 101 167
  see also gender relations
Mali 43, 47, 48, 49, 50, 53, 55, 57–8, 78
mandarins 2, 117
Maori women 130, 134
marginalization 42, 95, 103, 123, 150
market distortions 10, 11, 27, 40
markets/market forces 21, 28–9, 31, 114–15, 165
men/male 24, 47, 49, 51, 53, 72, 76, 139, 183
  see also gender; male domination; male-female relations; patriarchy
methodology 33, 34
Mexico Conference 54, 61, 112, 148
Middle East 38
ministries 57–60, 62–70, 117–18, 123, 130, 131
  see also location
missionaries 2, 117
monarchy 52, 72, 79, 90, 93, 105, 109
monitoring 63, 118, 149
monitoring units 56
Morocco 5–6, 9, 11, 38, 43, 48–55, 61, 67,

71–2, 79, 87–111
moudouana 79
multilateral institutions 13, 159, 161, 168, 172
Muslim *see* Islam

NAC [National Action Committee] [Canada] 18, 127, 128, 129
National Council of Women [Canada] 129
'national ownership' 14, 65–71, 154, 161
National Resistance Movement 60–1
naturalist arguments 106–7
negative effects/implications 122, 127, 180
neo-classical economics 26, 27, 28
networks/alliances 14, 21, 116, 117, 120, 124, 162–9
  see also co-operation
New Zealand 5, 113, 114, 129–35, 136
NGOs 12, 15–19, 121–2, 127, 168, 172–80, 183, 185, 187–8, 190–3
  see also INGOs; WINGOs
Nielson Task Force 124
Nordic countries 144
North-South divide 14, 15, 186
NRC [National Resistance Council] [Uganda] 74–5
NWC [National Women's Council] [Uganda] 74–5

One World Action 174, 179, 185, 186
opportunities 83–6
  see also equal opportunities
organizations 1, 21, 138, 139, 185, 187, 191
  culture 21, 22, 116, 145–69
  mandate 145, 146, 149, 164, 166, 167, 169
  see also bureaucracy; 'fit', organisational; institutions; location; mainstreaming; NGOs; umbrella organizations
OSW [Office of the Status of Women] [Australia] 116–21
outside-insider relations/dynamics 6–9, 12–19, 30, 71–80, 134, 141
oversight unit 56, 59
Oxfam 174, 177, 179, 183, 184, 185, 186

parental/maternity leave 68, 133
participation/participatory approaches 15–19, 88–90, 180–4
'patriarchal bargain' 101
patriarchy 79, 102
  see also male dominance; subordination
planning 65–71
policy advocacy 25, 26, 29, 30, 34, 37–41, 139, 148, 160, 162–70
policy analysis 70, 160, 169
policy issues 18, 23–6, 37–41, 116, 128, 159–61
policy making 21, 26–7, 31, 40, 54
'political'/'politics' 88, 89–90
political parties 75, 91, 93, 95, 96, 106–10, 113

women's movement 5–6, 8–9, 12–15, 30, 54, 87–8, 92, 94–7, 105–21, 125, 170–1
international 13, 55, 140–2
Women's Program 125, 126
women *see* feminists; femininity; femocrats; gender; female-male relations; reproduction; status of women

work 10, 65
see also employment; incomes; labour; reproductive work; unemployment; unpaid work
World Bank 18, 29–30, 32, 34–5, 138, 141–4, 146–52, 158–64, 169
WWF [Working Women's Forum] [India] 174, 177, 186, 189